Introduction to Clustering Large and High-Dimensional Data

There is a growing need for a more automated system of partitioning data sets into groups, or clusters. For example, as digital libraries and the World Wide Web continue to grow exponentially, the ability to find useful information increasingly depends on the indexing infrastructure or search engine. Clustering techniques can be used to discover natural groups in data sets and to identify abstract structures that might reside there, without having any background knowledge of the characteristics of the data. Clustering has been used in a variety of areas, including computer vision, VLSI design, data mining, bioinformatics (gene expression analysis), and information retrieval, to name just a few.

This book focuses on a few of the most important clustering algorithms, providing a detailed account of these major models in an information retrieval context. The beginning chapters introduce the classic algorithms in detail, while the later chapters describe clustering through divergences and show recent research for more advanced audiences.

Jacob Kogan is an Associate Professor in the Department of Mathematics and Statistics at the University of Maryland, Baltimore County. Dr. Kogan received his Ph.D. in Mathematics from the Weizmann Institute of Science and has held teaching and research positions at the University of Toronto and Purdue University, as well as a Fulbright Fellowship to Israel. His research interests include text and data mining, optimization, calculus of variations, optimal control theory, and robust stability of control systems. Dr. Kogan is the author of *Bifurcations of Extremals in Optimal Control* and *Robust Stability and Convexity: An Introduction* and coeditor of *Grouping Multidimensional Data: Recent Advances in Clustering.*

Introduction to Clustering Large and High-Dimensional Data

JACOB KOGAN

University of Maryland, Baltimore County

CAMBRIDGE
UNIVERSITY PRESS

CAMBRIDGE
UNIVERSITY PRESS

Shaftesbury Road, Cambridge CB2 8EA, United Kingdom

One Liberty Plaza, 20th Floor, New York, NY 10006, USA

477 Williamstown Road, Port Melbourne, VIC 3207, Australia

314–321, 3rd Floor, Plot 3, Splendor Forum, Jasola District Centre, New Delhi – 110025, India

103 Penang Road, #05–06/07, Visioncrest Commercial, Singapore 238467

Cambridge University Press is part of Cambridge University Press & Assessment, a department of the University of Cambridge.

We share the University's mission to contribute to society through the pursuit of education, learning and research at the highest international levels of excellence.

www.cambridge.org
Information on this title: www.cambridge.org/9780521617932

First published 2007

A catalogue record for this publication is available from the British Library

Library of Congress Cataloging-in-Publication data
Kogan, Jacob, 1954–
Introduction to clustering large and high-dimensional data / Jacob Kogan.
    p. cm.
Includes bibliographical references and index.
ISBN-13: 978-0-521-85267-8 (hardback)
ISBN-10: 0-521-85267-6 (hardback)
ISBN-13: 978-0-521-61793-2 (pbk.)
ISBN-10: 0-521-61793-6 (pbk.)
1. Cluster analysis – Data processing.   2. Cluster analysis – Computer programs.   3. Computer algorithms.   4. Dimensional analysis – Data processing.   5. Dimensional analysis – Computer programs.   I. Title.
QA278.K594   2007
519.5′3 – dc22   2006024381

ISBN   978-0-521-85267-8   Hardback
ISBN   978-0-521-61793-2   Paperback

God is a comedian playing to an audience
too afraid to laugh.

– Voltaire (1694–1778)

Contents

Foreword

Clustering is a fundamental data analysis task with broad seemingly distant applications that include psychology, biology, control and signal processing, information theory, and data mining, to name just a few. The term "clustering" has been used in a variety of contexts over the last 50 years. The recent dramatic increase in computing power brings renewed interest to this fascinating research discipline. The production of a comprehensive survey would be a monumental task given the extensive literature in this area.

This book is motivated by information retrieval applications that are typically characterized by large, sparse, and high-dimensional data. Rather than covering as many clustering techniques as possible, the book provides a more detailed account of a few important clustering algorithms. The exposition varies from an excellent coverage of introductory (more elementary) material for novice readers to more detailed discussions of recent research results involving sophisticated mathematics for graduate students and research experts.

The book focuses on k-means clustering, which is by far the most popular partitional algorithm widely used in applications. A detailed and elementary description of the classical quadratic k-means clustering algorithm provides a gentle introduction to clustering for undergraduate science majors, including engineering majors. Spherical k-means and information–theoretical k-means are introduced and connections between various versions of the algorithm are discussed. The relationship between the quadratic k-means clustering algorithm and deterministic annealing is described.

A unified approach to the creation of k-means algorithms through divergences is covered, along with a treatment of clustering problems as *continuous* optimization problems. This is in contrast to traditional search methods for the "best" partition of a finite set into a predefined number of groups.

The BIRCH and PDDP clustering algorithms are discussed in great detail. PDDP is designed to handle large and sparse data while BIRCH is capable of handling large and more general data sets. Kogan demonstrates how both algorithms can be used to generate initial partitions for k-means. A version of BIRCH with divergences (rather than with the squared Euclidean norm) is also described in the book.

At the end of each chapter, pointers to references relevant to the material of that chapter are provided. The bibliography contains several references to clustering results not covered in the book and should prove to be quite valuable for anyone interested in learning about or contributing to clustering-based research.

Michael W. Berry
University of Tennessee

Preface

Clustering is a fundamental problem that has numerous applications in many disciplines. Clustering techniques are used to discover natural groups in data sets and to identify abstract structures that might reside there, without having any background knowledge of the characteristics of the data. They have been used in a variety of areas, including bioinformatics; computer vision; VLSI design; data mining; gene expression analysis; image segmentation; information retrieval; information theory; machine learning, object, character, and pattern recognition; signal compression; text mining; and Web page clustering.

While grouping, or clustering, is a building block in a wide range of applications, this book is motivated by the document clustering problem. The problem is characterized by very high-dimensional and sparse data. This book illustrates in depth applications of mathematical techniques for clustering large, sparse, and high-dimensional data.

The book is based on a one-semester introductory course given at the University of Maryland, Baltimore County, in the fall of 2001 and repeated in the spring of 2004. The course introduces a mixed population of advanced undergraduate and graduate students to basic results in this research area. In the fall of 2005, the course was modified and offered to a class of undergraduate computer science students at Ort Braude Engineering College, Israel. A special effort has been made to keep the exposition as simple as possible.

The classical k-means clustering algorithm is introduced first with the squared Euclidean distance. Ability to work with quadratic functions of one scalar variable is the only mathematical skill needed to comprehend this material. Later in the book the algorithm with Bregman and Csiszar divergences is introduced, thus providing the instructor with an opportunity to calibrate the level of generality that fits a specific student population. Problems inserted in the body of the book facilitate understanding theoretical material;[1] suggested projects require minimal programming skills and help the student to grasp the reality of large high-dimensional data sets. Each chapter is concluded by a brief bibliography section. These sections attempt to direct an interested reader to references relevant to the material of the corresponding chapters.

Clustering is used in a number of traditionally distant fields to describe methods for grouping of unlabeled data. Different research communities have different terminologies for clustering and the context in which clustering techniques are used. In selecting the material the author has been following his own research interests. Time limitations of one-semester courses do not allow one to cover many important relevant results. The author believes in the following results due to G. Leitmann [95]:

Theorem. *There does not exist a best method, that is, one which is superior to all other methods, for solving all problems in a given class of problems.*

Proof: By contradiction.   □

Corollary. *Those who believe, or claim, that their method is the best one suffer from that alliterative affliction, ignorance/arrogance.*

Proof: By observation.   □

---

[1] While some of the problems are straightforward, others may require investment of time and effort.

Clustering has attracted research attention for more than 50 years, and many important results available in the literature are not covered in this book. A partial list of excellent publications on the subject is provided in Section 1.3 and [79]. This book's references stretch from the 1956 work of Steinhaus [125] to the recent work of Teboulle [128] (who brought [125] and a number of additional relevant references to the author's attention). Undoubtedly, many important relevant contributions are missing.

In spite of my efforts, many typos, errors, and mistakes surely remain in the book. While it is my unfortunate duty to accept full responsibility for them, I would like to encourage readers to email suggestions and comments to kogan@umbc.edu.

Acknowledgments

My first thanks go to Efim Gendler and Igal Lichtman, who introduced me to the fascinating area of text mining. I am indebted to Charles Nicholas for his support and collaboration.

I am grateful to Pavel Berkhin, Mike Berry, Dan Boley, Inderjit Dhillon, Joydeep Ghosh, and Zeev Volkovich for their help and influence. Special thanks go to Marc Teboulle who, over many years, has tirelessly tried to attract my attention to the beauty of optimization theory and its powerful techniques.

The productive environment at Ort Braude College developed by Shmaryahu Rozner, Rosa Azhari, and Zeev Barzilay has fostered a fruitful interaction between teaching and research that has been important to the development of this book. Special thanks go to Baruch Filhawari whose constant help made my stay at Ort Braude a pleasant experience and work on the book so productive.

Many thanks go to my students at UMBC and Ort Braude for their help in developing this book. Of the many fine people whom I have been associated with at Cambridge University Press, I would especially like to thank Lauren Cowles for her patience and assistance. Last but not least, I would like to express my thanks to Rouben Rostamian for his help with LaTeX-related issues.

I have also been aided by the research support of Northrop Grumman Mission Systems, the U.S. Department of Defense, the United States–Israel Binational Science Foundation, and the J. William Fulbright Foreign Scholarship Board. This support is gratefully acknowledged.

1 Introduction and motivation

For a given document collection $\mathcal{D} = \{D_1, D_2, \ldots, D_m\}$ and a query Q one often is concerned with the following basic problems:

1. Find documents in $\mathcal{D}$ "related" to the query. If, for example, a "distance" between two documents D_i and D_j is given by the function $d(D_i, D_j)$ and a threshold $\text{tol} > 0$ is specified one may be interested in identifying the document subset $\mathcal{D}_{\text{tol}} \subseteq \mathcal{D}$ defined by

$$\mathcal{D}_{\text{tol}} = \{D : D \in \mathcal{D}, \ d(Q, D) < \text{tol}\}. \qquad (1.0.1)$$

2. Partition the collection $\mathcal{D}$ into disjoint subcollections $\pi_1, \pi_2, \ldots, \pi_k$ (called clusters) so that the documents in a cluster are more similar to each other than to documents in other clusters. The number of clusters k also has to be determined.

When "tight" clusters $\pi_i, i = 1, \ldots, k$ are available "representatives" c_i of the clusters can be used instead of documents to identify $\mathcal{D}_{\text{tol}}$. The substitution of documents by representatives reduces the data set size and speeds up the search at the expense of accuracy. The "tighter" the clusters are the less accuracy is expected to be lost. Building "high quality" clusters is, therefore, of paramount importance to the first problem. Applications of clustering to IR are in particular motivated by *the Cluster Hypothesis* which states that "closely associated documents tend to be related to the same requests."

1

The World Wide Web provides a huge reservoir of information and the result of a query to a search engine can return thousand of pages. Clustering can be used to partition these results into groups each of which captures a particular aspect of the query. So that, for example, when the query is "virus" results related to "computer virus" will be placed in one cluster, while the results related to "viruses that cause colds" will be located in another one. A number of Internet search engines cluster search results thus providing a user with an efficient navigation tool.[1] Natural steps to approach the two above-mentioned problems are:

Step 1. Embed the documents and the query into a metric space.

Step 2. Handle problems 1 and 2 above as problems concerning points in the metric space.

This book discusses in detail a particular family of algorithms that clusters a finite data set $\mathcal{A}$ in a finite-dimensional Euclidean space. The problem first presented as a discrete optimization problem of finding the "optimal" k-cluster partition of the data set (as this is traditionally done in clustering literature). Next we state the clustering problem as a continuous optimization problem to which various optimization techniques are applied. The book also discusses different choices of "distance-like" functions with a particular emphasis on Bregman and Csiszar divergences that already found many useful applications in optimization and have been recently introduced in machine learning and clustering literature.

Document collections are often changing with time (new documents may be added to the existing collection and old documents may be discarded). It is, therefore, of interest to address the clustering problem under the assumption $\mathcal{D} = \mathcal{D}(t)$ (i.e., the document collection $\mathcal{D}$ is time-dependent).

---

[1] See, for example, http://www.groxis.com, http://www.iboogie.tv, http://www.kartoo.com, http://www.mooter.com/, and http://vivisimo.com

1.1. A way to embed ASCII documents into a finite-dimensional Euclidean space

A vector space model maps documents into vectors in a finite-dimensional Euclidean space. A brief description of perhaps the simplest vector space model is the following. First, a sorted list of words that occur in all the documents is built, this list serves as a dictionary. Words that belong to a stop list[2] are removed from the dictionary. If the number of distinct words in the dictionary is n, then a vector $\mathbf{a}_i \in \mathbf{R}^n$ is built for document D_i, $i = 1, \ldots, m$ as follows: the first coordinate $\mathbf{a}_i[1]$ of $\mathbf{a}_i$ is the number of times the first word of the dictionary occurs in D_i (if the word does not occur in D_i, then $\mathbf{a}_i[1] = 0$). The second coordinate $\mathbf{a}_i[2]$ is the number of times the second word of the dictionary occurs in D_i, and so on.

We illustrate the construction by a simple example. Consider the following collection[3]:

$D_1 = $ We expect a lot from our search engines.

$D_2 = $ We ask them vague questions about topics that we're unfamiliar with ourselves and in turn anticipate a concise, organize response.

$D_3 = $ We type in principal when we meant principle.

After the stop words removal the sorted dictionary contains 17 words:

anticipate, concise, engines, expect, lot, meant, organize, principal,
principle, questions, response, search, topics, turn, type, unfamiliar, vague.

---

[2] A stop list is a list of words that are believed to have a little or no value as search or discrimination terms. For example, the stop list from the SMART system at Cornell University can be found at ftp://ftp.cs.cornell.edu/pub/smart/english.stop
[3] The text is borrowed from [16]

The vector space dimension $n = 17$, and we will be building vectors in $\mathbf{R}^{17}$. For example, the vector $\mathbf{a}_1$ corresponding to the document D_1 is given by

$$\mathbf{a}_1 = (0, 0, 1, 1, 1, 0, 0, 0, 0, 0, 0, 1, 0, 0, 0, 0, 0)^T.$$

The simple example indicates that one can expect sparse high-dimensional vectors (this is indeed the case in IR applications). A "term by document" matrix is the $n \times m$ matrix with columns being the vectors $\mathbf{a}_i$, $i = 1, \ldots, m$. Each column of the matrix $A = [\mathbf{a}_1, \ldots, \mathbf{a}_m]$ represents a document and each row corresponds to a unique term in the collection. While this book is mainly concerned with document clustering, one can consider word/term clustering by focusing on rows of the "term by document" matrix. In fact simultaneous co-clustering of columns and rows may benefit separate clustering of columns only or rows only.

It is not uncommon that coordinates of $\mathbf{a}_i$ are weighted frequencies (and not just raw counts of word occurrences). Vectors $\mathbf{a}_i$ are usually L_2 normalized so that $\|\mathbf{a}_i\|_2 = (\sum \mathbf{a}_i^2[j])^{\frac{1}{2}} = 1$. Often words are stemmed, that is, suffixes and, sometimes, also prefixes are removed so that, for example, an application of Porter stemming algorithm to the words "study", "studying", and "studied" produces the term (not even an English word!) "studi." Porter stemming reduces the dictionary by about 30% and saves the memory space without seriously compromising clustering quality of English texts (handling Semitic languages like Arabic or Hebrew is much more different in this respect). In an attempt to further reduce the dimension of the vector space model often only a subset of most "meaningful" words is selected for the document–vectors construction.

A typical vector resulting from mapping a text into a finite-dimensional Euclidean space is high dimensional, sparse, and L_2 normalized. So, for example, the vector $\mathbf{a}_1$ after normalization becomes

$$\mathbf{a}_1 = \left(0, 0, \frac{1}{2}, \frac{1}{2}, \frac{1}{2}, 0, 0, 0, 0, 0, 0, \frac{1}{2}, 0, 0, 0, 0, 0\right)^T.$$

This book is concerned with clustering a finite set $\mathcal{A}$ of vectors in $\mathbf{R}^n$. Motivated by IR applications it is often (but not always) assumed that the vectors are L_2 normalized and their coordinates are nonnegative real numbers.

1.2. Clustering and this book

Unlike many books on the subject this book does not attempt to cover a wide range of clustering techniques, but focuses on only three basic crisp or exclusive clustering algorithms[4] and their extensions. These algorithms are:

1. k-means,
2. Principal Direction Divisive Partitioning (PDDP),
3. Balanced Iterative Reducing and Clustering using Hierarchies (BIRCH).

Most of the book is devoted to the k-means family of algorithms and their interconnections. Applications of the k-means algorithms equipped with a variety of distance-like functions are discussed in detail. In order to apply k-means one needs an initial partition of the data set. A common technique to address this problem is to perform multiple runs of k-means, each with a randomly selected initial centroids (which is by itself not a trivial task in a high-dimensional space), and then to select the "best" partition. We, however, advocate applications of algorithms like PDDP and BIRCH for building initial partitions for k-means.

Both PDDP and BIRCH are designed to generate partitions of large data sets. While PDDP is especially efficient with sparse and high-dimensional data (that, in particular, arises in IR applications), BIRCH is capable of handling general data sets residing in a finite-dimensional Euclidean space.

---

[4] That is, each object is assigned to a single cluster

The problem of the "right" choice of k, the number of clusters, is not discussed in the book.

Project 1.2.1. *For a given ASCII document D:*

1. *Build an alphabetical list of words that occur in D.*
2. *For each word compute and record the corresponding frequency.*

While the book is concerned with some mathematical techniques for clustering it is worthwhile to keep in mind that clustering is a real life problem that is difficult to cast in a mathematical formalism. El-Yaniv and Souroujon [52] illustrate the difficult choice facing clustering algorithms: "... consider a hypothetical data set containing articles by each of two authors such that half of the articles authored by each author discusses one topic, and the other half discusses another topic. There are two possible dichotomies of the data which could yield two different bi-partitions: one according to topic, and another according to writing style."

Often good clustering results depend on the "right" choice of similarity measure. Well, "a picture is worth ten thousand words," so we conclude this section with a picture of two very different object (see Figure 1.1). Should they belong in the same cluster? How to find the "right" similarity measure? What is the "goal" of a clustering procedure? While the book does not address these important questions it presents a number of techniques to generate different similarity measures and algorithms for clustering large high-dimensional data sets.

1.3. Bibliographic notes

The Cluster Hypothesis is introduced in [135]. The role of Bregman divergence in machine learning is discussed, for example, in [28, 76, 91, 92, 120]. A class of unsupervised statistical learning algorithms formulated in terms of minimizing Bregman divergences

Figure 1.1: Find the difference.

is presented in [136]. Clustering with Bregman divergence is reported in the award-winning paper [8], the extended version of the results is reported in [9]. Clustering with Csiszar divergence was introduced recently in [83–85].

For a description of document processing consult [16], for a detailed discussion see for example [58, 88, 89].

Simultaneous co-clustering of rows and columns of a matrix with nonnegative entries is considered in [122] via the information bottleneck method. Iterative double clustering built on ideas of [121] is proposed in [52]. An application of bipartite spectral graph partitioning for simultaneous co-clustering is suggested in [33]. In [15] the incremental k-means-type algorithm with Kullback–Leibler distance-like function is used to cluster rows and columns of the matrix, the batch counterpart of the algorithm is derived in [41].

A review of term weighting formulas for the vector space model is provided in [27]. For Porter stemming algorithm see [113]. For a partial list of general clustering-related references the reader is advised to consult, for example [2–4, 10, 14, 46, 48, 50, 54, 56, 59, 63–65, 68, 71, 72, 75, 79, 86, 87, 105, 106, 108, 124, 127, 137, 138] .

Finally, we would like to draw the reader's attention to the new emerging field of multiway clustering. The multiway clustering is motivated mainly by computer vision applications and the existing publications are a few (see e.g. [1, 62, 142, 149]).

2 Quadratic k-means algorithm

This chapter focuses on the basic version of the k-means clustering algorithm equipped with the quadratic Euclidean distance-like function. First, the classical batch k-means clustering algorithm with a general distance-like function is described and a "best representative" of a cluster, or centroid, is introduced. This completes description of the batch k-means with general distance-like function, and the rest of the chapter deals with k-means clustering algorithms equipped with the squared Euclidean distance.

Elementary properties of quadratic functions are reviewed, and the classical quadratic k-means clustering algorithm is stated. The following discussion of the algorithm's advantages and deficiencies results in the incremental version of the algorithm (the quadratic incremental k-means algorithm). In an attempt to address some of the deficiencies of batch and incremental k-means we merge both versions of the algorithm, and the combined algorithm is called the k-means clustering algorithm throughout the book.

The analysis of the computational cost associated with the merger of the two versions of the algorithm is provided and convexity properties of partitions generated by the batch k-means and k-means algorithms are discussed. Definition of "centroids" as affine subspaces of $\mathbf{R}^n$ and a brief discussion of connections between quadratic and spherical k-means (formally introduced in Chapter 4) complete the chapter.

2.1. Classical batch k-means algorithm

For a set of vectors $\mathcal{A} = \{a_1, \ldots, a_m\} \subset \mathbf{R}^n$, a prescribed subset $\mathcal{C}$ of $\mathbf{R}^n$ and a "distance" function $d(\mathbf{x}, \mathbf{a})$ define a centroid $\mathbf{c} = \mathbf{c}(\mathcal{A})$ of the set $\mathcal{A}$ as a solution of the minimization problem

$$\mathbf{c} = \arg\min \left\{ \sum_{\mathbf{a} \in \mathcal{A}} d(\mathbf{x}, \mathbf{a}), \ \mathbf{x} \in \mathcal{C} \right\}. \tag{2.1.1}$$

The quality of the set $\mathcal{A}$ is denoted by $Q(\mathcal{A})$ and is defined by

$$Q(\mathcal{A}) = \sum_{i=1}^{m} d(\mathbf{c}, \mathbf{a}), \quad \text{where } \mathbf{c} = \mathbf{c}(\mathcal{A}) \tag{2.1.2}$$

(we set $Q(\emptyset) = 0$ for convenience). Let $\Pi = \{\pi_1, \ldots, \pi_k\}$ be a partition of $\mathcal{A}$, that is,

$$\bigcup_i \pi_i = \mathcal{A}, \quad \text{and} \quad \pi_i \cap \pi_j = \emptyset \text{ if } i \neq j.$$

We abuse notations and define the quality of the partition Π by

$$Q(\Pi) = Q(\pi_1) + \cdots + Q(\pi_k). \tag{2.1.3}$$

We aim to find a partition $\Pi^{\min} = \{\pi_1^{\min}, \ldots, \pi_k^{\min}\}$ that *minimizes* the value of the objective function Q. The problem is known to be NP-hard, and we are looking for algorithms that generate "reasonable" solutions.

It is easy to see that centroids and partitions are associated as follows:

1. Given a partition $\Pi = \{\pi_1, \ldots, \pi_k\}$ of the set $\mathcal{A}$ one can define the corresponding centroids $\{\mathbf{c}(\pi_1), \ldots, \mathbf{c}(\pi_k)\}$ by:

$$\mathbf{c}(\pi_i) = \arg\min \left\{ \sum_{\mathbf{a} \in \pi_i} d(\mathbf{x}, \mathbf{a}), \ \mathbf{x} \in \mathcal{C} \right\}. \tag{2.1.4}$$

2. For a set of k "centroids" $\{\mathbf{c}_1, \ldots, \mathbf{c}_k\}$ one can define a partition $\Pi = \{\pi_1, \ldots, \pi_k\}$ of the set $\mathcal{A}$ by:

$$\pi_i = \{\mathbf{a} \ : \ \mathbf{a} \in \mathcal{A}, \ d(\mathbf{c}_i, \mathbf{a}) \leq d(\mathbf{c}_l, \mathbf{a}) \text{ for each } l = 1, \ldots, k\} \tag{2.1.5}$$

(we break ties arbitrarily). Note that, in general, $\mathbf{c}(\pi_i) \neq \mathbf{c}_i$.

The classical batch k-means algorithm is a procedure that iterates between the two steps described above to generate a partition Π' from a partition Π (see Algorithm 2.1.1). While Step 2 is pretty much straightforward, Step 1 requires to solve a constrained optimization problem. The degree of difficulty involved depends on the function $d(\cdot, \cdot)$ and the set $\mathcal{C}$. In addition, creation of an empty cluster at Step 2 of the procedure it is not unusual for iterations of batch k-means (see Example 2.1.1). The general accepted practice in this case is to start the procedure anew with a different choice of an initial partition/centroids. The entire procedure is essentially a gradient-based algorithm. We remark that a more general definition of a centroid that works with the two step batch k-means procedure is possible (see also Section 2.3.3).

In the rest of the chapter we focus on $\mathcal{C} = \mathbf{R}^n$, and the distance-like function

$$d(\mathbf{x}, \mathbf{a}) = \|\mathbf{x} - \mathbf{a}\|^2 = \left|\mathbf{x}[1] - \mathbf{a}[1]\right|^2 + \cdots + |\mathbf{x}[n] - \mathbf{a}[n]|^2,$$

where $\mathbf{x} = (\mathbf{x}[1], \ldots, \mathbf{x}[n])^T$. Note that while the function $d(\mathbf{x}, \mathbf{a}) = \|\mathbf{x} - \mathbf{a}\|^2$ is symmetric and nonnegative it fails to satisfy the triangle inequality, that is, for example, $1 = d(0, 1) > d(0, 0.5) + d(0.5, 1) = 0.5$. Most of the "dissimilarity" functions used in clustering fail to satisfy all the three standard requirements imposed on distance functions:

1. $d(\mathbf{x}, \mathbf{y}) \geq 0$, and $d(\mathbf{x}, \mathbf{y}) = 0$ if and only if $\mathbf{x} = \mathbf{y}$.
2. $d(\mathbf{x}, \mathbf{y}) = d(\mathbf{y}, \mathbf{x})$.
3. For each three vectors $\mathbf{x}$, $\mathbf{y}$, $\mathbf{z}$ the triangle inequality holds, that is,

$$d(\mathbf{x}, \mathbf{z}) \leq d(\mathbf{x}, \mathbf{y}) + d(\mathbf{y}, \mathbf{z}).$$

We refer to $d(\cdot, \cdot)$ as a "distance-like" function throughout the book.

2.1.1. Quadratic distance and centroids

To simplify the exposition first consider m scalars $a_1, \ldots, a_m$ and the quadratic function δ of a scalar variable x

$$\delta(x) = \sum_{i=1}^{m} |x - a_i|^2 = mx^2 - 2 \left(\sum_{i=1}^{m} a_i \right) x + \sum_{i=1}^{m} a_i^2. \qquad (2.1.6)$$

Note that for each x one has $\delta'(x) = 2mx - 2\sum_{i=1}^{m} a_i$. Since $\delta(x)$ is a convex function $\delta(c) = \min_x \delta(x)$ if and only if $0 = \delta'(c)$, hence

$$c = \frac{a_1 + \cdots + a_m}{m}. \qquad (2.1.7)$$

If

$$\sum_{i=1}^{m} ||\mathbf{x} - \mathbf{a}_i||^2 = \sum_{i=1}^{m} \sum_{j=1}^{n} [\mathbf{x}[j] - \mathbf{a}_i[j]]^2 = \sum_{j=1}^{n} \left(\sum_{i=1}^{m} [\mathbf{x}[j] - \mathbf{a}_i[j]]^2 \right), \qquad (2.1.8)$$

then application of (2.1.7) separately to each coordinate yields

$$\mathbf{c} = \mathbf{c}(\mathcal{A}) = \frac{\mathbf{a}_1 + \cdots + \mathbf{a}_m}{m}. \qquad (2.1.9)$$

Problem 2.1.1. *Consider m scalars $a_1, \ldots, a_m$ and the distance function $d(x, y) = |x - y|$. Identify centroids c of the set $\{a_1, \ldots, a_m\}$, that is, find solutions of the minimization problem*

$$\min_{x \in \mathbf{R}} \sum_{i=1}^{m} |x - a_i|. \qquad (2.1.10)$$

Problem 2.1.2. *Solve minimization problem (2.1.10) when the scalar set is substituted by the vector set $\{\mathbf{a}_1, \ldots, \mathbf{a}_m\}$ and $d(\mathbf{x}, \mathbf{y}) = |\mathbf{x}[1] - \mathbf{y}[1]| + \cdots + |\mathbf{x}[n] - \mathbf{y}[n]|$.*

Problem 2.1.3. *Solve Problem 2.1.2 with $d(\mathbf{x}, \mathbf{y}) = \max\{|\mathbf{x}[1] - \mathbf{y}[1]|, \ldots, |\mathbf{x}[n] - \mathbf{y}[n]|\}$.*

2.1. Classical batch k-means algorithm

2.1.2. Batch k-means clustering algorithm

Let $\Pi = \{\pi_1, \ldots, \pi_k\}$ be a partition of $\mathcal{A}$ with the corresponding centroids $\mathbf{c}_i = \mathbf{c}(\pi_i)$, $i = 1, \ldots, k$. Due to (2.1.3) the quality Q of the partition Π is

$$Q(\Pi) = \sum_{i=1}^{k} \sum_{\mathbf{a} \in \pi_i} ||\mathbf{c}_i - \mathbf{a}||^2. \qquad (2.1.11)$$

For $\mathbf{a} \in \pi_i \subseteq \mathcal{A}$ denote i, the index of π_i, by $\mathtt{present}(\mathbf{a})$, and the index j of the centroid nearest $\mathbf{a}$ by $\min(\mathbf{a})$ (that is $||\mathbf{c}_{\min(\mathbf{a})} - \mathbf{a}|| = ||\mathbf{c}_j - \mathbf{a}|| \le ||\mathbf{c}_l - \mathbf{a}||$, $l = 1, \ldots, k$). Define the partition $\mathtt{nextBKM}(\Pi) = \Pi' = \{\pi_1', \ldots, \pi_k'\}$ by:

$$\pi_i' = \{\mathbf{a} \; : \; \min(\mathbf{a}) = i\}.$$

We now show that

$$Q(\Pi) \ge Q(\mathtt{nextBKM}(\Pi)). \qquad (2.1.12)$$

Indeed,

$$Q(\Pi) = ||\mathbf{c}_{\mathtt{present}(\mathbf{a}_1)} - \mathbf{a}_1||^2 + \cdots + ||\mathbf{c}_{\mathtt{present}(\mathbf{a}_m)} - \mathbf{a}_m||^2.$$

If

$$q(\Pi) = ||\mathbf{c}_{\min(\mathbf{a}_1)} - \mathbf{a}_1||^2 + \cdots + ||\mathbf{c}_{\min(\mathbf{a}_m)} - \mathbf{a}_m||^2,$$

then, since $||\mathbf{c}_{\mathtt{present}(\mathbf{a}_i)} - \mathbf{a}_i||^2 \ge ||\mathbf{c}_{\min(\mathbf{a}_i)} - \mathbf{a}_i||^2$ for $i = 1, \ldots, k$, one has

$$Q(\Pi) \ge q(\Pi). \qquad (2.1.13)$$

For each $\mathbf{a} \in \pi_1'$ one has $\min(\mathbf{a}) = 1$, and $\mathbf{c}_{\min(\mathbf{a})} = \mathbf{c}_1$. Moreover

$$\sum_{\mathbf{a} \in \pi_1'} ||\mathbf{c}_{\min(\mathbf{a})} - \mathbf{a}||^2 = \sum_{\mathbf{a} \in \pi_1'} ||\mathbf{c}_1 - \mathbf{a}||^2 \ge \sum_{\mathbf{a} \in \pi_1'} ||\mathbf{c}(\pi_1') - \mathbf{a}||^2$$

$$= \sum_{\mathbf{a} \in \pi_1'} ||\mathbf{c}_1' - \mathbf{a}||^2 = Q(\pi_1').$$

Clearly, the same inequality holds when 1 is substituted by any index $l = 2, \ldots, k$. Hence

$$q(\Pi) = \sum_{l=1}^{k} \sum_{\mathbf{a} \in \pi_l'} ||\mathbf{c}_{\min(\mathbf{a})} - \mathbf{a}||^2 \geq \sum_{l=1}^{k} \sum_{\mathbf{a} \in \pi_l'} ||\mathbf{c}_l' - \mathbf{a}||^2$$

$$= Q(\texttt{nextBKM}(\Pi)). \tag{2.1.14}$$

Inequalities (2.1.13) and (2.1.14) complete the proof of (2.1.12). The classical quadratic batch k-means algorithm is given next.

Algorithm 2.1.1 (Quadratic batch k-means algorithm). *For a user supplied tolerance* `tol` ≥ 0 *do the following:*

1. *Start with an arbitrary partitioning* $\Pi^{(0)} = \{\pi_1^{(0)}, \ldots, \pi_k^{(0)}\}$. *Set the index of iteration* $t = 0$.

2. *Generate the partition* `nextBKM`$(\Pi^{(t)})$.
   if $[Q(\Pi^{(t)}) - Q(\texttt{nextBKM}(\Pi^{(t)})) > \texttt{tol}]$
       set $\Pi^{(t+1)} = \texttt{nextBKM}(\Pi^{(t)})$
       increment t *by 1.*
       go to 2

3. *Stop.*

Figures 2.1, 2.2, and 2.3 illustrate the basic steps of Algorithm 2.1.1.

2.1.3. Batch k-means: advantages and deficiencies

Under mild additional assumptions a final partition $\Pi = \{\pi_1, \ldots, \pi_k\}$ generated by Algorithm 2.1.1 with $\texttt{tol} = 0$ enjoys convexity properties. If the centroids $\{\mathbf{c}(\pi_1), \ldots, \mathbf{c}(\pi_k)\}$ are *distinct*, then for each pair of centroids $\mathbf{c}(\pi_i)$, $\mathbf{c}(\pi_j)$ there is a segment that connects the centroids. The hyperplane $\mathcal{H}_{ij}$ perpendicular to the segment and passing through its middle point $\frac{\mathbf{c}(\pi_i) + \mathbf{c}(\pi_j)}{2}$ divides the space into two subspaces $\mathcal{H}_{ij}^-$ and $\mathcal{H}_{ij}^+$ (see Figure 2.4). To simplify the exposition we assume that $\mathbf{c}_i = \mathbf{c}(\pi_i) \in \mathcal{H}_{ij}^-$ and $\mathbf{c}_j = \mathbf{c}(\pi_j) \in \mathcal{H}_{ij}^+$. Since $\texttt{tol} = 0$, an iteration of Algorithm 2.1.1 does not change the partition Π, that is, each $\mathbf{a} \in \pi_i$

2.1. Classical batch *k*-means algorithm

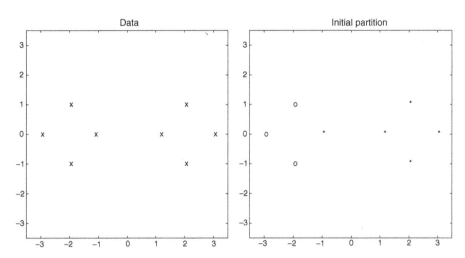

Figure 2.1: Vector set and initial two cluster partition, "zeros" are in the "left" cluster and "dots" are in the "right" cluster.

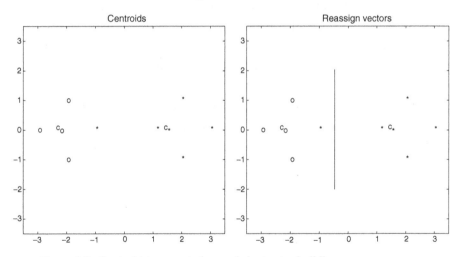

Figure 2.2: Centroids' computation and clusters' rebuilding.

belongs to $\mathcal{H}_{ij}^{-}$, and each $\mathbf{a} \in \pi_j$ belongs to $\mathcal{H}_{ij}^{+}$. If, in addition, we assume that *for each pair of indices i, j either π_i and $\mathcal{H}_{ij}$ or π_j and $\mathcal{H}_{ij}$ are disjoint*, then the following separation result follows.

Lemma 2.1.1. *For each $1 \leq i \neq j \leq k$ one has conv $\{\pi_i\} \cap$ conv $\{\pi_j\} = \emptyset$.*

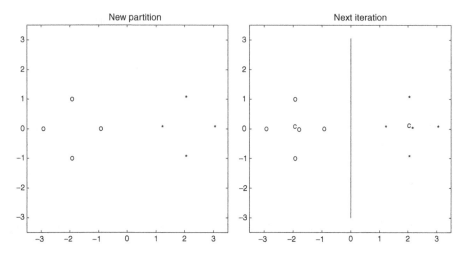

Figure 2.3: New partition generated by a single batch k-means iteration.

Under the "final partition k distinct centroids" assumption the entire space $\mathbf{R}^n$ is subdivided into k regions $\{\mathcal{V}_1, \ldots, \mathcal{V}_k\}$ so that $\mathbf{c}_i$ is the nearest centroid for the elements of $\mathcal{V}_i$. This set of regions is called Voronoi or Dirichlet partition defined by the centroids.

We remark that partitions generated by Algorithm 2.1.1 do not necessarily satisfy the two assumptions needed for Lemma 2.1.1, and may fail to be "separable" (see Example 2.3.1). Partitions generated by Algorithm 2.2.1 introduced in Section 2.2.2 always satisfy these assumptions and are "separable."

Note that there are 2^m possible partitions of the vector set $\mathcal{A} = \{\mathbf{a}_1, \ldots, \mathbf{a}_{m-1}, \mathbf{a}_m\}$ into two clusters. Let $\mathcal{A}^- = \{\mathbf{a}_1, \ldots, \mathbf{a}_{m-1}\}$.

Problem 2.1.4. *Show that*

$$Q(\mathcal{A}^-) = \sum_{i=1}^{m-1} ||\mathbf{c}(\mathcal{A}^-) - \mathbf{a}_i||^2$$

$$= \sum_{i=1}^{m-1} ||\mathbf{c}(\mathcal{A}) - \mathbf{a}_i||^2 - \frac{||\mathbf{c}(\mathcal{A}) - \mathbf{a}_m||^2}{m-1} \leq \sum_{i=1}^{m} ||\mathbf{c}(\mathcal{A}) - \mathbf{a}_i||^2.$$

Note that the right-hand side equals to the left-hand side if and only if $\mathbf{c}(\mathcal{A}) = \mathbf{a}_m$.

2.1. Classical batch k-means algorithm

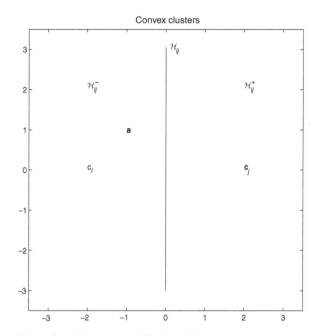

Figure 2.4: Convexity of final partition.

Next we turn to a special case of a scalar data set $\mathcal{A} = \{a_1 < a_2 < \cdots < a_m\}$. Let $\pi_1^l = \{a_1, \ldots, a_l\}$, $\pi_2^l = \{a_{l+1}, \ldots, a_m\}$, $l = 0, \ldots, m$. Due to Problem 2.1.4

$$Q\left(\{\pi_1^1, \pi_2^1\}\right) \le Q\left(\{\pi_1^0, \pi_2^0\}\right).$$

Furthermore, an optimal two cluster partition is $\{\pi_1^l, \pi_2^l\}$ for some $0 < l < m$ (see Figure 2.5).

Problem 2.1.5. *If* $f(l) = Q(\{\pi_1^l, \pi_2^l\})$, *show that*

$$f(0) = f(m), \quad \text{and } f(0) > f(l), l = 1, \ldots, m-1.$$

Problem 2.1.6. *Does the function* f *have additional interesting properties? True or False? If* $\{\pi_1^l, \pi_2^l\}$ *is the optimal partition, then* $x_l \le c(\mathcal{A}) \le x_{l+1}$. *(Building two clusters for scalar data* $\mathcal{A} = \{a_1 < a_2 < \cdots < a_m\}$ *separated by the mean, that is*

$$\pi_1 = \{a \ : \ a \le c(\mathcal{A})\}, \text{ and } \pi_2 = \{a \ : \ a > c(\mathcal{A})\}$$

is suggested in [20]).

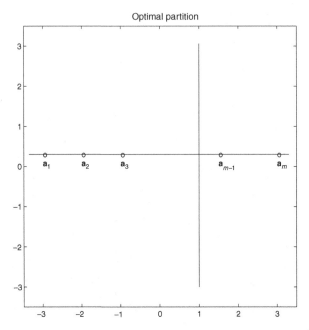

Figure 2.5: Optimal two cluster partition of a scalar data set.

Some prominent drawbacks of the batch k-means algorithm are:

1. The "right" number of clusters k should be supplied.
2. The initial partition $\Pi^{(0)} = \{\pi_1^{(0)}, \ldots, \pi_k^{(0)}\}$ should be supplied.
3. Although the initial partition contains k clusters the number of nonempty clusters in the batch k-means generated final partition may be less than k (see Example 2.1.1 and Figure 2.6).
4. Batch k-means often fails to generate an optimal partition (see Example 2.1.2 and Figure 2.7).

Example 2.1.1. *Consider the scalar data set* $\{-7, -5, -4, 4, 5, 7\}$ *and the initial three cluster partition* $\Pi^{(0)} = \{\pi_1^{(0)}, \pi_2^{(0)}, \pi_3^{(0)}\}$ *with*

$\pi_1^{(0)}$	$\pi_2^{(0)}$	$\pi_3^{(0)}$
$\{-7, -5\}$	$\{-4, 4\}$	$\{5, 7\}$

2.1. Classical batch k-means algorithm

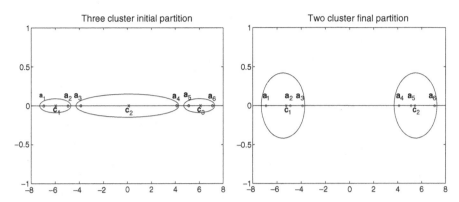

Figure 2.6: Example 2.1.1 provides initial (on the left) and final (on the right) partitions with different number of nonempty clusters.

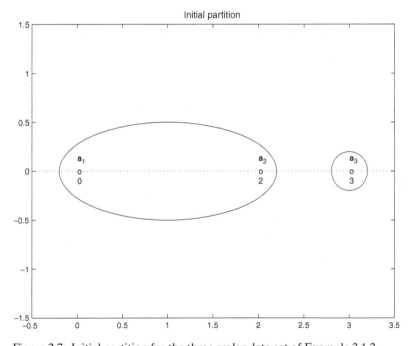

Figure 2.7: Initial partition for the three scalar data set of Example 2.1.2.

An iteration of batch k-means leads to the final partition $\Pi^{(1)} = \{\pi_1^{(1)}, \pi_2^{(1)}, \pi_3^{(1)}\}$, with

$\pi_1^{(1)}$	$\pi_2^{(1)}$	$\pi_3^{(1)}$
$\{-7, -5, -4\}$	$\emptyset$	$\{4, 5, 7\}$

so that the second cluster becomes empty, and the number of nonempty clusters is reduced from three to two.

Example 2.1.2. Consider the three scalar data set $\mathcal{A} = \{0, 2, 3\}$, and the initial partition $\Pi^{(0)} = \{\pi_1^{(0)}, \pi_2^{(0)}\}$ where $\pi_1^{(0)} = \{0, 2\}$, and $\pi_2^{(0)} = \{3\}$. An iteration of the batch k-means algorithm applied to $\Pi^{(0)}$ does not change the partition. On the other hand, the partition $\Pi^{(1)} = \{\{0\}, \{2, 3\}\}$ is superior to $\Pi^{(0)}$. The better partition $\Pi^{(1)}$ is undetected by the algorithm.

Project 2.1.1. Code the batch k-means algorithm. Keeping in mind sparsity of the data use the sparse format (a brief description of the format follows).

A compressed column storage (CCS), which is also called the Harwell-Boeing sparse matrix format, is specified by the arrays *value*, *rowind*, and *pointr*, where:

1. *value* stores the nonzero matrix entries,
2. *rowind* stores the row indices of each nonzero matrix entry (and the first index is 0),
3. *pointr* stores the index of the elements in *value* which start a column of the sparse matrix, the last entry of *pointr* is the total number of nonzero entries.

For example, if the matrix is

$$\begin{bmatrix} 0 & 3 \\ 1 & 2 \\ 7 & 0 \end{bmatrix},$$

then the corresponding arrays are:

1. *value* $\boxed{1\,|\,7\,|\,3\,|\,2}$,

2. *rowind* $\boxed{1\,|\,2\,|\,0\,|\,1}$,

3. *pointr* $\boxed{0\,|\,2\,|\,4}$.

Note that $pointr[i+1] - pointr[i]$ is the number of nonzero entries of column i. It is also convenient to store the matrixsize array that contains the following information.

3	number of rows
2	number of cols
4	number of nonzero entries

2.2. Incremental algorithm

In this section we describe the incremental quadratic k-means algorithm, and develop machinery for merging the batch and incremental versions of the quadratic k-means algorithms (the incremental k-means is introduced in Section 2.2.2). Although the technique of this section is custom tailored to quadratic functions it will become clear in Chapter 8 that analogous results hold for many k-means algorithms with entropy-like distances.

We begin with the following problem: Let $\mathcal{A} = \{\mathbf{a}_1, \ldots, \mathbf{a}_p\}$, $\mathcal{B} = \{\mathbf{b}_1, \ldots, \mathbf{b}_q\}$ be two disjoint vector sets in $\mathbf{R}^n$ with p and q vectors respectively. Express $Q(\mathcal{A} \bigcup \mathcal{B})$ by means of $Q(\mathcal{A})$ and $Q(\mathcal{B})$.

2.2.1. Quadratic functions

We return now to the quadratic function δ given by (2.1.6) for a set of scalars $\{a_1, \ldots, a_m\}$. Note that for each x one has

$$\delta'(x) = 2mx - 2\sum_{i=1}^{m} a_i, \quad \delta''(x) = 2m, \quad \text{and} \quad \frac{d^l}{dx^l}\delta(x) = 0, \; l = 3, 4, \ldots$$

Furthermore for $c = c(\{a_1, \ldots, a_m\})$ and each x one has

$$\sum_{i=1}^{m} |x - a_i|^2 = \delta(x) = \delta(c) + \delta'(x)(x - c) + \frac{1}{2}\delta''(x)(x - c)^2$$

$$= \sum_{i=1}^{m} |c - a_i|^2 + m|c - x|^2. \tag{2.2.1}$$

Applications of (2.2.1) to coordinates $i = 1, 2, \ldots, n$ yield:

$$\sum_{i=1}^{m} ||\mathbf{x} - \mathbf{a}_i||^2 = \sum_{i=1}^{m} ||\mathbf{c} - \mathbf{a}_i||^2 + m ||\mathbf{c} - \mathbf{x}||^2. \tag{2.2.2}$$

This identity, in particular, leads to the following result.

Lemma 2.2.1. *If* $\mathcal{A} = \{\mathbf{a}_1, \ldots, \mathbf{a}_p\}$, $\mathcal{B} = \{\mathbf{b}_1, \ldots, \mathbf{b}_q\}$ *are two disjoint subsets of* $\mathbf{R}^n$, *then*

$$Q\left(\mathcal{A}\bigcup\mathcal{B}\right) = Q(\mathcal{A}) + Q(\mathcal{B}) + p||\mathbf{c} - \mathbf{c}(\mathcal{A})||^2 + q||\mathbf{c} - \mathbf{c}(\mathcal{B})||^2, \tag{2.2.3}$$

where

$$\mathbf{c} = \mathbf{c}\left(\mathcal{A}\bigcup\mathcal{B}\right) = \frac{p}{p+q}\mathbf{c}(\mathcal{A}) + \frac{q}{p+q}\mathbf{c}(\mathcal{B}).$$

Proof:

$$Q\left(\mathcal{A}\bigcup\mathcal{B}\right) = \sum_{i=1}^{p} ||\mathbf{c} - \mathbf{a}_i||^2 + \sum_{i=1}^{q} ||\mathbf{c} - \mathbf{b}_i||^2$$

due to (2.2.2)

$$= \sum_{i=1}^{p} ||\mathbf{c}(\mathcal{A}) - \mathbf{a}_i||^2 + p||\mathbf{c} - \mathbf{c}(\mathcal{A})||^2 + \sum_{i=1}^{q} ||\mathbf{c}(\mathcal{B})$$

$$- \mathbf{b}_i||^2 + q||\mathbf{c} - \mathbf{c}(\mathcal{B})||^2$$

$$= Q(\mathcal{A}) + Q(\mathcal{B}) + p||\mathbf{c} - \mathbf{c}(\mathcal{A})||^2 + q||\mathbf{c} - \mathbf{c}(\mathcal{B})||^2.$$

This completes the proof. $\qquad\square$

2.2. Incremental algorithm

Problem 2.2.1. *Let A and B be two sets as in Lemma 2.2.1. If*

$$p||\mathbf{c} - \mathbf{c}(A)||^2 + q||\mathbf{c} - \mathbf{c}(B)||^2 = \min_{\mathbf{x} \in \mathbf{R}^n} \left\{ p||\mathbf{x} - \mathbf{c}(A)||^2 \right.$$
$$\left. + q||\mathbf{x} - \mathbf{c}(B)||^2 \right\},$$

then $\mathbf{c} = \frac{p}{p+q}\mathbf{c}(A) + \frac{q}{p+q}\mathbf{c}(B)$.

The following result is a corollary of Lemma 2.2.1.

Theorem 2.2.1. *If $A = \pi_1 \cup \pi_2 \cup \cdots \cup \pi_k$ with $m_i = |\pi_i|$ and $\mathbf{c}_i = \mathbf{c}(\pi_i)$, $i = 1, \ldots, k$; then*

$$\mathbf{c} = \mathbf{c}(A) = \frac{m_1}{m}\mathbf{c}_1 + \cdots + \frac{m_k}{m}\mathbf{c}_k, \text{ where } m = m_1 + \cdots + m_k.$$

If $\pi_i \cap \pi_j = \emptyset$ when $i \neq j$, then

$$Q(A) = \sum_{i=1}^{k} Q(\pi_i) + \sum_{i=1}^{k} m_i ||\mathbf{c} - \mathbf{c}_i||^2. \tag{2.2.4}$$

If

$$C = \{\underbrace{\mathbf{c}_1, \ldots, \mathbf{c}_1}_{m_1}, \ldots, \underbrace{\mathbf{c}_k, \ldots, \mathbf{c}_k}_{m_k}\}$$

is the set of centroids counted with appropriate weights, then (2.2.4) leads to the following

$$Q(A) - Q(C) = \sum_{i=1}^{k} Q(\pi_i).$$

We now focus on two special cases of Lemma 2.2.1. First, consider the set $B = \{\mathbf{b}\}$ being a singleton and denote the set $A \cup B = \{\mathbf{a}_1, \ldots, \mathbf{a}_p, \mathbf{b}\}$ by A^+. Due to Lemma 2.2.1 one has

$$Q(A^+) = Q(A) + p||\mathbf{c}(A^+) - \mathbf{c}(A)||^2 + ||\mathbf{c}(A^+) - \mathbf{b}||^2.$$

Keeping in mind that

$$\mathbf{c}(A^+) = \frac{p}{p+1}\mathbf{c}(A) + \frac{1}{p+1}\mathbf{b} \tag{2.2.5}$$

one gets

$$p\,||\mathbf{c}(\mathcal{A}^+) - \mathbf{c}(\mathcal{A})||^2 = \frac{p}{(p+1)^2}||\mathbf{c}(\mathcal{A}) - \mathbf{b}||^2$$

and

$$||\mathbf{c}(\mathcal{A}^+) - \mathbf{b}||^2 = \frac{p^2}{(p+1)^2}||\mathbf{c}(\mathcal{A}) - \mathbf{b}||^2$$

and finally

$$Q(\mathcal{A}^+) = Q(\mathcal{A}) + \frac{p}{p+1}||\mathbf{c}(\mathcal{A}) - \mathbf{b}||^2. \tag{2.2.6}$$

Next consider the set $\mathcal{B} = \{\mathbf{b}_1, \ldots, \mathbf{b}_{q-1}, \mathbf{b}_q\}$, remove vector $\mathbf{b}_q$ from $\mathcal{B}$, and denote the resulting set $\{\mathbf{b}_1, \ldots, \mathbf{b}_{q-1}\}$ by $\mathcal{B}^-$. An application of Lemma 2.2.1 yields:

$$Q(\mathcal{B}) = Q(\mathcal{B}^-) + (q-1)||\mathbf{c}(\mathcal{B}) - \mathbf{c}(\mathcal{B}^-)||^2 + ||\mathbf{c}(\mathcal{B}) - \mathbf{b}_q||^2.$$

Keeping in mind that

$$\mathbf{c}(\mathcal{B}^-) = \frac{q}{q-1}\mathbf{c}(\mathcal{B}) - \frac{1}{q-1}\mathbf{b}_q \tag{2.2.7}$$

one gets

$$(q-1)\,||\mathbf{c}(\mathcal{B}) - \mathbf{c}(\mathcal{B}^-)||^2 = \frac{1}{q-1}||\mathbf{c}(\mathcal{B}) - \mathbf{b}_q||^2$$

and

$$Q(\mathcal{B}) = Q(\mathcal{B}^-) + \frac{q}{q-1}||\mathbf{c}(\mathcal{B}) - \mathbf{b}_q||^2. \tag{2.2.8}$$

Remark 2.2.1. *Note that $\mathcal{B} = (\mathcal{B}^-)^+$ and due to (2.2.6)*

$$Q(\mathcal{B}) = Q((\mathcal{B}^-)^+) = Q(\mathcal{B}^-) + \frac{q-1}{q}||\mathbf{c}(\mathcal{B}^-) - \mathbf{b}_q||^2.$$

Due to (2.2.7) the expression $\mathbf{c}(\mathcal{B}^-) - \mathbf{b}_q$ can be substituted by $\frac{q}{q-1}[\mathbf{c}(\mathcal{B}) - \mathbf{b}_q]$. The substitution leads to (2.2.8).

Formula (2.2.6) and formula (2.2.8) lead to the following result.

Theorem 2.2.2. *Let* $\mathcal{A} = \{\mathbf{a}_1, \ldots, \mathbf{a}_p\}$, $\mathcal{B} = \{\mathbf{b}_1, \ldots, \mathbf{b}_q\}$ *are two disjoint subsets of* $\mathbf{R}^n$. *If* $\mathcal{A}^+ = \{\mathbf{a}_1, \ldots, \mathbf{a}_p, \mathbf{b}_q\}$, *and* $\mathcal{B}^- = \{\mathbf{b}_1, \ldots, \mathbf{b}_{q-1}\}$, *then*

$$[Q(\mathcal{A}) - Q(\mathcal{A}^+)] + [Q(\mathcal{B}) - Q(\mathcal{B}^-)] = \frac{q}{q-1} ||\mathbf{c}(\mathcal{B}) - \mathbf{b}_q||^2$$
$$- \frac{p}{p+1} ||\mathbf{c}(\mathcal{A}) - \mathbf{b}_q||^2. \qquad (2.2.9)$$

The expression (2.2.9) is the change in the objective function $Q(\mathcal{A}, \mathcal{B}) - Q(\mathcal{A}^+, \mathcal{B}^-)$ caused by removal of $\mathbf{b}_q$ from $\mathcal{B}$ and assignment of this vector to $\mathcal{A}$.

2.2.2. Incremental *k*-means algorithm

Motivated by Example 2.1.2 we now focus on formula (2.2.9). The decision whether a vector $\mathbf{a} \in \pi_i$ should be moved from cluster π_i with m_i vectors to cluster π_j with m_j vectors is made by the batch *k*-means algorithm based on examination of the expression $||\mathbf{c}(\pi_i) - \mathbf{a}|| - ||\mathbf{c}(\pi_j) - \mathbf{a}||$. The positive sign of

$$\Delta_k = ||\mathbf{c}(\pi_i) - \mathbf{a}||^2 - ||\mathbf{c}(\pi_j) - \mathbf{a}||^2,$$

may trigger the move. As (2.2.9) shows the change in the value of the objective function caused by the move is

$$\Delta = \frac{m_i}{m_i - 1} ||\mathbf{c}(\pi_i) - \mathbf{a}||^2 - \frac{m_j}{m_j + 1} ||\mathbf{c}(\pi_j) - \mathbf{a}||^2.$$

The difference between the expressions

$$\Delta - \Delta_k = \frac{1}{m_i - 1} ||\mathbf{c}(\pi_i) - \mathbf{a}||^2 + \frac{1}{m_j + 1} ||\mathbf{c}(\pi_j) - \mathbf{a}||^2 \geq 0 \quad (2.2.10)$$

is negligible when the clusters π_i and π_j are large. However, $\Delta - \Delta_k$ may become significant for small clusters. In particular, it is possible that Δ_k is negative, and the batch *k*-means iteration leaves $\mathbf{a}$ in cluster π_i. At the same time the value of Δ is positive, and reassigning $\mathbf{a}$ to π_j would decrease Q. Indeed, for the data set in Example 2.1.2 and $\mathbf{a} = \mathbf{a}_2$ one has

$$\Delta_k = ||\mathbf{c}_1 - \mathbf{a}_2||^2 - ||\mathbf{c}_2 - \mathbf{a}_2||^2 = 1 - 1 = 0,$$

and

$$\Delta = \frac{2}{1}\|\mathbf{c}_1 - \mathbf{a}_2\|^2 - \frac{1}{2}\|\mathbf{c}_2 - \mathbf{a}_2\|^2 = 2 - \frac{1}{2} = \frac{3}{2}.$$

This remark suggests a refinement of the batch k-means algorithm that incorporates the incremental step. This incremental step is formally introduced next.

Definition 2.2.1. *A first variation of a partition Π is a partition Π' obtained from Π by removing a single vector $\mathbf{a}$ from a cluster π_i of Π and assigning this vector to an existing cluster π_j of Π.*

Note, that:

1. The partition Π is a first variation of itself.
2. A first variation iteration (as well as an iteration of the k-means algorithm) may decrease the number of clusters in the partition. However, due to (2.2.6), first variation does this rarely.

Definition 2.2.2. *The partition* $\mathtt{nextFV}(\Pi)$ *is a first variation of Π so that for each first variation Π' one has*

$$Q(\mathtt{nextFV}(\Pi)) \le Q(\Pi'). \qquad (2.2.11)$$

The refinement of the batch k-means algorithm, which we shall refer to simply as the k-means clustering algorithm, is given next.

Algorithm 2.2.1 (The k-means clustering algorithm). *For a user supplied nonnegative tolerances* $\mathtt{tol_B}$ *and* $\mathtt{tol_I}$ *do the following:*

1. *Start with an arbitrary partitioning $\Pi^{(0)} = \{\pi_1^{(0)}, \ldots, \pi_k^{(0)}\}$. Set the index of iteration $t = 0$.*

2. *Generate the partition* $\mathtt{nextBKM}(\Pi^{(t)})$.
   if $[Q(\Pi^{(t)}) - Q(\mathtt{nextBKM}(\Pi^{(t)})) > \mathtt{tol_B}]$
       set $\Pi^{(t+1)} = \mathtt{nextBKM}(\Pi^{(t)})$
       increment t by 1.
       go to 2

3. *Generate the partition* $\texttt{nextFV}(\Pi^{(t)})$.
   $$if\,[Q(\Pi^{(t)}) - Q(\texttt{nextFV}(\Pi^{(t)})) > \texttt{tol}_I]$$
   set $\Pi^{(t+1)} = \texttt{nextFV}(\Pi^{(t)})$.
   increment t by 1.
   go to 2

4. *Stop.*

The above described "merger" of the batch and incremental versions of the k-means algorithm enjoys speed of the batch version and accuracy of the incremental version. We next apply Algorithm 2.2.1 to the initial partition provided in Example 2.1.2.

Example 2.2.1. *A single iteration of the first variation applied to* $\Pi^{(0)} = \{\{0, 2\}, \{3\}\}$ *generates the optimal partition* $\Pi^{(1)} = \{\pi_1^{(1)}, \pi_2^{(1)}\}$ *with* $\pi_1^{(1)} = \{0\}$, $\pi_2^{(1)} = \{2, 3\}$ *(see Figure 2.8).*

Note that all numerical computations associated with Step 3 of Algorithm 2.2.1 have been already performed at Step 2 (see (2.2.9)). The improvement over batch k-means comes, therefore, at virtually no additional computational expense.

Problem 2.2.2. *Show that the k-means clustering algorithm does not necessarily lead to the optimal partition.*

Problem 2.2.3. *Assume that the data set $\mathcal{A}$ contains two identical vectors* $\mathbf{a}' = \mathbf{a}''$.

1. *True or False? If* $\Pi = \{\pi_1, \ldots, \pi_k\}$ *is a k-means stable partition (see Definition 2.3.1),* $\mathbf{a}' \in \pi'$, $\mathbf{a}'' \in \pi''$, *and at least one of the clusters* π', π'' *is not a singleton, then* $\pi' = \pi''$.
2. *Show that the above result does not necessarily hold when k-means is substituted by* batch k-means. *In other words give an example of a data set $\mathcal{A}$ with identical vectors and an initial partition* $\Pi^{(0)}$ *so that application of the* batch k-means *to* $\Pi^{(0)}$ *generates a final partition in which identical vectors are assigned to different clusters.*

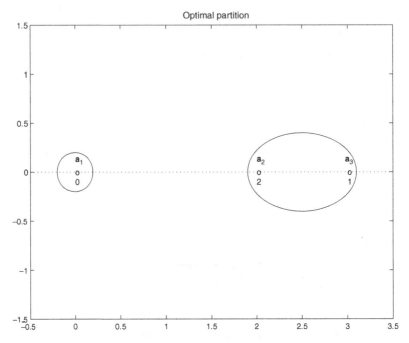

Figure 2.8: Optimal two cluster partition.

Throughout the book we assume that the data set contains distinct vectors only. This assumption does not hold in many practical applications. Assume that the data set $\mathcal{A}$ contains $w_i > 0$ "copies" of $\mathbf{a}_i$ (here w_i is just a positive scalar).

Problem 2.2.4. *Show that the solution* $\mathbf{c}(\mathcal{A})$ *to the problem*

$$\min_{\mathbf{x} \in \mathbf{R}^n} \sum_{i=1}^{m} w_i \|\mathbf{x} - \mathbf{a}_i\|^2, \ w_i > 0$$

is given by the arithmetic mean, that is

$$\mathbf{c}(\mathcal{A}) = \frac{1}{w} \sum w_i \mathbf{a}_i, \ where \ w = w_1 + \cdots + w_m.$$

Problem 2.2.5. *Let* $\pi = \{\mathbf{a}_1, \ldots, \mathbf{a}_p\}$, *with exactly* w_i *copies of* $\mathbf{a}_i$, $i = 1, \ldots, p$. *Suppose that* π^+ *is a cluster obtained from* π *by assigning* w'

28

copies of vector $\mathbf{a}'$ *to* π. *Show that*

$$Q(\pi^+) = Q(\pi) + \frac{w'w}{w + w'}\|\mathbf{c} - \mathbf{a}'\|^2, \text{ where } w = w_1 + \cdots + w_p.$$
(2.2.12)

Problem 2.2.6. *Let* $\pi = \{\mathbf{a}_1, \ldots, \mathbf{a}_{p-1}, \mathbf{a}'\}$, *with exactly* w_i *copies of* $\mathbf{a}_i$, $i = 1, \ldots, p - 1$ *and* w' *copies of* $\mathbf{a}'$. *Suppose that* π^- *is a cluster obtained from* π *by removing* w' *copies of vector* $\mathbf{a}'$ *from* π. *Use Problem 2.2.5 to show that*

$$Q\left(\pi^-\right) = Q(\pi) - \frac{w'w}{w - w'}\|\mathbf{c} - \mathbf{a}'\|^2, \text{ where } w = w_1 + \cdots + w_{p-1} + w'.$$
(2.2.13)

Problem 2.2.7. *True or False? Let* Π *be a two cluster partition* $\{\pi_1, \pi_2\}$ *of the data set* $\mathcal{A}$ *such that* $w' > 0$ *copies of* $\mathbf{a}$ *belong to* π_1, $w'' > 0$ *copies of* $\mathbf{a}$ *belong to* π_2, $\|\mathbf{c}(\pi_1) - \mathbf{a}\| = \|\mathbf{c}(\pi_2) - \mathbf{a}\|$, *and* π_1 *contains vectors other than* $\mathbf{a}$. *Let* Π' *be a two cluster partition* $\{\pi_1^-, \pi_2^+\}$ *obtained from* Π *by removing* w' *copies of* $\mathbf{a}$ *from* π_1 *and assigning them to* π_2. *Show that* $Q(\Pi) > Q(\Pi')$.

2.3. Quadratic k-means: summary

This section presents results of numerical experiments that illustrate the difference between the batch k-means algorithm, and the k-means algorithm (that combines batch and incremental iterations). We discuss properties of partitions generated by the two algorithms. Finally, we attempt to introduce an objective function *dependent* distance on the set of partitions generated by the k-means clustering algorithm.

2.3.1. Numerical experiments with quadratic k-means

The numerical experiments presented below compare performance of the batch k-means algorithm (Algorithm 2.1.1) to those of the k-means clustering algorithm (Algorithm 2.2.1). Both algorithms are applied to the same initial partitions. The initial partitions are generated by

Table 2.1: Medlars Collection: 1033 vectors of dimension 300

Algorithm	Input parameters	# of clusters	Q	Improvement
PDDP	cluster size ≤ 25	63	706.62	0%
batch *k*-means	$\mathtt{tol} = 0.005$	63	671.68	5%
k-means	$\mathtt{tol} = 0.005$	63	642.89	8%

Table 2.2: Cranfield Collection: 1398 vectors of dimension 100

Algorithm	Input parameters	# of clusters	Q	Improvement
PDDP	cluster size ≤ 25	79	777.47	0%
batch *k*-means	$\mathtt{tol} = 0.005$	79	711.09	8%
k-means	$\mathtt{tol} = 0.005$	79	688.32	11%

the Principal Direction Divisive Partitioning (PDDP, to be discussed in Section 5.1) with the maximal cluster size 25. We run the experiments on Medlars Collection and Cranfield Collection (available from http://www.cs.utk.edu/~lsi/). As a reference point we use the quality of partition generated by PDDP. A percentage of the decrease in the objective function Q is reported under "improvement" in Tables 2.1–2.3. In all the experiments we set $\mathtt{tol_B} = \mathtt{tol_I}$, and denote the tolerance by $\mathtt{tol}$.

In the next experiment we increase the vector space model dimension from 100 to 400, recompute vectors for the Cranfield Collection documents and run both algorithms on the initial partition generated by PDDP for 1398 Cranfield Collection vectors of dimension 100 (the quality of the initial partition Q is recomputed for vectors of dimension 400).

The results show that in all three cases Algorithm 2.2.1 outperforms Algorithm 2.1.1.

To underline the performance difference we also apply the algorithms to three clusters randomly generated from a document collection combining Medlars, CISI, and Cranfield Collections (total of

2.3. Quadratic k-means: summary

Table 2.3: Cranfield Collection: 1398 vectors of dimension 400

Algorithm	Input parameters	# of clusters	Q	Improvement
PDDP	cluster size ≤ 25	79	946.65	0%
batch k-means	`tol` $= 0.005$	79	880.69	7%
k-means	`tol` $= 0.005$	79	842.72	11%

3891 documents) with 600 "best" terms selected (see [37] for selection procedure details). The iteration statistics is reported below:

1. batch k-means (Algorithm 2.1.1) stops after 10 iterations,
2. k-means (Algorithm 2.2.1) stops after 1149 batch iterations and 984 first variation iterations.

Since an incremental iteration is executed only after a "failed" batch iteration the number of "successful" batch iterations performed by the k-means algorithm is only $1149 - 984 = 165$ (i.e., we observe batch iterations following a sequence of incremental iterations). Needless to say that the algorithms generate very different final partitions.

2.3.2. Stable partitions

We start with an illustrative example.

Example 2.3.1. *Let $\mathcal{A}$ be a four vector subset of $\mathbf{R}^2$ (see Figure 2.9)*

$$\mathbf{a}_1 = \begin{bmatrix} 1 \\ 0 \end{bmatrix}, \quad \mathbf{a}_2 = \begin{bmatrix} 0 \\ 1 \end{bmatrix}, \quad \mathbf{a}_3 = \begin{bmatrix} -1 \\ 0 \end{bmatrix}, \quad and \; \mathbf{a}_4 = \begin{bmatrix} 0 \\ -1 \end{bmatrix}.$$

An application of a batch k-means iteration to the two cluster partition

$$\Pi = \{\pi_1, \pi_2\} \; with \; \pi_1 = \{\mathbf{a}_1, \mathbf{a}_3\}, \quad and \; \pi_2 = \{\mathbf{a}_2, \mathbf{a}_4\} \qquad (2.3.1)$$

does not change Π. At the same time removal of $\mathbf{a}_2$ from π_2 and assignment of $\mathbf{a}_2$ to π_1 leads to a better quality partition. In particular, an application of Algorithm 2.2.1 does change Π and leads to the partition $\Pi' = \{\{\mathbf{a}_1, \mathbf{a}_2\}, \{\mathbf{a}_3, \mathbf{a}_4\}\}$.

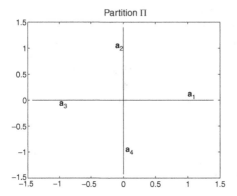

Figure 2.9: Batch *k*-means stable partition.

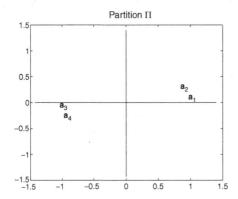

Figure 2.10: Batch *k*-means stable partition.

Moreover, even when

$$\mathcal{A} = \left\{ \mathbf{a}_1 = \begin{bmatrix} 1 \\ 0 \end{bmatrix}, \quad \mathbf{a}_2 = \begin{bmatrix} \cos\left(\frac{\pi}{12}\right) \\ \sin\left(\frac{\pi}{12}\right) \end{bmatrix}, \quad \mathbf{a}_3 = \begin{bmatrix} -1 \\ 0 \end{bmatrix}, \right.$$

$$\left. \text{and } \mathbf{a}_4 = \begin{bmatrix} \cos\left(\frac{13\pi}{12}\right) \\ \sin\left(\frac{13\pi}{12}\right) \end{bmatrix} \right\}$$

batch *k*-means does not change the two cluster partition $\Pi = \{\{\mathbf{a}_1, \mathbf{a}_3\}, \{\mathbf{a}_2, \mathbf{a}_4\}\}$ (see Figure 2.10).

This example motivates the following definition.

Definition 2.3.1. *Let* CA *be a clustering algorithm. A partition* Π *is called* CA *stable if an application of* CA *to* Π *does not change* Π.

It is clear that partition Π in Example 2.3.1 is batch k-means stable, and not incremental k-means stable.

Consider now a two cluster partition $\Pi = \{\pi_1, \pi_2\}$ so that $|\pi_1| = q > 1$ and $|\pi_2| = p \geq 1$. Assume that $\mathbf{c}(\pi_1) = \mathbf{c}(\pi_2) = \mathbf{c}$, pick $\mathbf{a} \in \pi_1$ so that $\mathbf{a} \neq \mathbf{c}$, and build a partition $\Pi' = \{\pi_1^-, \pi_2^+\}$ by removing $\mathbf{a}$ from π_1 and assigning it to π_2. Due to (2.2.9) one has

$$Q(\Pi') = Q(\Pi) - \left[\frac{q}{q-1} - \frac{p}{p+1}\right] \|\mathbf{c} - \mathbf{a}\|^2 < Q(\Pi).$$

This shows that when $\mathbf{c}(\pi_1) = \mathbf{c}(\pi_2) = \mathbf{c}$ the partition Π may not be k-means stable, and centroids $\mathbf{c}(\pi_1), \mathbf{c}(\pi_2)$ of a stable k-means two cluster partition $\Pi = \{\pi_1, \pi_2\}$ with $|\pi_1| > 1$ do not coincide.

Since the assumption $\mathbf{a}_i \neq \mathbf{a}_j$ when $i \neq j$ holds throughout the text the result does not depend on the assumption $|\pi_1| > 1$. Indeed, if $p = q = 1$, then the clusters are singletons, and $\mathbf{c}(\pi_1) \neq \mathbf{c}(\pi_2)$. If at least one cluster, say π_1, contains more than one vector, then the choice of a vector different from the centroid $\mathbf{c}(\pi_1)$ is possible. The above discussion leads to the following result.

Lemma 2.3.1. *If* $\Pi = \{\pi_1, \pi_2\}$ *is k-means stable, then* $\mathbf{c}(\pi_1) \neq \mathbf{c}(\pi_2)$.

Generalization of this result to the case of k cluster partition is straightforward.

Theorem 2.3.1. *If* $\Pi = \{\pi_1, \dots, \pi_k\}$ *is k-means stable, then* $\mathbf{c}(\pi_i) \neq \mathbf{c}(\pi_j)$ *when* $i \neq j$.

This result implies that conv $\pi_i \cap$ conv $\pi_j = \emptyset$ when $i \neq j$ (the details of the proof are left to the reader as an exercise, see Lemma 2.1.1).

Definition 2.3.2. *A partition* Π_{12} *is a product of a p cluster partition* $\Pi_1 = \{\pi_1^1, \dots, \pi_p^1\}$ *and a q cluster partition* $\Pi_2 = \{\pi_1^2, \dots, \pi_q^2\}$ *if clusters* *of Π_{12} are all nonempty intersections $\pi_i^1 \cap \pi_j^2$ of clusters from Π_1 and Π_2.*

Example 2.3.2. *Let $\mathcal{A} = \{\mathbf{a}_1, \ldots, \mathbf{a}_8\} \subset \mathbf{R}^2$ where the first four vectors are the same as in Example 2.3.1, and $\mathbf{a}_{4+i} = \mathbf{a}_i + [\begin{smallmatrix} 3 \\ 0 \end{smallmatrix}], i = 1, \ldots, 4$. If*

$$\Pi_1 = \{\{\mathbf{a}_1, \mathbf{a}_2, \mathbf{a}_3, \mathbf{a}_4\}, \{\mathbf{a}_5, \mathbf{a}_7\}, \{\mathbf{a}_6, \mathbf{a}_8\}\}$$

and

$$\Pi_2 = \{\{\mathbf{a}_5, \mathbf{a}_6, \mathbf{a}_7, \mathbf{a}_8\}, \{\mathbf{a}_1, \mathbf{a}_3\}, \{\mathbf{a}_2, \mathbf{a}_4\}\},$$

then

$$\Pi_{12} = \{\{\mathbf{a}_1, \mathbf{a}_3\}, \{\mathbf{a}_2, \mathbf{a}_4\}, \{\mathbf{a}_5, \mathbf{a}_7\}, \{\mathbf{a}_6, \mathbf{a}_8\}\}$$

with $Q(\Pi_1) = Q(\Pi_2) = Q(\Pi_{12}) = 4$.

Theorem 2.2.1 implies $Q(\Pi_1) - Q(\Pi_{12}) \geq 0$. The next result provides sufficient conditions for strict inequality.

Theorem 2.3.2. *Let $\Pi_1 = \{\pi_1^1, \ldots, \pi_p^1\}$ and $\Pi_2 = \{\pi_1^2, \ldots, \pi_q^2\}$ be two k-means stable partitions of the data set $\mathcal{A}$. If $\Pi_1 \neq \Pi_{12}$, then $Q(\Pi_1) - Q(\Pi_{12}) > 0$.*

Proof: Since $\Pi_1 \neq \Pi_{12}$ there is $\pi_l^1 \in \Pi_1$ that is not entirely contained in a single cluster of Π_2, that is, there are two clusters π_i^2 and π_j^2 so that

$$\pi_l^1 \cap \pi_i^2 \neq \emptyset \quad \text{and} \quad \pi_l^1 \cap \pi_j^2 \neq \emptyset.$$

Due to Theorem 2.3.1 one has $\mathbf{c}(\pi_i^2) \neq \mathbf{c}(\pi_j^2)$, and there is a hyperplane $\mathcal{H}_{ij}$ that separates the space into two disjoint half spaces $\mathcal{H}_{ij}^-$ and $\mathcal{H}_{ij}^+$ so that

$$\pi_l^1 \cap \pi_i^2 \subseteq \pi_i^2 \subset \mathcal{H}_{ij}^- \quad \text{and} \quad \pi_l^1 \cap \pi_j^2 \subseteq \pi_j^2 \subset \mathcal{H}_{ij}^+.$$

This yields $\mathbf{c}(\pi_l^1 \cap \pi_i^2) \in \mathcal{H}_{ij}^-$, and $\mathbf{c}(\pi_l^1 \cap \pi_j^2) \in \mathcal{H}_{ij}^+$. In particular, $\mathbf{c}(\pi_l^1 \cap \pi_i^2) \neq \mathbf{c}(\pi_l^1 \cap \pi_j^2)$, and at least one of the centroids is different from $\mathbf{c}(\pi_l^1)$. To simplify the presentation we assume that

$\mathbf{c}(\pi_l^1) \neq \mathbf{c}(\pi_l^1 \cap \pi_i^2)$. To complete the proof we use Theorem 2.2.1 to obtain

$$Q(\Pi_1) - Q(\Pi_{12}) = \sum_{r=1}^{p} \left[\sum_{s=1}^{q} |\pi_r^1 \cap \pi_s^2| \cdot \left\| \mathbf{c}(\pi_r^1) - \mathbf{c}(\pi_r^1 \cap \pi_s^2) \right\|^2 \right]$$

$$\geq |\pi_l^1 \cap \pi_i^2| \cdot \left\| \mathbf{c}(\pi_l^1) - \mathbf{c}(\pi_l^1 \cap \pi_i^2) \right\|^2 > 0.$$

The proof is now completed. □

The above discussion motivates introduction of the "distance" $d(\Pi_1, \Pi_2)$ between two k-means stable partitions Π_1 and Π_2 as follows:

$$d(\Pi_1, \Pi_2) = [Q(\Pi_1) - Q(\Pi_{12})] + [Q(\Pi_2) - Q(\Pi_{12})].$$

Note that if Π_1 and Π_2 are k-means stable partitions, then:

1. $d(\Pi_1, \Pi_2) \geq 0$, and $d(\Pi_1, \Pi_2) = 0$ if and only if $\Pi_1 = \Pi_2$.
2. $d(\Pi_1, \Pi_2) = d(\Pi_2, \Pi_1)$.

Problem 2.3.1. *Use Theorem 2.3.2 to prove the first distance property listed above.*

Problem 2.3.2. *Investigate whether or not the triangle inequality holds for three k-means stable partitions Π_1, Π_2, and Π_3.*

2.3.3. Quadratic k-means

We conclude discussion of the classical k-means algorithm by noticing that Algorithm 2.2.1 can be applied also in the case when centroids are defined as geometric objects other than vectors. For example, for a vector $\mathbf{a}$ and a line $\mathbf{l}$ denote by $d(\mathbf{l}, \mathbf{a})$ the shortest distance from the vector $\mathbf{a}$ to the line $\mathbf{l}$. Define the "distance" from the set $\mathcal{A} = \{\mathbf{a}_1, \ldots, \mathbf{a}_m\}$ to the line $\mathbf{l}$ as

$$\sum_{i=1}^{m} d(\mathbf{l}, \mathbf{a}_i). \tag{2.3.2}$$

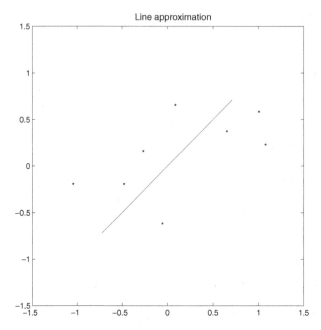

Figure 2.11: Multidimensional data set and "centroid."

Define now centroid $\mathbf{c} = \mathbf{c}(\mathcal{A})$ as a line in $\mathbf{R}^n$ so that

$$\sum_{i=1}^{m} d(\mathbf{c}, \mathbf{a}_i) \leq \sum_{i=1}^{m} d(\mathbf{l}, \mathbf{a}_i) \text{ for each line } \mathbf{l} \text{ in } \mathbf{R}^n \qquad (2.3.3)$$

(see Figure 2.11). This definition can be extended to affine subspaces of any dimension. Approximation of a vector set by a one-dimensional line leads to a very fast clustering algorithm (to be discussed in detail in Section 5.3.1).

Finally, we note that the quadratic quality $Q(\Pi)$ of the partition $\Pi = \{\pi_1, \ldots, \pi_k\}$ can be written in the form

$$Q(\Pi) = \sum_{i=1}^{k}\sum_{\mathbf{a}\in\pi_i} \|\mathbf{c}_i - \mathbf{a}\|^2 = \sum_{i=1}^{k}\sum_{\mathbf{a}\in\pi_i} (\mathbf{a} - \mathbf{c}_i)^T(\mathbf{a} - \mathbf{c}_i) = \sum_{i=1}^{k}\sum_{\mathbf{a}\in\pi_i} (\mathbf{a} - \mathbf{c}_i)^T\mathbf{a}$$

$$= \sum_{\mathbf{a}\in\mathcal{A}} \|\mathbf{a}\|^2 - \sum_{i=1}^{k}\sum_{\mathbf{a}\in\pi_i} \mathbf{a}^T\mathbf{c}_i.$$

36

Hence the problem of *minimizing* $Q(\Pi)$ can be stated as the problem of finding a partition Π that *maximizes* the quality function

$$\sum_{i=1}^{k} \sum_{\mathbf{a} \in \pi_i} \mathbf{a}^T \mathbf{c}_i \text{ subject to } \mathbf{c}_i = \frac{1}{|\pi_i|} \sum_{\mathbf{a} \in \pi_i} \mathbf{a}.$$

For a set $\pi = \{\mathbf{a}_1, \ldots, \mathbf{a}_p\}$ we denote $\|\sum_{\mathbf{a} \in \pi} \mathbf{a}\|$ by a and observe that if centroid of π is defined as a solution of the *maximization* problem

$$\mathbf{c} = \arg\max \left\{ \sum_{\mathbf{a} \in \pi} \mathbf{a}^T \mathbf{x} : \mathbf{x} \in \mathbf{R}^n, \ \|\mathbf{x}\| = \frac{a}{p} \right\}, \qquad (2.3.4)$$

then $\mathbf{c} = \frac{1}{p} \sum_{\mathbf{a} \in \pi} \mathbf{a}$. This observation motivates a clustering algorithm introduced in Chapter 4.

2.4. Spectral relaxation

While k-means outperforms batch k-means it is worth exploring how far from optimal partitions generated by the clustering algorithms might be. While $\Pi^{\min}$ and $Q(\Pi^{\min})$ are not available we can obtain a lower bound for $Q(\Pi^{\min})$. Let $\Pi = \{\pi_1, \ldots, \pi_k\}$ be a k-cluster partition of the data set $\mathcal{A} = \{\mathbf{a}_1, \ldots, \mathbf{a}_m\}$. Rearranging the vectors in $\mathcal{A}$ if needed we assume that the first $m_1 = |\pi_1|$ vectors $\mathbf{a}_1, \ldots, \mathbf{a}_{m_1}$ belong to cluster π_1, the next $m_2 = |\pi_2|$ vectors belong to cluster π_2 and so on. A straightforward computation leads to the following formula

$$Q(\Pi) = \text{trace}(A^T A) - \text{trace}(Y^T A^T A Y),$$

where

$$Y = \begin{bmatrix} \frac{\mathbf{e}_{m_1}}{\sqrt{m_1}} & \cdots & \cdots & \\ \cdots & \frac{\mathbf{e}_{m_2}}{\sqrt{m_2}} & \cdots & \cdots \\ \cdots & \cdots & \cdots & \cdots \\ \cdots & \cdots & \cdots & \frac{\mathbf{e}_{m_k}}{\sqrt{m_k}} \end{bmatrix}. \qquad (2.4.5)$$

To minimize $Q(\Pi)$ one has to maximize $\text{trace}(Y^T A^T A Y)$ over matrices Y given by (2.4.5). We note that $Y^T Y = I_k$, substitute special matrices given by (2.4.5) by orthonormal matrices, and consider a relaxed problem

$$\max\{\text{trace}(Y^T A^T A Y) \; : \; Y^T Y = I_k\}. \tag{2.4.6}$$

Solution to this problem is given by the next statement.

Theorem 2.4.1. (Ky Fan). *If H is a symmetric matrix with eigenvalues*

$$\lambda_1 \geq \lambda_2 \geq \cdots \geq \lambda_n,$$

then

$$\max_{Y^T Y = I_k} \text{trace}(Y^T H Y) = \lambda_1 + \lambda_2 + \cdots + \lambda_k.$$

This result immediately leads to a lower bound for $Q(\Pi^{\min})$:

$$Q(\Pi^{\min}) \geq \text{trace}(A^T A) - \max_{Y^T Y = I_k} \text{trace}(Y^T A^T A Y)$$

$$= \sum_{i=k+1}^{\min\{m,n\}} \sigma_i^2(A).$$

2.5. Bibliographic notes

For discussion of means see, for example, the classical monograph [67], and [13, 132]. The classical "quadratic" batch k-means algorithm is attributed to [57], the problem is mentioned already in the work of Hugo Steinhaus [125]. The incremental version of the algorithm is discussed in [47] and the combination of the two versions is described in [66, 78, 145]. The idea of changing cluster affiliation for a subset of the data set A only as well as modification of the objective function that penalizes partitions with large number of clusters is also discussed in [78].

The compressed column storage format (CCS), which is also called the Harwell-Boeing sparse matrix format is given in [49]. For an *objective function independent* distance on the set of partitions of a given data set A see [104].

Approximation of a vector set by a line leads to very fast clustering algorithm introduced in [20] (this algorithm is discussed in detail in Section 5.3.1). A centroid of a vector set $\mathcal{A} \subset \mathbf{R}^n$ that is an affine subspace of $\mathbf{R}^n$ is discussed in [23], a representative of a set of categorical objects ("mode of a set") is defined in [70]. Representation of a cluster by a solution of an optimization problem goes back to work of Diday (see, e.g., [42, 43]).

Computational shortcuts to accelerate the batch k-means algorithm with a distance–like function $d(\mathbf{x}, \mathbf{y})$ that satisfies the triangle inequality are discussed in [53] and references therein. Speeding up k-means clustering by bootstrap techniques is suggested in [30]. Additional k-means acceleration ideas are reported, for example, in [111].

The exposition of spectral relaxation follows [143]. For complexity of clustering problems consult, for example [25].

3 BIRCH

Many clustering algorithms, including k-means, require an access to the entire data set. When the data set is very large and does not fit into available memory one has to "squash" the dataset to make applications of k-means-like algorithms possible. The Balanced Iterative Reducing and Clustering algorithm (BIRCH) is a clustering algorithm designed to operate under the assumption "the amount of memory available is limited, whereas the dataset can be arbitrary large" [147]. The algorithm does the "squashing," or generates "a compact dataset summary" minimizing I/O cost involved in clustering the dataset. BIRCH thus reduces the problem of clustering the original very large data set into the one of clustering the set of "summaries" which has the potential to be much smaller. In the next section we briefly describe the basic idea behind BIRCH, and then use this idea to describe a version of k-means that can be applied to partitions generated by BIRCH.

3.1. Balanced iterative reducing and clustering algorithm

For a data set $\mathcal{A} = \{\mathbf{a}_1, \ldots, \mathbf{a}_m\}$ too large to fit into the available computer memory consider a partition $\Pi = \{\pi_1, \ldots, \pi_M\}$ of $\mathcal{A}$. We would like to consider each cluster $\pi_i \in \Pi$ as a single "feature" in such a way that for each subset of p clusters $\pi_{i_1}, \ldots, \pi_{i_p}$ in Π computation of

$$Q(\pi_{i_1} \cup \cdots \cup \pi_{i_p}) \tag{3.1.1}$$

41

is possible. The question now is: "what information concerning the partition Π is needed to compute (3.1.1)?" The answer to this question is provided by Theorem 2.2.1. Indeed, if for $i = 1, \ldots, M$

1. $m_i = |\pi_i|$ the size of π_i,
2. $q_i = Q(\pi_i)$ the quality of π_i,
3. $\mathbf{b}_i = \mathbf{c}(\pi_i) = \frac{1}{m_i} \sum_{\mathbf{a} \in \pi_i} \mathbf{a}$ the centroid of π_i,

then

$$Q\left(\pi_{i_1} \cup \cdots \cup \pi_{i_p}\right) = \sum_{j=1}^{p} q_{i_j} + \sum_{j=1}^{p} m_{i_j} \|\mathbf{c} - \mathbf{b}_{i_j}\|^2,$$

$$\text{where } \mathbf{c} = \frac{m_{i_1} \mathbf{b}_{i_1} + \cdots + m_{i_p} \mathbf{b}_{i_p}}{m_{i_1} + \cdots + m_{i_p}}. \tag{3.1.2}$$

Given a positive real constant R (that controls the "spread" of a cluster) and an integer L (that controls the size of a cluster) the following is a strategy to cluster the dataset $\mathcal{A}$:

1. Set $t = 0$, $\mathcal{A}^{(t)} = \mathcal{A}$, and $\Pi^{(t)} = \emptyset$.
2. Remove $\mathbf{a} \in \mathcal{A}^{(t)}$ from $\mathcal{A}^{(t)}$, set $\pi_1^{(t+1)} = \{\mathbf{a}\}$, $\Pi^{(t+1)} = \{\pi_1^{(t+1)}\}$.
   Set $\mathcal{A}^{(t+1)} = \mathcal{A}^{(t)} - \{\mathbf{a}\}$, $t = t + 1$.
   If $[\mathcal{A}^{(t)} = \emptyset]$
      Stop.
3. Remove $\mathbf{a} \in \mathcal{A}^{(t)}$ from $\mathcal{A}^{(t)}$, and assign $\mathbf{a}$ to the "nearest" cluster $\pi_i^{(t)}$ of $\Pi^{(t)}$.
4. If $[Q(\pi_i^{(t)} \cup \{\mathbf{a}\}) \leq R^2(|\pi_i^{(t)}| + 1)$ and $|\pi_i^{(t)}| + 1 \leq L]$
   then
      set $\Pi^{(t+1)} = \left\{\pi_1^{(t)}, \ldots, \pi_{i-1}^{(t)}, \pi_i^{(t)} \cup \{\mathbf{a}\}, \pi_{i+1}^{(t)}, \ldots, \pi_p^{(t)}\right\}$
   else
      set $\pi_{p+1}^{(t+1)} = \{\mathbf{a}\}$, $\pi_i^{(t+1)} = \pi_i^{(t)}$, $i = 1, \ldots, p$
      set $\Pi^{(t+1)} = \left\{\pi_1^{(t+1)}, \ldots, \pi_p^{(t+1)}, \pi_{p+1}^{(t+1)}\right\}$
5. Set $\mathcal{A}^{(t+1)} = \mathcal{A}^{(t)} - \{\mathbf{a}\}$.
6. If $[\mathcal{A}^{(t+1)} \neq \emptyset]$

3.1. Balanced iterative reducing and clustering algorithm

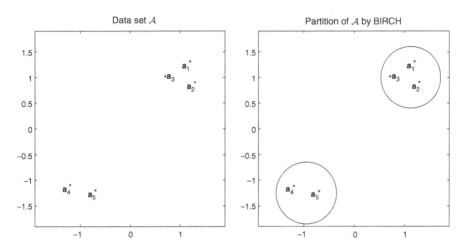

Figure 3.1: Partition of the data set $\mathcal{A}$.

then

$$\text{set } t = t + 1$$
$$\text{go to Step 3}$$

7. Stop.

The above clustering scheme requires a single scan of the data set and its I/O cost is linear with the data set size. We denote the final partition generated by this scheme by

$$\Pi = \{\pi_1, \ldots, \pi_M\}. \tag{3.1.3}$$

In the next section we introduce a k-means-like algorithm that clusters $\mathcal{A}$ using M vectors $\mathbf{b}_i = \mathbf{c}(\pi_i)$ and M pairs of scalars $q_i = Q(\pi_i)$, and $m_i = |\pi_i|$ only. (See Figures 3.1 and 3.2 that show the original data set $\mathcal{A}$ and the summary $\mathcal{B}$).

Problem 3.1.1. *Let* $\pi = \{\mathbf{a}_1, \ldots, \mathbf{a}_p\}$, $\mathbf{c} = \mathbf{c}(\pi)$, *and* $\pi^+ = \pi \cup \{\mathbf{a}\} = \{\mathbf{a}_1, \ldots, \mathbf{a}_p, \mathbf{a}\}$. *If* $Q(\pi) < R^2 p$ *and* $\|\mathbf{c} - \mathbf{a}\| < R$, *then* $Q(\pi^+) < R^2 (p + 1)$.

43

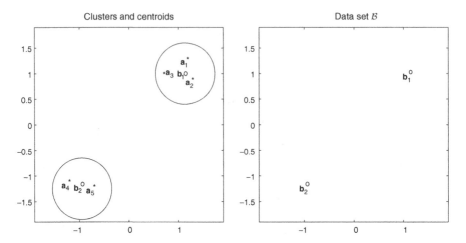

Figure 3.2: Reduced data set $\mathcal{B}$.

Problem 3.1.2. *Let* $\pi = \{\mathbf{a}_1, \ldots, \mathbf{a}_p\}$, $\mathbf{c} = \mathbf{c}(\pi)$. *Define the radius* $R(\pi)$ *and the diameter* $D(\pi)$ *of* π *by*

$$R = R(\pi) = \left(\frac{1}{p} \sum_{i=1}^{p} \|\mathbf{c} - \mathbf{a}_i\|^2 \right)^{\frac{1}{2}}$$

$$\text{and } D = D(\pi) = \left(\frac{1}{p(p-1)} \sum_{i,j=1}^{p} \|\mathbf{a}_j - \mathbf{a}_i\|^2 \right)^{\frac{1}{2}}.$$

Show that $2pR^2 = (p-1)D^2$.

3.2. BIRCH-like k-means

In this section we shall be concerned with the data set $\mathcal{A} = \{\mathbf{a}_1, \ldots, \mathbf{a}_m\}$, the partition $\Pi = \{\pi_1, \ldots, \pi_M\}$ of $\mathcal{A}$, and the data set $\mathcal{B} = \{\mathbf{b}_1, \ldots, \mathbf{b}_M\}$ where $\mathbf{b}_i = \mathbf{c}(\pi_i)$. The subset $\{\mathbf{b}_1, \mathbf{b}_2\} \subseteq \mathcal{B}$ can be associated with a subset $\pi_1 \cup \pi_2 \subseteq \mathcal{A}$. In general, the M cluster partition $\{\pi_1, \ldots, \pi_M\}$ of $\mathcal{A}$ associates each subset $\pi^{\mathcal{B}} \subseteq \mathcal{B}$ with a subset $\pi^{\mathcal{A}} \subseteq \mathcal{A}$ through

$$\pi^{\mathcal{A}} = \bigcup_{\mathbf{b}_j \in \pi^{\mathcal{B}}} \pi_j.$$

Hence a k-cluster partition $\Pi_{\mathcal{B}} = \{\pi_1^B, \ldots, \pi_k^B\}$ of the set $\mathcal{B}$ can be associated with a k-cluster partition $\Pi_{\mathcal{A}} = \{\pi_1^A, \ldots, \pi_k^A\}$ of the set $\mathcal{A}$ as follows:

$$\pi_i^A = \bigcup_{\mathbf{b}_j \in \pi_i^B} \pi_j, \ i = 1, \ldots, k. \tag{3.2.1}$$

Provided M is small enough so that the set $\mathcal{B} = \{\mathbf{b}_1, \ldots, \mathbf{b}_M\}$ and the scalars m_i and $q_i, i = 1, \ldots, M$ fit into the available computer memory we would like to run a k-means-like algorithm that clusters the data set $\mathcal{A}$ using M vectors $\mathbf{b}_i$ and $2M$ scalars m_i and q_i. The algorithm starts with an initial partition $\Pi_{\mathcal{B}}^{(0)}$ and generates a sequence of partitions

$$\Pi_{\mathcal{B}}^{(t)}, \ t = 1, 2, \ldots \text{ so that } Q\left(\Pi_{\mathcal{A}}^{(0)}\right) \geq Q\left(\Pi_{\mathcal{A}}^{(1)}\right) \geq \cdots \geq Q\left(\Pi_{\mathcal{A}}^{(t)}\right)$$
$$\geq Q\left(\Pi_{\mathcal{A}}^{(t+1)}\right) \geq \cdots$$

where $\Pi_{\mathcal{A}}^{(t)}$ is a partition of $\mathcal{A}$ associated with $\Pi_{\mathcal{B}}^{(t)}$ through (3.2.1). Theorem 2.2.1 and formula (3.1.2) furnish the technical tools for the algorithm design. Keeping in mind the partition Π of $\mathcal{A}$ given by (3.1.3) for a cluster $\pi^B = \{\mathbf{b}_1, \ldots, \mathbf{b}_p\}$ we define the centroid $\mathbf{c}(\pi^B)$ as $\mathbf{c}(\pi^A)$, that is

$$\mathbf{c}\left(\pi^B\right) = \frac{m_1 \mathbf{b}_1 + \cdots + m_p \mathbf{b}_p}{m_1 + \cdots + m_p} \text{ so that } \mathbf{c}\left(\pi^B\right)$$
$$= \arg\min\left\{\sum_{i=1}^{p} m_i \|\mathbf{x} - \mathbf{b}_i\|^2 : \mathbf{x} \in \mathbf{R}^n\right\}. \tag{3.2.2}$$

We follow notations introduced in Section 2.1. Let $\Pi_{\mathcal{B}} = \{\pi_1^B, \ldots, \pi_k^B\}$, for $\mathbf{b} \in \pi_i^B \subseteq \mathcal{B}$ denote i, the index of π_i^B, by $\texttt{present}(\mathbf{b})$, and the index j of the centroid $\mathbf{c}_j = \mathbf{c}(\pi_j^B)$ nearest $\mathbf{b}$ by $\texttt{min}(\mathbf{b})$, so that $\|\mathbf{b} - \mathbf{c}_{\texttt{min}(\mathbf{b})}\| = \|\mathbf{b} - \mathbf{c}_j\| \leq \|\mathbf{b} - \mathbf{c}_l\|, l = 1, \ldots, k$. Define the partition $\texttt{nextBKM}(\Pi_{\mathcal{B}}) = \Pi'_{\mathcal{B}} = \{(\pi_1^B)', \ldots, (\pi_k^B)'\}$ by

$$\left(\pi_i^B\right)' = \left\{\mathbf{b} : \texttt{min}(\mathbf{b}) = i\right\}.$$

Definition 3.2.1. *Define the quality $Q_B(\pi^B)$ of a cluster $\pi^B \subseteq B$ by*

$$Q_B(\pi^B) = \sum_{\mathbf{b}_j \in \pi^B} m_j \|\mathbf{c}(\pi^B) - \mathbf{b}_j\|^2, \qquad (3.2.3)$$

and the quality of a partition $\Pi_B = \{\pi_1^B, \ldots, \pi_k^B\}$ by

$$Q_B(\Pi_B) = \sum_{i=1}^{k} Q_B(\pi_i^B). \qquad (3.2.4)$$

Lemma 3.2.1. *If Π_B be a partition of the data set B, then $Q_B(\Pi_B) + Q(\Pi) = Q(\Pi_A)$.*

Proof: Let $\pi_i^A \in \Pi_A$. Due to (3.1.2) one has

$$Q(\pi_i^A) = \sum_{\mathbf{b}_j \in \pi_i^B} \left[Q(\pi_j) + m_j \|\mathbf{c}(\pi_i^B) - \mathbf{b}_j\|^2 \right].$$

Hence for the partition $\Pi_B = \{\pi_1^B, \ldots, \pi_k^B\}$ and the associated partition $\Pi_A = \{\pi_1^A, \ldots, \pi_k^A\}$ one has

$$Q(\Pi_A) = \sum_{i=1}^{k} Q(\pi_i^A) = \sum_{i=1}^{k} \left[\sum_{\mathbf{b}_j \in \pi_i^B} \left[Q(\pi_j) + m_j \|\mathbf{c}(\pi_i^B) - \mathbf{b}_j\|^2 \right] \right]$$

$$= \sum_{i=1}^{k} \sum_{\mathbf{b}_j \in \pi_i^B} Q(\pi_j) + \sum_{i=1}^{k} \sum_{\mathbf{b}_j \in \pi_i^B} m_j \|\mathbf{c}(\pi_i^B) - \mathbf{b}_j\|^2$$

$$= Q(\Pi) + Q_B(\Pi_B).$$

$\square$

The next statement mimics the corresponding statement about iterations of the quadratic batch k-means algorithm introduced in Section 2.1.

Theorem 3.2.1. *Let Π_B be a partition of the data set B. If $\Pi_B' = \text{nextBKM}(\Pi_B)$, then $Q_B(\Pi_B) \geq Q_B(\Pi_B')$. If Π_A' is a partition of A associated with Π_B', then $Q(\Pi_A) \geq Q(\Pi_A')$.*

Proof: The proof of the first statement is identical to that given in Section 2.1 for iterations of the quadratic batch k-means. The second statement follows from the first one and Lemma 3.2.1. $\square$

We shall denote by $\mathrm{nextBKM}_\mathcal{B}\,(\Pi_\mathcal{A})$ the partition of $\mathcal{A}$ associated with $\mathrm{nextBKM}\,(\Pi_\mathcal{B})$. To state the clustering algorithm we need an additional definition.

Definition 3.2.2. *The partition* $\mathrm{nextFV}\,(\Pi_\mathcal{B})$ *is a first variation of* $\Pi_\mathcal{B}$ *such that for each first variation* $\Pi'_\mathcal{B}$ *of* $\Pi_\mathcal{B}$ *one has* $Q_\mathcal{B}\,(\mathrm{nextFV}\,(\Pi_\mathcal{B})) \leq Q_\mathcal{B}\,(\Pi'_\mathcal{B})$. *The partition of* $\mathcal{A}$ *associated with* $\mathrm{nextFV}\,(\Pi_\mathcal{B})$ *is denoted by* $\mathrm{nextFV}_\mathcal{B}\,(\Pi_\mathcal{A})$.

We note the following:

1. in general, $\mathrm{nextFV}\,(\Pi_\mathcal{A})$ and $\mathrm{nextFV}_\mathcal{B}\,(\Pi_\mathcal{A})$ are different partitions,
2. if $\Pi'_\mathcal{B}$ is a first variation of $\Pi_\mathcal{B}$, and $\Pi'_\mathcal{A}$ is a partition of $\mathcal{A}$ associated with $\Pi'_\mathcal{B}$, then $Q\,(\mathrm{nextFV}_\mathcal{B}\,(\Pi_\mathcal{A})) \leq Q\,(\Pi'_\mathcal{A})$.

Algorithm 3.2.1 (The quadratic BIRCH k-means clustering algorithm). *For a user supplied nonnegative tolerances* $\mathrm{tol_B}$ *and* $\mathrm{tol_I}$ *do the following:*

1. *Start with an arbitrary k-cluster partition* $\Pi_\mathcal{B}^{(0)}$ *of the data set* $\mathcal{B}$. *Set the index of iteration* $t = 0$.
2. *Generate the partition* $\mathrm{nextBKM}(\Pi_\mathcal{B}^{(t)})$.
   if $[Q_\mathcal{B}(\Pi_\mathcal{B}^{(t)}) - Q_\mathcal{B}(\mathrm{nextBKM}(\Pi_\mathcal{B}^{(t)})) > \mathrm{tol_B}]$
     set $\Pi_\mathcal{B}^{(t+1)} = \mathrm{nextBKM}(\Pi_\mathcal{B}^{(t)})$
     increment t by 1.
     go to 2
3. *Generate the partition* $\mathrm{nextFV}(\Pi_\mathcal{B}^{(t)})$.
   if $[Q(\Pi_\mathcal{B}^{(t)}) - Q(\mathrm{nextFV}(\Pi_\mathcal{B}^{(t)})) > \mathrm{tol_I}]$
     set $\Pi_\mathcal{B}^{(t+1)} = \mathrm{nextFV}(\Pi_\mathcal{B}^{(t)})$.
     increment t by 1.
     go to 2
4. *Stop.*

At each iteration the algorithm generates partition $\Pi_B^{(t+1)}$ from the partition $\Pi_B^{(t)}$ so that $Q_B(\Pi_B^{(t)}) \geq Q_B(\Pi_B^{(t+1)})$ and, due to Lemma 3.2.1, $Q(\Pi_A^{(t)}) \geq Q(\Pi_A^{(t+1)})$. This yields the concluding statement.

Theorem 3.2.2. *Let* $\Pi_B^{(t)}$, $t = 0, 1, \ldots$ *be the sequence of partitions generated by Algorithm 3.2.1. If* $\Pi_A^{(t)}$, $t = 0, 1, \ldots$ *are the associated partitions of* A, *then* $\{Q(\Pi_A^{(t)})\}$ *is a nonincreasing sequence of nonnegative numbers.*

To implement Step 3 of the algorithm one would need a convenient analogue of formula (2.2.9). Specifically, consider clusters

$$\pi^B = \{\mathbf{b}_1, \ldots, \mathbf{b}_p\} \quad \text{and} \quad \pi^{B^+} = \{\mathbf{b}_1, \ldots, \mathbf{b}_p, \mathbf{b}_{p+1}\}.$$

Let $m = m_1 + \cdots + m_p, m_+ = m + m_{p+1}$, and $\mathbf{c} = \mathbf{c}(\pi^B)$. A straightforward computation leads to the following expression

$$Q_B(\pi^{B^+}) - Q_B(\pi^B) = \frac{m \cdot m_{p+1}}{m_+} ||\mathbf{c} - \mathbf{b}_{p+1}||^2. \tag{3.2.5}$$

Analogously, if

$$\pi^B = \{\mathbf{b}_1, \ldots, \mathbf{b}_p\} \quad \text{and} \quad \pi^{B^-} = \{\mathbf{b}_1, \ldots, \mathbf{b}_{p-1}\},$$

and $m_- = m - m_p$, then

$$Q_B\left(\pi^B\right) - Q_B(\pi^{B^-}) = \frac{m \cdot m_p}{m_-} ||\mathbf{c} - \mathbf{b}_p||^2. \tag{3.2.6}$$

For a vector $\mathbf{b}_i$ we denote the numbers q_i and m_i by $q(\mathbf{b}_i)$ and $m(\mathbf{b}_i)$. Consider now two clusters π_1^B and π_2^B. Let $M_1 = \sum_{\mathbf{b} \in \pi_1^B} m(\mathbf{b})$, and $M_2 = \sum_{\mathbf{b} \in \pi_2^B} m(\mathbf{b})$. Select $\mathbf{b} \in \pi_2^B$. The formula

$$\left[Q_B(\pi_1^B) - Q_B(\pi_1^{B^+}) \right] + \left[Q_B(\pi_2^B) - Q_B(\pi_2^{B^-}) \right]$$
$$= \frac{M_2 \cdot m(\mathbf{b})}{M_2 - m(\mathbf{b})} ||\mathbf{c}(\pi_2^B) - \mathbf{b}_p||^2$$
$$- \frac{M_1 \cdot m(\mathbf{b})}{M_1 + m(\mathbf{b})} ||\mathbf{c}(\pi_1^B) - \mathbf{b}_p||^2. \tag{3.2.7}$$

follows straightforward from (3.2.5) and (3.2.6).

Problem 3.2.1. *Show that*

1. $Q_B(\pi_1^B) - Q_B(\pi_1^{B+}) = -q(\mathbf{b}) - \frac{M_1 \cdot m(\mathbf{b})}{M_1 + m(\mathbf{b})} ||\mathbf{c}(\pi_1^B) - \mathbf{b}_p||^2.$
2. $Q_B(\pi_2^B) - Q_B(\pi_2^{B-}) = q(\mathbf{b}) + \frac{M_2 \cdot m(\mathbf{b})}{M_2 - m(\mathbf{b})} ||\mathbf{c}(\pi_2^B) - \mathbf{b}_p||^2.$

3.3. Bibliographic notes

The BIRCH was introduced by Zhang, Ramakrishnan, and Livny in [146, 147]. These papers introduce "clustering features," that is, for a cluster π the clustering feature is defined as a triple $(|\pi|, \sum_{\mathbf{a} \in \pi} \mathbf{a}, \sum_{\mathbf{a} \in \pi} ||\mathbf{a}||^2)$. The batch version of BIRCH k-means that clusters "clustering features" or "sufficient statistics" is provided by Bradley, Fayyad, and Reina in [22]. The sufficient statistics is defined in this work as a triple $(\sum_{\mathbf{a} \in \pi} \mathbf{a}, \sum_{\mathbf{a} \in \pi} ||\mathbf{a}||^2, |\pi|)$.

Problem 3.3.1. *Show that the triplets $(|\pi|, Q(\pi), \mathbf{c}(\pi))$ and $(|\pi|, \sum_{\mathbf{a} \in \pi} \mathbf{a}, \sum_{\mathbf{a} \in \pi} ||\mathbf{a}||^2)$ contain identical information. That is, show that if one triplet is available, then the other one can be computed.*

4 Spherical k-means algorithm

This chapter describes a clustering algorithm designed to handle l_2 unit norm vectors. The algorithm is reminiscent to the quadratic k-means algorithm (Algorithm 2.1.1), however the "distance" between two unit vectors $\mathbf{x}$ and $\mathbf{y}$ is measured by $d(\mathbf{x}, \mathbf{y}) = \mathbf{x}^T \mathbf{y}$ (so that the two unit vectors $\mathbf{x}$ and $\mathbf{y}$ are equal if and only if $d(\mathbf{x}, \mathbf{y}) = 1$). We define the set $\mathcal{C}$ housing centroids as a union of the unit $n - 1$-dimensional l_2 sphere

$$\mathcal{S}_2^{n-1} = \{\mathbf{x} \; : \; \mathbf{x} \in \mathbf{R}^n, \; \mathbf{x}^T \mathbf{x} = 1\}$$

centered at the origin and the origin (when it does not lead to ambiguity we shall denote the sphere just by $\mathcal{S}$).

The chapter is structured similar to Chapter 2. First, we introduce the batch spherical k-means algorithm, then the incremental version of the algorithm is described. Finally, the batch and incremental iterations are combined to generate the spherical k-means algorithm. We conclude the chapter with a short discussion that relates quadratic and spherical k-means algorithms.

4.1. Spherical batch k-means algorithm

To introduce centroids one has to modify formula (2.1.1). For a set of vectors $\mathcal{A} = \{\mathbf{a}_1, \ldots, \mathbf{a}_m\} \subset \mathbf{R}^n$, and the "distance-like" function $d(\mathbf{x}, \mathbf{a}) = \mathbf{a}^T \mathbf{x}$ define centroid $\mathbf{c} = \mathbf{c}(\mathcal{A})$ of the set $\mathcal{A}$ as a solution of the *maximization* problem

$$
\mathbf{c} = \begin{cases} \arg\max \left\{ \sum_{\mathbf{a} \in \mathcal{A}} \mathbf{x}^T \mathbf{a}, \ \mathbf{x} \in \mathcal{S} \right\} & \text{if } \mathbf{a}_1 + \cdots + \mathbf{a}_m \neq 0, \\ 0 & \text{otherwise.} \end{cases} \tag{4.1.1}
$$

Formula (4.1.1) immediately yields

$$
\mathbf{c}(\mathcal{A}) = \begin{cases} \dfrac{\mathbf{a}_1 + \cdots + \mathbf{a}_m}{\|\mathbf{a}_1 + \cdots + \mathbf{a}_m\|} & \text{if } \mathbf{a}_1 + \cdots + \mathbf{a}_m \neq 0, \\ 0 & \text{otherwise.} \end{cases} \tag{4.1.2}
$$

Note that:

1. For $\mathcal{A} \subset \mathbf{R}_+^n$ (which is typical for many IR applications) the sum of the vectors in $\mathcal{A}$ is never 0, and $\mathbf{c}(\mathcal{A})$ is a unit length vector.
2. The quality of the set $\mathcal{A}$ is just $Q(\mathcal{A}) = \sum_{\mathbf{a} \in \mathcal{A}} \mathbf{a}^T \mathbf{c}(\mathcal{A}) = \|\mathbf{a}_1 + \cdots + \mathbf{a}_m\|$.
3. While the motivation for spherical k-means is provided by IR applications dealing with vectors with nonnegative coordinates residing on the unit sphere, formula (4.1.2) provides solutions to maximization problem (4.1.1) for *any* set $\mathcal{A} \subset \mathbf{R}^n$.

Problem 4.1.1. *Let $d(\mathbf{x}, \mathbf{a}) = (\mathbf{x}^T \mathbf{a})^2$. Define centroid $\mathbf{c} = \mathbf{c}(\pi)$ as a solution of the maximization problem*

$$
\arg\max \left\{ \sum_{\mathbf{a} \in \pi} d(\mathbf{x}, \mathbf{a}), \ \mathbf{x} \in \mathcal{S} \right\}.
$$

Identify $\mathbf{c}$.

The goal now is to find a partition $\Pi^{\max} = \{\pi_1^{\max}, \ldots, \pi_k^{\max}\}$ that *maximizes*

$$
Q(\Pi) = \sum_{i=1}^{k} \left\| \sum_{\mathbf{a} \in \pi_i} \mathbf{a} \right\|. \tag{4.1.3}
$$

In what follows we describe the batch spherical k-means algorithm which is an iterative process that starts with an initial partition $\Pi^{(0)}$

and generates a sequence of partitions

$$\Pi^{(1)}, \ldots, \Pi^{(l)}, \Pi^{(l+1)} \ldots \text{ with } Q(\Pi^{(l)}) \leq Q(\Pi^{(l+1)}), \ l = 0, 1, \ldots$$

To emphasize the relationship between the partitions $\Pi^{(l)}$ and $\Pi^{(l+1)}$ we shall abuse notations and again denote $\Pi^{(l+1)}$ by $\texttt{nextBKM}(\Pi^{(l)})$. For a partition $\Pi = \{\pi_1, \ldots, \pi_k\}$ with centroids $\{\mathbf{c}_1, \ldots, \mathbf{c}_k\}$ and a vector $\mathbf{a} \in \pi_i$ we denote by $\texttt{max}(\mathbf{a})$ the index of the centroid nearest to $\mathbf{a}$, that is

$$j = \texttt{max}(\mathbf{a}) \text{ if and only if } \mathbf{a}^T \mathbf{c}_j \geq \mathbf{a}^T \mathbf{c}_l, \quad l = 1, \ldots, k.$$

The batch spherical k-means algorithm is given next.

Algorithm 4.1.1. (Spherical batch k-means clustering algorithm). *Given a user supplied tolerance $\texttt{tol}_B \geq 0$ do the following:*

1. *Start with an arbitrary partitioning $\Pi^{(0)}$. Set the index of iteration $t = 0$.*

2. *Compute $\Pi^{(t+1)} = \texttt{nextBKM}(\Pi^{(t)})$ induced by:*

$$\pi_l^{(t+1)} = \{\mathbf{a} \in \mathcal{A} \ : \ l = \texttt{max}(\mathbf{a})\}, \ 1 \leq l \leq k\}. \tag{4.1.4}$$

3. *If $[Q(\texttt{nextBKM}(\Pi^{(t)})) - Q(\Pi^{(t)}) > \texttt{tol}_B]$*
   set $\Pi^{(t+1)} = \texttt{nextBKM}(\Pi^{(t)})$
   increment t by 1
   go to Step 2 above.

4. *Stop.*

4.1.1. Spherical batch k-means: advantages and deficiencies

Algorithm 4.1.1 is a gradient-ascent scheme, that is, the objective function value does not decrease from one iteration to the next. However, like any other gradient-ascent scheme, the spherical batch k-means algorithm does not necessarily lead to the optimal solution. A simple example below illustrates this statement.

Example 4.1.1. *Let* $\mathcal{A} = \{\mathbf{a}_1, \mathbf{a}_2, \mathbf{a}_3\}$ *with* $\mathbf{a}_1 = (1,0)^T$, $\mathbf{a}_2 = (\cos\frac{\pi}{3},$ $\sin\frac{\pi}{3})^T$, *and* $\mathbf{a}_3 = (0,1)^T$. *Consider the initial partition* $\Pi^{(0)} = \{\pi_1^{(0)},$ $\pi_2^{(0)}\}$ *with* $\pi_1^{(0)} = \{\mathbf{a}_1, \mathbf{a}_2\}$, $\pi_2^{(0)} = \{\mathbf{a}_3\}$. *An application of the spherical*

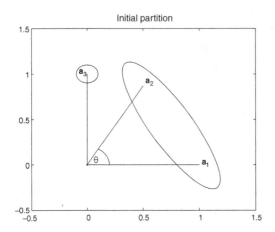

Initial partition

batch k-means algorithm does not change the initial partition $\{\pi_1^{(0)}, \pi_2^{(0)}\}$. *At the same time it is clear that the partition* $\{\pi_1', \pi_2'\}$ *with* $\pi_1' = \{\mathbf{a}_1\}$, $\pi_2' = \{\mathbf{a}_2, \mathbf{a}_3\}$ *is "better" than the initial partition.*

Let $\Pi = \{\pi_1, \pi_2\}$ be an output of Algorithm 4.1.1. Assume that $\mathbf{c}_1 = \mathbf{c}(\pi_1) \neq \mathbf{c}(\pi_2) = \mathbf{c}_2$. Since

$$\mathbf{a}^T\mathbf{c}_1 \leq \mathbf{a}^T\mathbf{c}_2 \text{ if and only if } \|\mathbf{a} - \mathbf{c}_1\|^2 \geq \|\mathbf{a} - \mathbf{c}_2\|^2$$

there exists a hyperplane passing through the origin and cutting the sphere $\mathcal{S}$ into the two semispheres $\mathcal{S}^-$ and $\mathcal{S}^+$ so that $\pi_1 \subset \mathcal{S}^-$ and $\pi_2 \subset \mathcal{S}^+$.

When the data set resides in a plane the separating hyperplane becomes a straight line passing through the origin (see Figure 4.1). We remark that the assumption $\mathbf{c}_1 \neq \mathbf{c}_2$ can be removed, and the sets conv π_1 and conv π_2 become disjoint when Algorithm 4.1.1 is augmented by incremental iterations (see Algorithm 4.3.2).

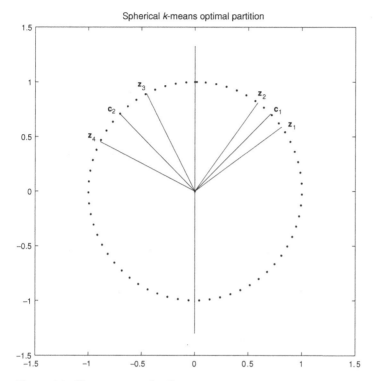

Figure 4.1: Cluster separating line.

4.1.2. Computational considerations

This section discusses some computational shortcuts associated with the spherical batch k-means algorithm. Note that for any unit vector $\mathbf{a}$, and vectors $\mathbf{c}$ and $\mathbf{c}'$ one has $||\mathbf{a}^T\mathbf{c} - \mathbf{a}^T\mathbf{c}'|| \leq ||\mathbf{c} - \mathbf{c}'||$, and

$$\mathbf{a}^T\mathbf{c} - ||\mathbf{c} - \mathbf{c}'|| \leq \mathbf{a}^T\mathbf{c}' \leq \mathbf{a}^T\mathbf{c} + ||\mathbf{c} - \mathbf{c}'||. \qquad (4.1.5)$$

In particular, when $\mathbf{c} = \mathbf{c}_l^{(t)} = \mathbf{c}(\pi_l^{(t)})$, and $\mathbf{c}' = \mathbf{c}_l^{(t+1)} = \mathbf{c}(\pi_l^{(t+1)})$ one has

$$\mathbf{a}^T\mathbf{c}_l^{(t)} - \left|\left|\mathbf{c}_l^{(t)} - \mathbf{c}_l^{(t+1)}\right|\right| \leq \mathbf{a}^T\mathbf{c}_l^{(t+1)} \leq \mathbf{a}^T\mathbf{c}_l^{(t)} + \left|\left|\mathbf{c}_l^{(t)} - \mathbf{c}_l^{(t+1)}\right|\right|. \qquad (4.1.6)$$

The right-hand side of (4.1.6) opens a door for computational savings. Repeated applications of the inequality lead to the upper bound for $\mathbf{a}^T \mathbf{c}_l^{(t+m)}$, $m = 1, \dots$. Indeed

$$\mathbf{a}^T \mathbf{c}_l^{(t+m)} \leq \mathbf{a}^T \mathbf{c}_l^{(t)} + \sum_{i=0}^{m-1} \left\| \mathbf{c}_l^{(t+i)} - \mathbf{c}_l^{(t+i+1)} \right\| . \qquad (4.1.7)$$

We store the upper bounds for vectors $\mathbf{a}_i$ and centroids $\mathbf{c}_j$ in a $m \times k$ matrix B with

$$B_{ij} = \mathbf{a}_i^T \mathbf{c}_j^{(t)} + \sum_{l=0}^{m-1} \left\| \mathbf{c}_j^{(t+l)} - \mathbf{c}_j^{(t+l+1)} \right\| , \quad i = 1, \dots, d; \ j = 1, \dots, k$$

so that

$$\mathbf{a}_i^T \mathbf{c}_j^{(t+m)} \leq B_{ij}. \qquad (4.1.8)$$

Assume now that the partition $\Pi^{(t+m)}$ is already available. To compute the new partition $\Pi^{(t+m+1)} = \mathtt{nextBKM}(\Pi^{(t+m)})$ Step 2 of the algorithm requires to compute $\max(\mathbf{a})$ for each $\mathbf{a} \in \mathcal{A}$ (see (4.1.4)). If for $\mathbf{a}_i$ one has

$$B_{ij} \leq \mathbf{a}_i^T \mathbf{c}_{\mathtt{present}(t+m,\mathbf{a}_i)} \text{ for each } j \neq \mathtt{present}(t+m, \mathbf{a}_i), \qquad (4.1.9)$$

then

$$\mathbf{a}_i^T \mathbf{c}_j \leq B_{ij} \leq \mathbf{a}_i^T \mathbf{c}_{\mathtt{present}(t+m,\mathbf{a}_i)} \text{ for each } j \neq \mathtt{present}(t+m, \mathbf{a}_i),$$

and $\mathtt{present}(t + m, \mathbf{a}_i) = \max(t + m, \mathbf{a}_i)$. In such a case $\mathbf{a}_i$ remains in the cluster $\pi_{\mathtt{present}(t+m,\mathbf{a}_i)}$. During the course of the algorithm it turns out that the first few iterations lead to a lot of vector movement between clusters. However, after a few iterations the clusters become more and more "stable" with only few vectors moving from cluster to cluster (the described behavior is typical for many versions of k-means). In this case inequality (4.1.9) helps to avoid expensive computation of dot products between vectors and "far away" centroids. This observation may lead to significant computational savings.

If for some j the inequality (4.1.9) is violated, then the dot product $\mathbf{a}_i^T \mathbf{c}_j^{(t+m)}$ should be computed, and the ij entry of the matrix should be updated $B_{ij} = \mathbf{a}_i^T \mathbf{c}_j^{(t+m)}$.

We now substitute Step 2 of the spherical k-means algorithm by a step that activates the saving procedure described above after first t_{min} iterations.

For each vector $\mathbf{a}_i$

if $(t \leq t_{min})$

  perform Step 2 of the spherical k-means algorithm

  if $(t = t_{min})$

    set $B_{ij} = \mathbf{a}_i^T \mathbf{c}_j^{(t)}$, $j = 1, \ldots, k$

if $(t > t_{min})$

  set $B_{ij} = B_{ij} + ||\mathbf{c}_j^{(t-1)} - \mathbf{c}_j^{(t)}||$, $j = 1, \ldots, k$

  compute $\mathbf{a}_i^T \mathbf{c}_{present(\mathbf{a}_i)}^{(t)}$

  if $(B_{ij} > \mathbf{a}_i^T \mathbf{c}_{present(\mathbf{a}_i)}^{(t)})$

    compute $\mathbf{a}_i^T \mathbf{c}_j^{(t)}$ and set $B_{ij} = \mathbf{a}_i^T \mathbf{c}_j^{(t)}$

  From among all $\mathbf{a}_i^T \mathbf{c}_j^{(t)}$ computed above find $\max(\mathbf{a}_i)$

  Build new partition $\Pi^{(t+1)} = \texttt{nextBKM}(\Pi^{(t1)})$.

Project 4.1.1. *Design a "computational shortcut" scheme for the k-means algorithm with the distance-like function $d(\mathbf{x}, \mathbf{y}) = ||\mathbf{x} - \mathbf{y}||^2$.*

4.2. Spherical two-cluster partition of one-dimensional data

This section deals with building an optimal two cluster partition for vector sets residing on a one-dimensional unit circle. While the algorithm capable of finding this partition is presented below, it turns out not to be as straightforward as the one that finds the optimal two cluster partition for one-dimensional data sets in the case of quadratic objective function discussed in Chapter 2.

4.2.1. One-dimensional line vs. the unit circle

Consider the following problem: Given a set of unit vectors $\mathcal{Z} = \{\mathbf{z}_1, \ldots, \mathbf{z}_m\} \subset \mathbf{R}^2$ partition $\mathcal{Z}$ into two "optimal" clusters π_1^{max} and

$\pi_2^{\max}$. A straightforward imitation of Boley's construction (see Problem 2.1.6) leads to the following solution: If $\mathbf{z} = \mathbf{z}_1 + \cdots + \mathbf{z}_m \neq 0$, then the line defined by $\mathbf{z}$ cuts the plane into two half-planes. The subset of $\mathcal{Z}$ that belongs to the "left" half-plane is denoted by $\mathcal{Z}_-$, and the subset of $\mathcal{Z}$ that belongs to the "right" half-plane is denoted by $\mathcal{Z}_+$. If $\mathbf{z}$ is zero, then, in order to generate the partition, we choose an arbitrary line passing through the origin.

Lack of robustness is, probably, the most prominent drawback of the suggested partitioning. Indeed, let $\{\mathbf{z}_1, \ldots, \mathbf{z}_m\}$ be a set of unit vectors concentrated around, say, the vector $\mathbf{e}_1 = (1, 0)^T$. If the set $\mathcal{Z}$ contains vectors $\{\mathbf{z}_1, \ldots, \mathbf{z}_m\}$ and their negatives $\{-\mathbf{z}_1, \ldots, -\mathbf{z}_m\}$, then $\mathbf{z} = 0$. This $\mathbf{z}$ does not do much to recover "good" clusters (although $\Pi = \{\pi_1, \pi_2\}$ with $\pi_1 = \{\mathbf{z}_1, \ldots, \mathbf{z}_m\}$, and $\pi_2 = \{-\mathbf{z}_1, \ldots, -\mathbf{z}_m\}$ looks like a reasonable partition, see Figure 4.2). Things get worse when $\mathbf{e}_1$ is assigned to the vector set $\mathcal{Z}$, that is,

$$\mathcal{Z} = \{\mathbf{z}_1, \ldots, \mathbf{z}_m, -\mathbf{z}_1, \ldots, -\mathbf{z}_m, \mathbf{e}_1\}.$$

Now $\mathbf{z} = \mathbf{e}_1$, and regardless of how "densely" the vectors $\{\mathbf{z}_1, \ldots, \mathbf{z}_m\}$ are concentrated around $\mathbf{e}_1$ the clusters $\mathcal{Z}_+$ and $\mathcal{Z}_-$ most probably contain vectors from both sets $\{\mathbf{z}_1, \ldots, \mathbf{z}_m\}$ and $\{-\mathbf{z}_1, \ldots, -\mathbf{z}_m\}$. This poor partition is illustrated in Figure 4.3.

Due to convexity of the optimal partition $\Pi^{\max} = \{\pi_1^{\max}, \pi_2^{\max}\}$ there is a nonzero vector $\mathbf{x}^o$ so that the clusters $\pi_1^{\max}$ and $\pi_2^{\max}$ are separated by the line passing through the origin and defined by $\mathbf{x}^o$ (see Figure 4.4). Since each unit vector $\mathbf{z} \in \mathbf{R}^2$ can be uniquely represented by $e^{i\theta}$ with $0 \leq \theta < 2\pi$ the associated clustering problem is essentially one-dimensional. We denote $\mathbf{z}_j$ by $e^{i\theta_j}$, and assume (without any loss of generality), that

$$0 \leq \theta_1 \leq \theta_2 \leq \cdots \leq \theta_m < 2\pi.$$

As in the case of clustering points on a line, it is tempting to assume that for some j a line passing through the origin and midway between

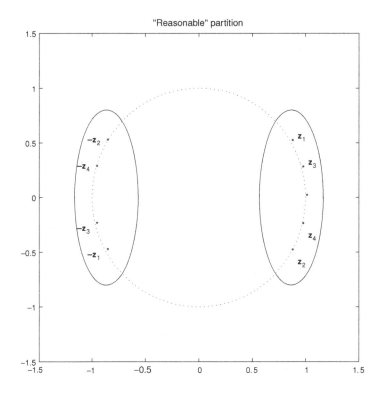

Figure 4.2: Poor "mean generated" partition.

z_j and z_{j+1} recovers the optimal partition. The next example shows that this is not necessarily the case.

Example 4.2.1. *Let* $z_1 = (1, 0)^T$, $z_2 = (\cos(\frac{2\pi}{3} - \epsilon), \sin(\frac{2\pi}{3} - \epsilon))^T$, $z_3 = -z_1$, *and* $z_4 = (\cos(-\frac{2\pi}{3} + \epsilon), \sin(-\frac{2\pi}{3} + \epsilon))^T$. *It is easy to see that when* $\epsilon = 0$ *the optimal partition is* $\Pi^{\max} = \{\{z_1\}, \{z_2, z_3, z_4\}\}$ *with* $Q(\Pi^{\max}) = 3$. *While a small positive* ϵ *(for example* $\epsilon = \frac{\pi}{36}$*) does not change the optimal partition, the four "midpoint" lines generate clusters containing two vectors each (a partition i is generated by a line passing through the origin and the "midpoint" between* z_i *and* z_{i+1}*). These partitions do not contain the optimal partition* $\{\pi_1^{\max}, \pi_2^{\max}\}$. *Figures 4.5 and 4.6 show the four "midpoint line" partitions with* $\epsilon = \frac{\pi}{36}$.

59

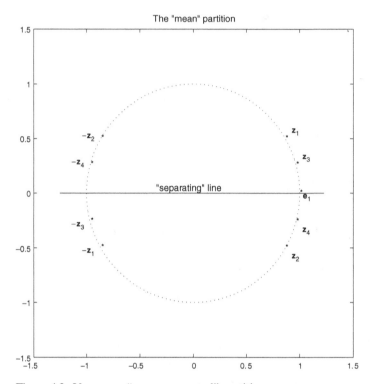

Figure 4.3: Very poor "mean generated" partition.

4.2.2. Optimal two cluster partition on the unit circle

To analyze the failure of Example 4.2.1, and to propose a remedy we introduce the formal definition of the "left" and "right" half-planes generated by a vector $\mathbf{x}$, and describe a procedure that computes the optimal "separator" $\mathbf{x}^o$.

- For a nonzero vector $\mathbf{x} \in \mathbf{R}^2$ we denote by $\mathbf{x}^\perp$ the vector obtained from $\mathbf{x}$ by rotating it clockwise by an angle of $90°$, that is,

$$\mathbf{x}^\perp = \begin{bmatrix} 0 & 1 \\ -1 & 0 \end{bmatrix} \mathbf{x}.$$

- For a nonzero vector $\mathbf{x} \in \mathbf{R}^2$, and a set of vectors $\mathcal{Z} = \{\mathbf{z}_1, \dots, \mathbf{z}_m\} \subset \mathbf{R}^2$ define two subsets of $\mathcal{Z}$ – the "positive" $\mathcal{Z}_+(\mathbf{x}) = \mathcal{Z}_+$, and the

4.2. Spherical two-cluster partition of one-dimensional data

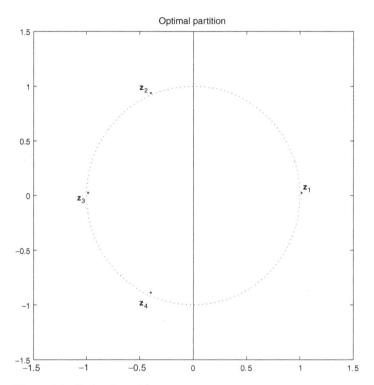

Figure 4.4: Optimal partition.

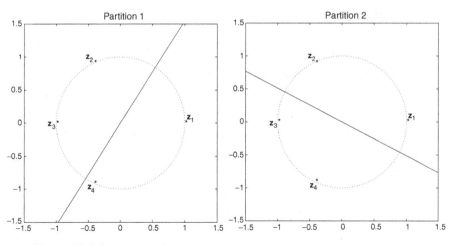

Figure 4.5: Midway partitions.

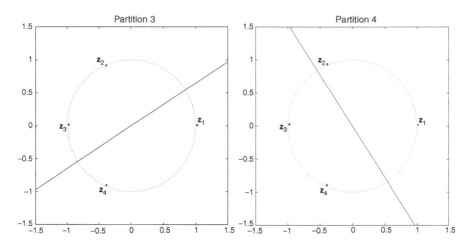

Figure 4.6: Midway partitions.

"negative" $\mathcal{Z}_-(\mathbf{x}) = \mathcal{Z}_-$ as follows:

$$\mathcal{Z}_+=\{\mathbf{z} : \mathbf{z} \in \mathcal{Z},\ \mathbf{z}^T\mathbf{x}^\perp \geq 0\}, \quad \text{and} \quad \mathcal{Z}_-=\{\mathbf{z} : \mathbf{z} \in \mathcal{Z},\ \mathbf{z}^T\mathbf{x}^\perp < 0\}.$$
(4.2.1)

- For two unit vectors $\mathbf{z}' = e^{i\theta'}$ and $\mathbf{z}'' = e^{i\theta''}$ we denote the "midway" vector $e^{i\frac{\theta'+\theta''}{2}}$ by $\mathrm{mid}\,(\mathbf{z}', \mathbf{z}'')$.

As the "optimal" separating line in Example 4.2.1 is rotated clockwise from $\mathbf{z}_2$ to $\mathrm{mid}\,(\mathbf{z}_2, \mathbf{z}_1)$ it crosses $\mathbf{z}_4$ changing cluster affiliation of this vector (see Figure 4.7). This could have been prevented if instead of rotating the "optimal" separating line all the way to $\mathrm{mid}\,(\mathbf{z}_2, \mathbf{z}_1)$ one would rotate it to $\mathrm{mid}\,(\mathbf{z}_2, -\mathbf{z}_4)$. The "optimal" separating line and the line passing through $\mathrm{mid}\,(\mathbf{z}_2, -\mathbf{z}_4)$ and the origin generate identical partitions (see Figure 4.8). In general, if the set $\mathcal{Z} = \{\mathbf{z}_1 = e^{i\theta_1}, \ldots, \mathbf{z}_m = e^{i\theta_m}\}$ is symmetric with respect to the origin, (i.e., for each $\mathbf{z}_i \in \mathcal{Z}$ there exists $\mathbf{z}_l \in \mathcal{Z}$ such that $\mathbf{z}_i = -\mathbf{z}_l$), then for

$$\mathbf{x}' = e^{i\theta'}, \quad \mathbf{x}'' = e^{i\theta''}, \quad \text{with } \theta_j < \theta' \leq \theta'' < \theta_{j+1}.$$

4.2. Spherical two-cluster partition of one-dimensional data

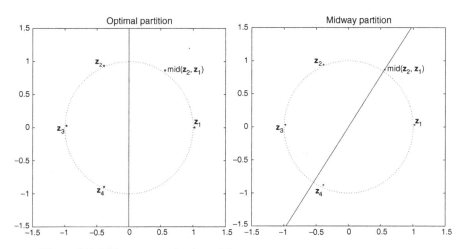

Figure 4.7: Midway vs. optimal partitions.

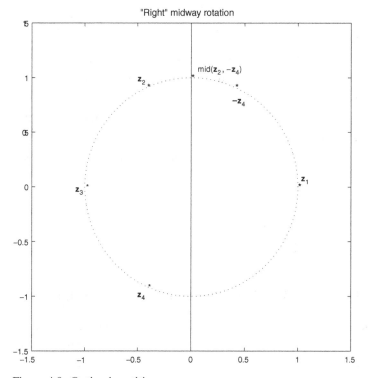

Figure 4.8: Optimal partition.

the partitions

$$\{\mathcal{Z}_+ (\mathbf{x}'), \mathcal{Z}_- (\mathbf{x}')\}, \quad \text{and} \quad \{\mathcal{Z}_+ (\mathbf{x}''), \mathcal{Z}_- (\mathbf{x}'')\}$$

are identical. This observation suggests the following simple procedure for recovering the optimal partition $\{\pi_1^{\max}, \pi_2^{\max}\}$:

1. Let $\mathbf{W} = \{\mathbf{w}_1, \ldots, \mathbf{w}_m, \mathbf{w}_{m+1}, \ldots, \mathbf{w}_{2m}\}$ be a set of two-dimensional vectors defined as follows:

   $\mathbf{w}_i = \mathbf{z}_i$ for $i = 1, \ldots, m$, and $\mathbf{w}_i = -\mathbf{z}_i$ for $i = m+1, \ldots, 2m$.

2. If needed reassign indices so that

   $$\mathbf{w}_j = e^{i\theta_j}, \quad \text{and} \quad 0 \le \theta_1 \le \theta_2 \le \cdots \le \theta_{2m} < 2\pi.$$

3. With each subscript j associate a partition $\{\pi_1^j, \pi_2^j\}$ of $\mathcal{Z}$ as follows:
   (a) set $\mathbf{x} = \frac{\mathbf{w}_j + \mathbf{w}_{j+1}}{2}$
   (b) set $\pi_1^j = \mathcal{Z}_+(\mathbf{x})$, and $\pi_2^j = \mathcal{Z}_-(\mathbf{x})$.
   Note that:
   (a) The indices j and $j + m$ generate identical partitions. We, therefore, have to consider at most m distinct partitions generated by $j = 1, \ldots, m$.
   (b) The optimal partition that maximizes (4.1.3) is among the generated ones.

4. With each partition $\{\pi_1^j, \pi_2^j\}$ associate the value of the objective function

   $$Q^j = Q(\{\pi_1^j, \pi_2^j\}), \quad j = 1, \ldots, m.$$

   If $Q^k = \max_{j=1,\ldots,m} Q^j$, then the desired partition of $\mathcal{Z}$ is $\{\pi_1^{\max}, \pi_2^{\max}\} = \{\pi_1^k, \pi_2^k\}$.

4.3. Spherical batch and incremental clustering algorithms

The incremental version of Algorithm 4.1.1 (the spherical batch k-means clustering algorithm) based on "first variation" iterations is capable of "fixing" Example 4.1.1. A combination of the two algorithms with an incremental step following a sequence of batch steps has the potential to improve final partitions generated by the spherical batch k-means alone. A discussion of the computational burden associated with the combined algorithm completes this section.

4.3.1. First variation for spherical k-means

The definition of the first variation $\texttt{nextFV}\,(\Pi)$ (see Definition 2.2.1) remains valid with the obvious reverse of the inequality in (2.2.11), that is

Definition 4.3.1. *The partition* $\texttt{nextFV}\,(\Pi)$ *is a first variation of* Π *so that for each first variation* Π' *one has*

$$Q(\texttt{nextFV}\,(\Pi)) \geq Q(\Pi'). \tag{4.3.1}$$

The proposed first variation algorithm starts with an arbitrary initial partition $\Pi^{(0)}$ and generates a sequence of partitions

$$\Pi^{(0)},\ \Pi^{(1)}, \ldots,\ \Pi^{(t)},\ \Pi^{(t+1)}, \ldots \text{ so that } \Pi^{(t+1)}$$
$$= \texttt{nextFV}\big(\Pi^{(t)}\big),\ t = 0, 1, \ldots.$$

We now pause briefly to illustrate differences between first variation iterations and iterations of the batch spherical k-means algorithm. To simplify the presentation we consider two sets $\mathcal{A} = \{\mathbf{a}_1, \ldots, \mathbf{a}_p\}$ and $\mathcal{B} = \{\mathbf{b}_1, \ldots, \mathbf{b}_q\}$. Our goal is to examine whether a single vector, say $\mathbf{b}_q$, should be removed from $\mathcal{B}$, and assigned to $\mathcal{A}$. We denote the resulting sets by $\mathcal{B}^-$ and $\mathcal{A}^+$, that is

$$\mathcal{A}^+ = \{\mathbf{a}_1, \ldots, \mathbf{a}_p, \mathbf{b}_q\} \quad \text{and} \quad \mathcal{B}^- = \{\mathbf{b}_1, \ldots, \mathbf{b}_{q-1}\}.$$

Note that an application of the batch spherical k-means algorithm to the two-cluster partition $\{\mathcal{A}, \mathcal{B}\}$ examines the quantity

$$\Delta_k = \mathbf{b}_q^T \left[\mathbf{c}(\mathcal{A}) - \mathbf{c}(\mathcal{B})\right].$$

If $\Delta_k > 0$, then the batch spherical k-means algorithm moves $\mathbf{b}_q$ from $\mathcal{B}$ to $\mathcal{A}$. Otherwise $\mathbf{b}_q$ remains in $\mathcal{B}$.

Unlike the batch spherical *k*-means algorithm, the incremental spherical algorithm computes

$$\Delta = [Q(\mathcal{B}^-) - Q(\mathcal{B})] + [Q(\mathcal{A}^+) - Q(\mathcal{A})].$$

A straightforward computation shows

$$\Delta = \left[\sum_{i=1}^{q-1} \mathbf{b}_i^T \mathbf{c}(\mathcal{B}^-) - \sum_{i=1}^{q-1} \mathbf{b}_i^T \mathbf{c}(\mathcal{B}) - \mathbf{b}_q^T \mathbf{c}(\mathcal{B}) \right]$$

$$+ \left[\sum_{i=1}^{p} \mathbf{a}_i^T \mathbf{c}(\mathcal{A}^+) + \mathbf{b}_q^T \mathbf{c}(\mathcal{A}^+) - \sum_{i=1}^{p} \mathbf{a}_i^T \mathbf{c}(\mathcal{A}) \right] = \sum_{i=1}^{q-1} \mathbf{b}_i^T \left[\mathbf{c}(\mathcal{B}^-) - \mathbf{c}(\mathcal{B}) \right]$$

$$+ \left\{ \sum_{i=1}^{p} \mathbf{a}_i^T [\mathbf{c}(\mathcal{A}^+) - \mathbf{c}(\mathcal{A})] + \mathbf{b}_q^T [\mathbf{c}(\mathcal{A}^+) - \mathbf{c}(\mathcal{A})] \right\}$$

$$+ \mathbf{b}_q^T [\mathbf{c}(\mathcal{A}) - \mathbf{c}(\mathcal{B})].$$

In other words

$$\Delta = \sum_{i=1}^{q-1} \mathbf{b}_i^T [\mathbf{c}(\mathcal{B}^-) - \mathbf{c}(\mathcal{B})]$$

$$+ \left\{ \sum_{i=1}^{p} \mathbf{a}_i^T [\mathbf{c}(\mathcal{A}^+) - \mathbf{c}(\mathcal{A})] + \mathbf{b}_q^T [\mathbf{c}(\mathcal{A}^+) - \mathbf{c}(\mathcal{A})] \right\} + \Delta_k. \quad (4.3.2)$$

By definition $\sum_{\mathbf{b} \in \mathcal{B}^-} \mathbf{b}^T \mathbf{c}(\mathcal{B}^-) \geq \sum_{\mathbf{b} \in \mathcal{B}^-} \mathbf{b}^T \mathbf{c}(\mathcal{B})$, and, therefore, $\sum_{i=1}^{q-1} \mathbf{b}_i^T [\mathbf{c}(\mathcal{B}^-) - \mathbf{c}(\mathcal{B})] \geq 0$. For the same reason

$$\left\{ \sum_{i=1}^{p} \mathbf{a}_i^T [\mathbf{c}(\mathcal{A}^+) - \mathbf{c}(\mathcal{A})] + \mathbf{b}_q^T [\mathbf{c}(\mathcal{A}^+) - \mathbf{c}(\mathcal{A})] \right\} \geq 0.$$

These two inequalities along with (4.3.2) imply $\Delta \geq \Delta_k$. The last inequality shows that even when $0 \geq \Delta_k$, and cluster affiliation of $\mathbf{b}_q$ is not changed by the batch spherical *k*-means algorithm the quantity Δ may still be positive. Thus, while $Q(\{\mathcal{B}^-, \mathcal{A}^+\}) > Q(\{\mathcal{B}, \mathcal{A}\})$, the partition $\{\mathcal{B}^-, \mathcal{A}^+\}$ will be missed by the batch spherical *k*-means algorithm (see Example 4.1.1).

4.3. Spherical batch and incremental clustering algorithms

We now turn to the magnitude of $\Delta - \Delta_k$. For a vector set $\mathcal{X} = \{\mathbf{x}_1, \ldots, \mathbf{x}_r\}$ denote $\mathbf{x}_1 + \cdots + \mathbf{x}_r$ by $\mathbf{s}(\mathbf{X})$. Due to (4.3.2) one has

$$0 \leq \Delta - \Delta_k = \mathbf{s}(\mathcal{B}^-)^T[\mathbf{c}(\mathcal{B}^-) - \mathbf{c}(\mathcal{B})] + \mathbf{s}(\mathcal{A}^+)^T[\mathbf{c}(\mathcal{A}^+) - \mathbf{c}(\mathcal{A})].$$
(4.3.3)

Since the vectors $\mathbf{s}(\mathcal{B}^-)$ and $\mathbf{c}(\mathcal{B}^-)$ are proportional the larger the difference $\mathbf{c}(\mathcal{B}^-) - \mathbf{c}(\mathcal{B})$ is the larger the dot product $\mathbf{s}(\mathcal{B}^-)^T[\mathbf{c}(\mathcal{B}^-) - \mathbf{c}(\mathcal{B})]$ becomes. A similar argument holds true for the second term of the right-hand side of (4.3.3). Hence we can expect a "substantial" difference between Δ and Δ_k when removing a single vector from cluster $\mathcal{B}$ and assigning it to cluster $\mathcal{A}$ "significantly" changes locations of the corresponding centroids. This phenomenon is unlikely to happen when the clusters are large. However, incremental iterations become efficient when a partition contains small clusters (in our experiments clusters of size 100 or less).

The incremental version of the spherical batch algorithm is the following:

Algorithm 4.3.2. (Incremental spherical k-means algorithm). *Given user supplied tolerance* $\mathtt{tol_I} \geq 0$ *do the following:*

1. *Start with a partitioning* $\Pi^{(0)}$. *Set the index of iteration* $t = 0$.
2. *Generate* $\mathtt{nextFV}(\Pi^{(t)})$.
3. *If* $[Q(\mathtt{nextFV}(\Pi^{(t)}t)) - Q(\Pi^{(t)}) > \mathtt{tol_I}]$
     set $\Pi^{(t+1)} = \mathtt{nextFV}(\Pi^{(t)})$.
     increment t *by 1*
     go to 2
4. *Stop.*

It is easy to see that a single "spherical incremental" iteration applied to the initial partition of Example 4.1.1 generates the "optimal partition". (see Figure 4.9).

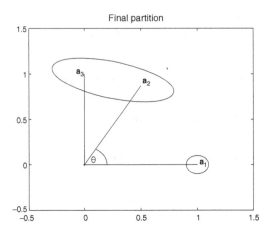

Figure 4.9: Optimal partition generated by merger of batch and incremental algorithms.

4.3.2. Spherical incremental iterations–computations complexity

We now briefly address the computational complexity associated with spherical incremental iterations. The time and memory complexity of spherical incremental iterations are basically the same as those of the batch spherical k-means algorithm. For each $\mathbf{a} \in \pi_l$ and cluster π_j the algorithm computes

$$\delta_j(\mathbf{a}) = [Q(\pi_l^-) - Q(\pi_l)] + [Q(\pi_j^+) - Q(\pi_j)],$$

where $\pi_l^- = \pi_l - \{\mathbf{a}\}$, and $\pi_j^+ = \pi_j \cup \{\mathbf{a}\}$. If $\delta_j(\mathbf{a}) \leq 0$ the vector $\mathbf{a}$ should not be moved to the cluster π_j. Evaluation of

$$Q(\pi_l^-) - Q(\pi_l) \quad \text{and} \quad Q(\pi_j^+) - Q(\pi_j)$$

for all the vectors $\mathbf{a} \in \mathcal{A}$ is the computational bottleneck of spherical incremental iterations. Note that

$$Q(\pi_l^-) - Q(\pi_l) = \sqrt{||\mathbf{s}(\pi_l)||^2 - 2||\mathbf{s}(\pi_l)||\mathbf{a}^T\mathbf{c}(\pi_l) + 1} - ||\mathbf{s}(\pi_l)||$$

$$(4.3.4)$$

and

$$Q(\pi_j^+) - Q(\pi_j) = \sqrt{||\mathbf{s}(\pi_j)||^2 + 2||\mathbf{s}(\pi_j)||\mathbf{a}^T\mathbf{c}(\pi_j) + 1} - ||\mathbf{s}(\pi_j)||.$$
(4.3.5)

We remark that computation of the quantities $||\mathbf{s}(\pi_l)||$, and $\mathbf{a}^T\mathbf{c}(\pi_l)$, $\mathbf{a} \in \mathcal{A}, l = 1, \ldots, k$ are needed for iterations of the spherical batch k-means algorithm as well. Furthermore, a straightforward computation shows that

$$Q(\pi_j^+) - Q(\pi_j) = \frac{2}{1 + \sqrt{1 + 2\mathbf{a}^T \frac{\mathbf{c}(\pi_j)}{|\mathbf{s}(\pi_j)|} + \frac{1}{|\mathbf{s}(\pi_j)|^2}}} \mathbf{a}^T \mathbf{c}(\pi_j)$$
$$+ \frac{1}{|\mathbf{s}(\pi_j)|} \frac{1}{1 + \sqrt{1 + 2\mathbf{a}^T \frac{\mathbf{c}(\pi_j)}{|\mathbf{s}(\pi_j)|} + \frac{1}{|\mathbf{s}(\pi_j)|^2}}}$$

and

$$Q(\pi_j^+) - Q(\pi_j) \leq \mathbf{a}^T\mathbf{c}(\pi_j) + \frac{1}{2|\mathbf{s}(\pi_j)|}.$$
(4.3.6)

Hence, if $\mathbf{a} = \mathbf{a}_i$ and

$$B_{ij} + \frac{1}{2|\mathbf{s}(\pi_j)|} \leq -\left[Q(\pi_i^-) - Q(\pi_i)\right]$$
(4.3.7)

(see Section 4.1.2, inequality (4.1.8)), then $\delta_j(\mathbf{a}_i) \leq 0$, and by storing the matrix B and the scalars $||\mathbf{s}(\pi_l)||, l = 1, \ldots, k$ one can avoid some computational burden associated with evaluation of $\delta_j(\mathbf{a}_i)$.

4.3.3. The "ping-pong" algorithm

While a single iteration of incremental spherical k-means computes the exact change of the objective function, changing a single vector cluster affiliation generally leads to a small increase in the objective function value. On the other hand, batch spherical k-means iterations typically lead to larger increases. To achieve best results we "combine" batch spherical k-means and incremental spherical k-means. The "ping-pong" refinement algorithm is a two-step procedure. The first step of the procedure runs spherical batch *k*-means iterations. When the first step fails to alter a partition, the second step runs a single incremental spherical *k*-means iteration. The proposed refinement algorithm is given next.

Algorithm 4.3.3. (The spherical *k*-means clustering algorithm). *For a user supplied nonnegative tolerances* $\mathtt{tol_B}$ *and* $\mathtt{tol_I}$ *do the following:*

1. *Start with an arbitrary partitioning* $\Pi^{(0)} = \{\pi_1^{(0)}, \ldots, \pi_k^{(0)}\}$. *Set the index of iteration* $t = 0$.

2. *Generate the partition* $\mathtt{nextBKM}(\Pi^{(t)})$.
   if $[Q(\mathtt{nextBKM}(\Pi^{(t)})) - Q(\Pi^{(t)}) > \mathtt{tol_B}]$
       set $\Pi^{(t+1)} = \mathtt{nextBKM}(\Pi^{(t)})$
       increment t by 1.
       go to 2

3. *Generate the partition* $\mathtt{nextFV}(\Pi^{(t)})$.
   if $[Q(\mathtt{nextFV}(\Pi^{(t)})) - Q(\Pi^{(t)}) > \mathtt{tol_I}]$
       set $\Pi^{(t+1)} = \mathtt{nextFV}(\Pi^{(t)})$.
       increment t by 1.
       go to 2

4. *Stop.*

We emphasize that most of the computations associated with Step 3 above have been already performed in Step 2, see (4.3.4) and (4.3.5). Hence the computational price of running a first variation iteration just after an iteration of the spherical *k*-means algorithm is negligible.

Problem 4.3.1. *Let* **a**, **b** *be two nonzero vectors in* $\mathbf{R}^n$. *Show that the following holds:*

1. $|\|\mathbf{a}\| - \|\mathbf{b}\|| \leq \|\mathbf{a} + \mathbf{b}\| \leq |\|\mathbf{a}\| + \|\mathbf{b}\||$.
2. $|\|\mathbf{a}\| - \|\mathbf{b}\|| = \|\mathbf{a} + \mathbf{b}\|$ *if and only if* $\mathbf{a} = \lambda\mathbf{b}$, $\lambda < 0$.
3. $\|\mathbf{a} + \mathbf{b}\| = |\|\mathbf{a}\| + \|\mathbf{b}\||$ *if and only if* $\mathbf{a} = \lambda\mathbf{b}$, $\lambda > 0$.

Problem 4.3.2. *If $\{\pi_1, \pi_2\}$ is a two-cluster stable spherical k-means partition, then $\mathbf{c}(\pi_i) \neq 0$, $i = 1, 2$.*

Problem 4.3.3. *If $\{\pi_1, \pi_2\}$ is a two-cluster stable spherical k-means partition, then $\mathbf{s}(\pi_1) \neq \mathbf{s}(\pi_2)$.*

Problem 4.3.4. *Let $\{\pi_1, \pi_2\}$ be a two-cluster stable spherical k-means partition with $\mathbf{c}(\pi_1) = \mathbf{c}(\pi_2)$. If $\|\mathbf{s}(\pi_1)\| < \|\mathbf{s}(\pi_2)\|$, then $\mathbf{a}^T\mathbf{c}(\pi_1) \geq 0$ for each $\mathbf{a} \in \pi_1$.*

Problem 4.3.5. *Give an example of a two-cluster stable spherical k-means partition $\{\pi_1, \pi_2\}$ with $\mathbf{a} \in \pi_1$ such that $\mathbf{a}^T\mathbf{c}(\pi_1) < 0$.*

Problem 4.3.6. *If $\{\pi_1, \pi_2\}$ is a two-cluster stable spherical k-means partition, then $\mathbf{c}(\pi_1) \neq \mathbf{c}(\pi_2)$.*

Problem 4.3.7. *Identify correct statements:*

1. *If $\Pi = \{\pi_1, \ldots, \pi_k\}$ is a spherical batch k-means stable partition, then for each pair of indices $1 \leq i < j \leq k$ one has $\mathrm{conv}\,\pi_i \cap \mathrm{conv}\,\pi_j = \emptyset$.*
2. *If $\Pi = \{\pi_1, \ldots, \pi_k\}$ is a spherical k-means stable partition, then for each pair of indices $1 \leq i < j \leq k$ one has $\mathrm{conv}\,\pi_i \cap \mathrm{conv}\,\pi_j = \emptyset$.*

4.3.4. Quadratic and spherical k-means

Consider a "new" k-means algorithm equipped with the quadratic distance-like function $d(\mathbf{x}, \mathbf{y}) = \|\mathbf{x} - \mathbf{y}\|^2$ and with the set $\mathcal{C}$ being the unit $n - 1$-dimensional sphere S_2^{n-1}. As in the case of the spherical k-means the data $\mathcal{A} = \{\mathbf{a}_1, \ldots, \mathbf{a}_m\}$ is L_2 normalized, that is, $\|\mathbf{a}_i\|_2 = 1$. To simplify the presentation we also assume (as it is customary done in IR applications) that each data vector $\mathbf{a}$ has only nonnegative coordinates.

Formula (2.1.1) in this case becomes the following:

$$\mathbf{c} = \mathbf{c}(\mathcal{A}) = \arg\min\left\{\sum_{\mathbf{a}\in\mathcal{A}} \|\mathbf{x} - \mathbf{a}\|^2, \ \|\mathbf{x}\|^2 = 1\right\}. \tag{4.3.8}$$

Problem 4.3.8. *Show that solutions for the minimization problem (4.3.8) are the same as solutions for the following maximization problem*

$$\mathbf{c} = \mathbf{c}(\mathcal{A}) = \arg\max\left\{\sum_{\mathbf{a}\in\mathcal{A}} \mathbf{x}^T\mathbf{a}, \ \|\mathbf{x}\|^2 = 1\right\}. \qquad (4.3.9)$$

Hence, when constrained to the unit sphere, centroids for the quadratic and spherical k-means coincide. Since for the unit length vectors $\mathbf{a}$ and $\mathbf{x}$ one has

$$\|\mathbf{x} - \mathbf{a}\| = 2 - 2\mathbf{x}^T\mathbf{a}$$

it is easy to see that the spherical k-means is a special particular case of the quadratic k-means clustering algorithm.

Problem 4.3.9. *Drop the assumption $\mathbf{a}_i \in \mathbf{R}_+^n$, $i = 1, \ldots, m$ and investigate whether or not the spherical k-means algorithm can be stated as a quadratic k-means clustering algorithm.*

This discussion leads to the question: "What are additional distance-like functions and regions in $\mathbf{R}^n$ where the data $\mathcal{A}$ and centroids can be located so that k-means-like clustering algorithms can be devised?" This question is partially addressed in Chapter 6 and Chapter 8.

4.4. Bibliographic notes

The batch spherical k-means clustering algorithm for L_2 unit vectors with nonnegative coordinates is motivated by IR applications and was introduced by Dhillon and Modha in [39]. Computational shortcuts for the spherical batch k-means algorithm are reported in [34]. The "ping-pong" refinement algorithm (combining both the batch and the incremental algorithms) is discussed in [35, 36]. Building optimal two cluster partitions for one-dimensional data sets is discussed in [37].

The equivalence of quadratic k-means and "constrained" spherical k-means is pointed out in [107].

5 Linear algebra techniques

This chapter is devoted to a number of Linear Algebra techniques for clustering. In what follows the central place is occupied by the Principal Direction Divisive Partitioning algorithm (PDDP). This remarkable algorithm is especially efficient when applied to sparse high-dimensional data.

5.1. Two approximation problems

For a vector $\mathbf{a}$ and a line $\mathbf{l}$ in $\mathbf{R}^n$ denote by $\mathrm{P}_{\mathbf{l}}(\mathbf{a})$ the orthogonal projection of $\mathbf{a}$ on $\mathbf{l}$. For a set of vectors $\mathcal{A} = \{\mathbf{a}_1, \ldots, \mathbf{a}_m\}$ and a line $\mathbf{l}$ in $\mathbf{R}^n$ denote by $\mathrm{P}_{\mathbf{l}}(\mathcal{A})$ the set of projections $\{\mathrm{P}_{\mathbf{l}}(\mathbf{a}_1), \ldots, \mathrm{P}_{\mathbf{l}}(\mathbf{a}_m)\}$.

Problem 5.1.1. *Let $\mathcal{A} = \{\mathbf{a}_1, \ldots, \mathbf{a}_m\}$ be a set of vectors in $\mathbf{R}^n$. Find the lines $\mathbf{l}_d$ and $\mathbf{l}_v$ such that for each line $\mathbf{l}$ in $\mathbf{R}^n$ one has:*

$$\sum_{i=1}^{m} ||\mathbf{a}_i - \mathrm{P}_{\mathbf{l}_d}(\mathbf{a}_i)||^2 \leq \sum_{i=1}^{m} ||\mathbf{a}_i - \mathrm{P}_{\mathbf{l}}(\mathbf{a}_i)||^2 \tag{5.1.1}$$

and

$$\sum_{i=1}^{m} ||\mathrm{P}_{\mathbf{l}_v}(\mathbf{a}_i) - \mathbf{c}\,(\mathrm{P}_{\mathbf{l}_v}(\mathcal{A}))\,||^2 \geq \sum_{i=1}^{m} ||\mathrm{P}_{\mathbf{l}}(\mathbf{a}_i) - \mathbf{c}\,(\mathrm{P}_{\mathbf{l}}(\mathcal{A}))\,||^2. \tag{5.1.2}$$

Problem 5.1.2. *Find out how the lines $\mathbf{l}_d$ and $\mathbf{l}_v$ are related.*

73

5.2. Nearest line

A line $\mathbf{l}$ in $\mathbf{R}^n$ can be described by the parametric equation $\mathbf{y} + \mathbf{x} \cdot t$ where $\mathbf{y}, \mathbf{x} \in \mathbf{R}^n$, $\|\mathbf{x}\| = 1$, $\mathbf{y}^T \mathbf{x} = 0$, and t is a scalar parameter. In what follows we fix a line $\mathbf{l}$ and compute the distance from a point $\mathbf{a} \in \mathbf{R}^n$ to $\mathbf{l}$. To simplify the notations we shall denote the projection $P_{\mathbf{l}}(\mathbf{a})$ just by $P(\mathbf{a})$. The projection $P(\mathbf{a})$ is given by $\mathbf{x}\mathbf{x}^T\mathbf{a} + \mathbf{y}$. The squared distance from $\mathbf{a}$ to $\mathbf{l}$ is, therefore,

$$\|\mathbf{a} - P(\mathbf{a})\|^2 = \|\mathbf{a} - \mathbf{y}\|^2 - \|\mathbf{x}^T\mathbf{a}\|^2. \tag{5.2.1}$$

The line $\mathbf{l}$ that solves Problem 5.1.1 solves the following constrained optimization problem

$$\min_{\mathbf{x}, \mathbf{y}} \left\{ \sum_{i=1}^m (\|\mathbf{a}_i - \mathbf{y}\|^2 - \|\mathbf{x}^T\mathbf{a}_i\|^2), \text{ subject to } \|\mathbf{x}\| = 1, \ \mathbf{y}^T\mathbf{x} = 0 \right\}. \tag{5.2.2}$$

We assume now that $\mathbf{x}$ is known, and will try to identify $\mathbf{y} = \mathbf{y}(\mathbf{x})$. The assumption about $\mathbf{x}$ reduces (5.2.2) to

$$\min_{\mathbf{y}} \left\{ \sum_{i=1}^m (\|\mathbf{a}_i - \mathbf{y}\|^2 - \|\mathbf{x}^T\mathbf{a}_i\|^2), \text{ subject to } \mathbf{y}^T\mathbf{x} = 0 \right\}. \tag{5.2.3}$$

Introduction of a Lagrange multiplier λ reduces (5.2.3) to the equation

$$\nabla_{\mathbf{y}} \left(\sum_{i=1}^m (\|\mathbf{a}_i - \mathbf{y}\|^2 - \|\mathbf{x}^T\mathbf{a}_i\|^2) + \lambda \mathbf{y}^T\mathbf{x} \right) = 0, \tag{5.2.4}$$

where $\nabla_{\mathbf{y}}$ is the gradient with respect to $\mathbf{y}$. The solution $\mathbf{y} = \mathbf{y}(\mathbf{x})$ is given by

$$\mathbf{y} = \mathbf{y}(\mathbf{x}) = \frac{1}{m} \sum_{i=1}^m \mathbf{a}_i - \mathbf{x}\mathbf{x}^T \left(\frac{1}{m} \sum_{i=1}^m \mathbf{a}_i \right). \tag{5.2.5}$$

We note that the vector $\mathbf{m} = \frac{1}{m} \sum_{i=1}^m \mathbf{a}_i$ is the arithmetic mean of the data set $\mathcal{A}$, and (5.2.5) shows that the "optimal" line

$$\mathbf{l} = \{\mathbf{y}(\mathbf{x}) + \mathbf{x} \cdot t \ : -\infty < t < \infty\} = \{\mathbf{m} + \mathbf{x} \cdot (t - \mathbf{x}^T\mathbf{m}) : -\infty < t < \infty\}$$

passes through the mean. We now turn to (5.2.2) that after the substitution $\mathbf{y} = \mathbf{m} - \mathbf{x}\mathbf{x}^T\mathbf{m}$ becomes

$$\min_{\mathbf{x}} \left\{ \sum_{i=1}^{m} (\|(\mathbf{a}_i - \mathbf{m}) + \mathbf{x}\mathbf{x}^T\mathbf{m}\|^2 - \|\mathbf{x}^T\mathbf{a}_i\|^2), \quad \text{subject to } \|\mathbf{x}\| = 1 \right\}.$$
(5.2.6)

Note that

$$\|(\mathbf{a} - \mathbf{m}) + \mathbf{x}\mathbf{x}^T\mathbf{m}\|^2 - \|\mathbf{x}^T\mathbf{a}\|^2 = \|\mathbf{a} - \mathbf{m}\|^2 - \|(\mathbf{a} - \mathbf{m})^T\mathbf{x}\|^2,$$

and (5.2.6) becomes

$$\sum_{i=1}^{m} \|(\mathbf{a}_i - \mathbf{m})\|^2 - \max_{\|\mathbf{x}\|=1} \sum_{i=1}^{m} \|(\mathbf{a}_i - \mathbf{m})^T\mathbf{x}\|^2.$$

Hence solution to (5.2.2) can be found by solving the *maximization* problem

$$\max_{\|\mathbf{x}\|=1} \sum_{i=1}^{m} \|(\mathbf{a}_i - \mathbf{m})^T\mathbf{x}\|^2 = \max_{\|\mathbf{x}\|=1} \mathbf{x}^T \left(\sum_{i=1}^{m} (\mathbf{a}_i - \mathbf{m})(\mathbf{a}_i - \mathbf{m})^T \right) \mathbf{x}.$$

Note that for a matrix

$$B = [\mathbf{b}_1, \ldots, \mathbf{b}_m], \ \mathbf{b}_i \in \mathbf{R}^n \text{ one has } BB^T = \sum_{i=1}^{m} \mathbf{b}_i \mathbf{b}_i^T.$$

Hence with $B = [\mathbf{a}_1 - \mathbf{m}, \ldots, \mathbf{a}_m - \mathbf{m}] = A - \mathbf{m}\mathbf{e}^T$ the original optimization problem (5.2.2) can be written as

$$\max_{\mathbf{x}} \{\mathbf{x}^T BB^T \mathbf{x} : \text{subject to } \|\mathbf{x}\| = 1\}.$$
(5.2.7)

Introduction of Lagrange multipliers leads to the equation

$$\nabla_{\mathbf{x}}(\mathbf{x}^T BB^T \mathbf{x} - \lambda(\mathbf{x}^T\mathbf{x} - 1)) = 0,$$
(5.2.8)

that is, $BB^T\mathbf{x} = \lambda\mathbf{x}$ and $\mathbf{x}^T\mathbf{x} = 1$. That is $\mathbf{x}$ is an eigenvector of BB^T with the corresponding eigenvalue λ, and

$$\mathbf{x}^T BB^T \mathbf{x} = \lambda^2.$$
(5.2.9)

Since BB^T is a symmetric and positive semidefinite matrix the n eigenvalues of BB^T are real and nonnegative

$$\lambda_n \geq \lambda_{n-1} \geq \cdots \geq \lambda_1 \geq 0.$$

It is clear now that to maximize (5.2.9) one needs the eigenvector $\mathbf{x}$
corresponding to the largest eigenvalue λ_n.

A similar analysis shows that the "best" least squares approximation of a vector set $\mathcal{A}$ by a two-dimensional plain is given by the para-
metric equation

$$\left\{ \mathbf{m} + \mathbf{x}_1 \cdot t_1 + \mathbf{x}_2 \cdot t_2 \; : \; \mathbf{x}_i^T \mathbf{x}_j = \delta_{ij}, \; \infty < t_i < \infty, \; i, j = 1, 2 \right\}$$

where $\mathbf{x}_1$ and $\mathbf{x}_2$ are the eigenvectors of BB^T corresponding to the two
largest eigenvalues λ_1 and λ_2.

A generalization of this result to k-dimensional affine subspace
of $\mathbf{R}^n$ is straightforward. This generalization also leads to a lower
bound for $Q(\Pi)$ with $d(\mathbf{x}, \mathbf{y}) = \|\mathbf{x} - \mathbf{y}\|^2$ (see (2.1.3)). Indeed, suppose
that the optimal k-cluster partition $\Pi^{\min} = \{\pi_1^{\min}, \ldots, \pi_k^{\min}\}$ has been
identified. Denote by $\mathbf{V}$ the affine hull of the corresponding centroids
$\mathbf{c}(\pi_1^{\min}), \ldots, \mathbf{c}(\pi_k^{\min})$. We denote the squared Euclidean distance from
$\mathbf{a} \in \mathbf{R}^n$ to $\mathbf{V}$ by $d(\mathbf{a}, \mathbf{V})$ (that is $d(\mathbf{a}, \mathbf{V}) = \|\mathbf{a} - P_\mathbf{V}(\mathbf{a})\|^2$ where $P_\mathbf{V}(\mathbf{a})$ is
the orthogonal projection of $\mathbf{a}$ on $\mathbf{V}$). Note that for each $i = 1, \ldots, k$
one has $d(\mathbf{a}, \mathbf{V}) \leq d(\mathbf{a}, \mathbf{c}(\pi_i^{\min}))$, and

$$\sum_{i=1}^{m} d(\mathbf{a}_i, \mathbf{V}) \leq Q(\Pi^{\min}). \tag{5.2.10}$$

Let $\mathbf{V}_{k-1}$ be the $k-1$-dimensional affine subspace of $\mathbf{R}^n$ that provides
the best least squares approximation to $\mathcal{A}$. This subspace is determined
by the mean vector $\mathbf{m}$ and the $k-1$ eigenvectors of the matrix BB^T
corresponding to the $k-1$ largest eigenvalues $\lambda_n, \ldots, \lambda_{n-k+1}$. Moreover

$$\sum_{i=1}^{m} d(\mathbf{a}_i, \mathbf{V}_{k-1}) \leq \sum_{i=1}^{m} d(\mathbf{a}_i, \mathbf{V}), \text{ and due to (5.2.10)}$$

$$\sum_{i=1}^{m} d(\mathbf{a}_i, \mathbf{V}_{k-1}) \leq Q(\Pi^{\min}).$$

To address Problem 5.1.2 we note that due to (5.2.1) the distance between projections of two vectors $\mathbf{a}$ and $\mathbf{b}$ is

$$||P(\mathbf{a}) - P(\mathbf{b})||^2 = ||\mathbf{x}\mathbf{x}^T(\mathbf{a} - \mathbf{b})||^2$$

depends on the direction vector $\mathbf{x}$ only, and independent of $\mathbf{y}$. We choose $\mathbf{y} = \mathbf{m}$ for convenience, and, due to the Pythagoras theorem (see e.g. [17]), obtain the following for a line $\mathbf{l}$ passing through $\mathbf{m}$ with a direction vector $\mathbf{x}$:

$$\sum_{i=1}^{m} ||\mathbf{a}_i - P(\mathbf{a}_i)||^2 + \sum_{i=1}^{m} ||P(\mathbf{a}_i) - \mathbf{m}||^2 = \sum_{i=1}^{m} ||\mathbf{a}_i - \mathbf{m}||^2.$$

It should now be clear that the line $\mathbf{l}$ that *maximizes* $\sum_{i=1}^{m} ||P(\mathbf{a}_i) - \mathbf{m}||^2$ is the same line that *minimizes* $\sum_{i=1}^{m} ||\mathbf{a}_i - P(\mathbf{a}_i)||^2$, and if we request $\mathbf{l}_v$ to pass through $\mathbf{m}$, then $\mathbf{l}_d = \mathbf{l}_v$.

5.3. Principal directions divisive partitioning

In this section we present two clustering algorithms based on principal directions. Both algorithms are memory efficient and fast. The algorithms take advantage of sparsity of the "term by document" matrix.

5.3.1. Principal direction divisive partitioning (PDDP)

The algorithm divides the entire collection into two clusters by using the principal direction. Each of these two clusters will be divided into two subclusters using the same process recursively. The subdivision of a cluster is stopped when the cluster satisfies a certain "quality" criterion. Cluster variance and size are two examples of the stopping criteria (in numerical experiments with PDDP reported in this book cluster size serves as the stopping criterion).

Clustering of a set of vectors in $\mathbf{R}^n$ is, in general, a difficult task. There is, however, an exception. When $n = 1$, and all the vectors belong to a one-dimensional line, clustering becomes relatively easy (see Problem 2.1.6). In many cases a good partition of a one-dimensional set $\mathcal{P}$

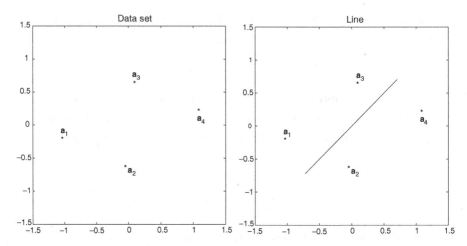

Figure 5.1: The multidimensional data set and the "best" line.

into two subsets $\mathcal{P}_1$ and $\mathcal{P}_2$ amounts to a selection of a number, say μ, so that

$$\mathcal{P}_1 = \{p \,:\, p \in \mathcal{P}, \ p \le \mu\}, \quad \text{and} \quad \mathcal{P}_2 = \{p \,:\, p \in \mathcal{P}, \ p > \mu\}$$
(5.3.1)

For example, the arithmetic mean is a good candidate for μ (see Problem 2.1.6).

The basic idea of the Principal Direction Divisive Partitioning algorithm (PDDP) is the following:

1. Given a set of vectors $\mathcal{A}$ in $\mathbf{R}^n$ determine the one-dimensional line $\mathbf{l}$ that provides the "best" approximation to $\mathcal{A}$ (see Figure 5.1).
2. Project $\mathcal{A}$ onto $\mathbf{l}$, and denote the projection of the set $\mathcal{A}$ by $\mathcal{P}$ (note that $\mathcal{P}$ is just a set of scalars, see Figure 5.2). Denote the projection of a vector $\mathbf{a}$ by p.
3. Partition $\mathcal{P}$ into two subsets $\mathcal{P}_1$ and $\mathcal{P}_2$ as described by (5.3.1).
4. Generate the induced partition $\{\mathcal{A}_1, \mathcal{A}_2\}$ of $\mathcal{A}$ as follows:

$$\mathcal{A}_1 = \{\mathbf{a} \,:\, p \in \mathcal{P}_1\}, \quad \text{and} \quad \mathcal{A}_2 = \{\mathbf{a} \,:\, p \in \mathcal{P}_2\} \qquad (5.3.2)$$

(the two last steps are illustrated by Figure 5.3).

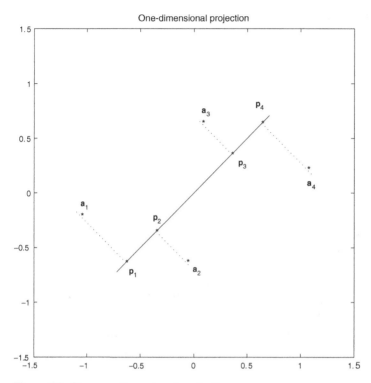

Figure 5.2: The one-dimensional projections.

PDDP selects the line that maximizes variance of the projections as the best one-dimensional approximation of an n-dimensional set. The direction of the line is defined by the eigenvector of the covariance matrix BB^T (see Section 5.2) corresponding to the largest eigenvalue. Since BB^T is symmetric and positive semidefinite all the eigenvalues λ_i, $i = 1, 2, \ldots, n$ of the matrix are real and nonnegative, that is, $\lambda_n \geq \lambda_{n-1} \geq \cdots \geq \lambda_1 \geq 0$. Furthermore, while the "scatter" value of the document set is $\lambda_1 + \lambda_2 + \cdots + \lambda_n$, the "scatter" value of the one-dimensional projection is only λ_n. The quantity

$$\frac{\lambda_n}{\lambda_1 + \lambda_2 + \cdots + \lambda_n} \tag{5.3.3}$$

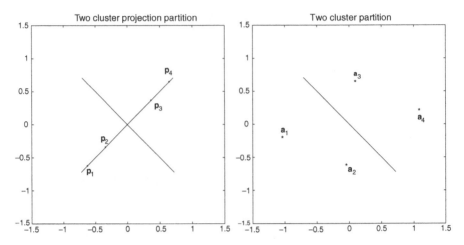

Figure 5.3: Two cluster partitions.

may, therefore, be considered as the fraction of information preserved under the projection (in contrast with the "lost" information $\frac{\lambda_1 + \cdots + \lambda_{n-1}}{\lambda_1 + \lambda_2 + \cdots + \lambda_n}$). Inspite of the fact that the numerator of (5.3.3) contains only one eigenvalue of a large matrix the algorithm generates remarkable results.

Problem 5.3.1. *Let* $\{\mathbf{a}_1, \ldots, \mathbf{a}_m\} \subset \mathbf{R}^n$, $\mathbf{m} = \frac{\mathbf{a}_1 + \cdots + \mathbf{a}_m}{m}$, $B = [\mathbf{a}_1 - \mathbf{m}, \ldots,$
$\mathbf{a}_m - \mathbf{m}]$ *and* $\lambda_n \geq \cdots \geq \lambda_1 \geq 0$ *are the eigenvalues of the matrix* BB^T.
Show that

$$\sum_{i=1}^m \|\mathbf{a}_i - \mathbf{m}\|^2 = \operatorname{tr}\left(BB^T\right) = \lambda_n + \cdots + \lambda_1.$$

5.3.2. Spherical principal directions divisive partitioning (sPDDP)

In this section we combine the simple and elegant PDDP idea with clustering one-dimensional circle technique developed in Section 4.2.1. First, a set of unit vectors $\mathcal{A} \subset \mathbf{R}^n$ is approximated by a one-dimensional great circle of $\mathbf{S}^{n-1}$ (a great circle is represented by an intersection of $\mathbf{S}^{n-1}$ and a two-dimensional subspace $\mathbf{P}$ of $\mathbf{R}^n$). Next the approximation is divided into two clusters. The stopping criterion for this algorithm is the same as for PDDP (cluster size is the stopping criterion for sPDDP-related experiments reported in this book). The proposed algorithm is the following:

Algorithm 5.3.1. *The Spherical Principal Directions Divisive Partitioning (sPDDP) clustering algorithm.*

1. *Given a set of unit vectors $\mathcal{A}$ in $\mathbf{R}^n$ determine the two-dimensional plane $\mathbf{P}$ that provides the best least squares approximation for $\mathcal{A}$.*

2. *Project $\mathcal{A}$ onto $\mathbf{P}$. Denote the projection of the set $\mathcal{A}$ by $\mathcal{P}$, and the projection of a vector $\mathbf{a}$ by $\mathbf{p}$ (note that $\mathbf{p}$ is two-dimensional).*

3. *If $\mathbf{p} \in \mathcal{P}$ is a nonzero vector, then "push" $\mathbf{p}$ to the great circle. Denote the corresponding vector by $\mathbf{z} = \frac{\mathbf{p}}{\|\mathbf{p}\|}$. Denote the constructed set by $\mathcal{Z}$.*

4. *Partition $\mathcal{Z}$ into two clusters $\mathcal{Z}_1$ and $\mathcal{Z}_2$. Assign projections $\mathbf{p}$ with $\|\mathbf{p}\| = 0$ to $\mathcal{Z}_1$.*

5. *Generate the induced partition $\{\mathcal{A}_1, \mathcal{A}_2\}$ of $\mathcal{A}$ as follows:*

$$\mathcal{A}_1 = \{\mathbf{a} : \mathbf{z} \in \mathcal{Z}_1\}, \quad and \quad \mathcal{A}_2 = \{\mathbf{a} : \mathbf{z} \in \mathcal{Z}_2\}. \qquad (5.3.4)$$

If the best two-dimensional approximation of the document set is the plane $\mathbf{P}$ that maximizes variance of the projections, then $\mathbf{P}$ is defined by two eigenvectors of the covariance matrix BB^T (see Section 5.2) corresponding to the largest eigenvalues λ_n and λ_{n-1}. The "preserved" information under this projection is

$$\frac{\lambda_n + \lambda_{n-1}}{\lambda_1 + \lambda_2 + \cdots + \lambda_n}. \qquad (5.3.5)$$

Note that the quantity given by (5.3.5) may be almost twice as much as the "preserved" information under the projection on the one-dimensional line given by (5.3.3). As we show later in this section this may lead to a significant improvement over results provided by PDDP.

Table 5.1: Spherical k-means generated "confusion" matrix with **69** "misclassified" documents using 4099 words

	Medlars	CISI	Cranfield
cluster 0	1004	5	4
cluster 1	18	1440	16
cluster 2	11	15	1380

5.3.3. Clustering with PDDP and sPDDP

Consider the data set that contains the document collections (classic3)

- DC0 (Medlars Collection 1033 medical abstracts)
- DC1 (CISI Collection 1460 information science abstracts)
- DC2 (Cranfield Collection 1398 aerodynamics abstracts)

already described in Section 2.3.1 (and available from http://www.utk.edu/~lsi/).

Partitioning the entire collection into three clusters by batch spherical k-means generates the confusion matrix given by Table 5.1. The entry ij is the number of documents that belong to cluster i and document collection j. Note that there is no a priori connection between document collection j and cluster i. Hence, one cannot expect the "confusion" matrix to have diagonal structure unless rows (or columns) of the matrix are suitably permuted. A good clustering procedure should be able to produce a "confusion" matrix with a single "dominant" entry in each row. We regard the other entries in a row as "misclassification" (so, e.g., the first row misclassifications are $9 = 5 + 4$). The number of "misclassified" documents is the sum of the misclassifications, which is 69 in this experiment. The confusion matrix shows that less that 2% of the entire collection have been "misclassified" by the algorithm.

We denote the overall collection of 3891 documents by DC. After stop-word removal (see ftp://ftp.cs.cornell.edu/pub/smart/english.stop), and stemming the data set contains 15,864 unique terms.

Our first goal is to select "good" index terms. We argue that for recovering the three document collections the term "blood" is much more useful than the term "case". Indeed, while the term "case" occurs in 253 Medlars documents, 72 CISI documents, and 365 Cranfield documents, the term "blood" occurs in 142 Medlars documents, 0 CISI documents, and 0 Cranfield documents. With each term t we associate a three dimensional "direction" vector $\mathbf{d(t)} = (d_0(\mathbf{t}), d_1(\mathbf{t}), d_2(\mathbf{t}))^T$, so that $d_i(\mathbf{t})$ is the number of documents in a collection DCi containing the term t. So, for example, $\mathbf{d}(\text{"case"}) = (253, 72, 365)^T$, and $\mathbf{d}(\text{"blood"}) = (142, 0, 0)^T$. In addition to "blood" terms like "layer" ($\mathbf{d}(\text{"layer"}) = (6, 0, 358)^T$), or "retriev" ($\mathbf{d}(\text{"retriev"}) = (0, 262, 0)^T$) seem to be much more useful than the terms "case", "studi" and "found" with $\mathbf{d}(\text{"studi"}) = (356, 341, 238)^T$, and $\mathbf{d}(\text{"found"}) = (211, 93, 322)^T$ respectively.

When only the "combined" collection DC of 3891 documents is available the above described construction of "direction" vectors is not possible and we employ a simple term selection algorithm based on term occurrence across a document collection. To exploit statistics of term occurrence throughout the corpus we remove terms that occur in less than r sentences across the collection, and denote the remaining terms by slice(r) (r should be collection dependent, the experiments in this chapter are performed with $r = 20$). The first l best quality terms that belong to slice(r) define the dimension of the vector space model.

We denote the frequency of a term t in the document $\mathbf{d}_j$ by f_j and measure the quality of the term t by

$$q(\mathbf{t}) = \sum_{j=1}^{m} f_j^2 - \frac{1}{m} \left[\sum_{j=1}^{m} f_j \right]^2, \qquad (5.3.6)$$

where m is the total number of documents in the collection (note that $q(\mathbf{t})$ is proportional to the term frequency variance). Tables 5.2 and 5.3 present 15 "best", and 15 "worst" terms for slice(20) in our collection of 3891 documents.

Table 5.2: 15 "best" terms in slice(20) according to q

Term	$q(t)$	$d_0(t)$	$d_1(t)$	$d_2(t)$
flow	7687.795	35	34	714
librari	7107.937	0	523	0
pressur	5554.151	57	12	533
number	5476.418	92	204	568
cell	5023.158	210	2	2
inform	4358.370	28	614	44
bodi	3817.281	84	23	276
system	3741.070	82	494	84
wing	3409.713	1	0	216
effect	3280.777	244	159	539
method	3239.389	121	252	454
layer	3211.331	6	0	358
jet	3142.879	1	0	92
patient	3116.628	301	3	0
shock	3085.249	4	1	224

Table 5.3: 15 "worst" terms in slice(20) according to q

Term	$q(t)$	$d_0(t)$	$d_1(t)$	$d_2(t)$
suppos	21.875	6	7	9
nevertheless	21.875	6	11	5
retain	21.875	9	4	9
art	21.875	0	20	2
compos	21.875	5	5	12
ago	21.875	2	18	2
elabor	21.875	3	16	3
obviou	21.897	4	9	6
speak	20.886	6	12	3
add	20.886	3	14	4
understood	20.886	2	14	5
pronounc	20.886	18	0	3
pertain	19.897	3	8	9
merit	19.897	1	9	10
provis	19.897	1	18	1

5.3. Principal directions divisive partitioning

Table 5.4: PDDP generated "confusion" matrix with **470** "misclassified" documents using 600 best q terms

	DC0	DC1	DC2
cluster 0	272	9	1379
cluster 1	4	1285	11
cluster 2	757	166	8
"empty" documents			
cluster 3	0	0	0

Table 5.5: Number of documents "misclassified" by PDDP and PDDP + quadratic k-means for term selection based on q

# of terms	500	600	700	1000	1300
PDDP	1062	470	388	236	181
PDDP + k-means	989	69	63	55	53

To evaluate the impact of feature selection by q on clustering we conduct the following experiment. The best quality **600** terms are selected, and unit norm vectors for the 3891 documents are built (we use the tfn scheme to construct document vectors). The document vectors are partitioned into three clusters with PDDP (see Table 5.4) or sPDDP (see Table 5.6). For the summary of results consult Tables 5.5 and 5.7 respectively.

Table 5.5 presents results for various choices of terms selected by q. The first row of Table 5.5 lists the number of selected terms, the second row presents the corresponding number of documents "misclassified" by PDDP, and the third row lists the number of documents "misclassified" by PDDP followed by quadratic k-means. The displayed results indicate that the algorithm "collapses" when the number of selected terms drops below 600. The table indicates that with 1300 selected terms (i.e., only about 30% of the 4,099 terms reported in Table 5.1) the number of "misclassified" documents is slightly lower than the number reported in Table 5.1.

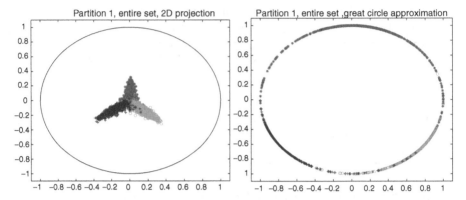

Figure 5.4: Classic3 two-dimensional projection $\mathcal{P}$ (left), and one-dimensional "circular" image $\mathcal{Z}$ of $\mathcal{P}$ (right).

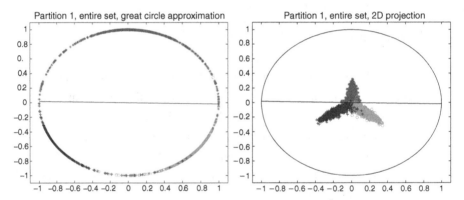

Figure 5.5: Two-cluster partition $\{\mathcal{Z}_1, \mathcal{Z}_2\}$ of the "circular" set $\mathcal{Z}$ (left), and induced two-cluster partition of the two-dimensional classic3 projection $\mathcal{P}$ (right).

We now turn to the spherical principal directions divisive partitioning algorithm. We start with illustration of the first iteration of the algorithm. Figure 5.4 depicts Step 2 and Step 3 of Algorithm 5.3.1. Vectors of three different colors represent the two-dimensional projections of the three different collections. Figure 5.5 shows the optimal two-cluster partition $\{\mathcal{Z}_1, \mathcal{Z}_2\}$, and the induced partition of the data set two-dimensional projection $\mathcal{P}$.

Table 5.6: sPDDP generated "confusion" matrix with **68** "misclassified" documents using 600 best q terms

	DC0	DC1	DC2
cluster 0	1000	3	1
cluster 1	8	10	1376
cluster 2	25	1447	21
"empty" documents cluster 3	0	0	0

Table 5.7: Number of documents "misclassified" by sPDDP and sPDDP + quadratic k-means for term selection based on q

# of terms	300	400	500	600
sPDDP	228	88	76	68
sPDDP + k-means	100	80	62	62

The confusion matrix for the three-cluster partition generated by sPDDP given in Table 5.6. While the quality of the confusion matrix is similar to that reported in Table 5.1, the dimension of the vector space model, **600**, is about only 15% of the vector space dimension reported in Table 5.1. We remark that the confusion matrix is a significant improvement over the result presented in Table 5.4.

Table 5.7 summarizes clustering results for sPDDP and sPDDP followed by quadratic k-means for different choices of index terms (all term selections are based on the q criterion). Note that while the PDDP algorithm "collapses" when the number of selected terms drops below 600 (see Table 5.5), the sPDDP algorithm performs reasonably well even when the number of selected terms is only 300.

5.4. Largest eigenvector

The results already presented in this chapter lead to the following problem: Let M be a symmetric and positive semidefinite $n \times n$ matrix. Denote by $\lambda_n \geq \lambda_{n-1} \geq \cdots \geq \lambda_1$ the eigenvalues of M, and by

$\mathbf{v}_n, \mathbf{v}_{n-1}, \ldots, \mathbf{v}_1$ the corresponding eigenvectors. *For a given integer l,* $1 \le l \le n$ *find* $\mathbf{v}_n, \ldots, \mathbf{v}_{n+1-l}$, *the eigenvectors corresponding to the first l largest eigenvalues* $\lambda_n, \ldots, \lambda_{n+1-l}$.

In this section we recall one of the simplest methods that recovers $\mathbf{v}_n$ and then provide an additional IR-related application that requires computation of $\mathbf{v}_n$.

5.4.1. Power method

A simple method that computes the largest eigenvalue λ_n along with the corresponding eigenvector $\mathbf{v}_n$ of the matrix M is described below.

Select a nonzero vector $\mathbf{x}$ and to consider the sequence

$$\frac{\mathbf{x}}{||\mathbf{x}||}, \quad \frac{M\mathbf{x}}{||M\mathbf{x}||}, \quad \ldots, \quad \frac{M^k\mathbf{x}}{||M^k\mathbf{x}||}, \quad \ldots$$

The vector $\mathbf{x} = c_1\mathbf{v}_1 + c_2\mathbf{v}_2 + \cdots + c_n\mathbf{v}_n$, and

$$M^k\mathbf{x} = \lambda_1^k c_1 \mathbf{v}_1 + \lambda_2^k c_2 \mathbf{v}_2 + \cdots + \lambda_n^k c_n \mathbf{v}_n$$
$$= \lambda_n^k c_n \left[\left(\frac{\lambda_1}{\lambda_n}\right)^k \frac{c_1}{c_n} \mathbf{v}_1 + \cdots + \left(\frac{\lambda_{n-1}}{\lambda_n}\right)^k \frac{c_{n-1}}{c_n} \mathbf{v}_{n-1} + \mathbf{v}_n \right].$$

Hence if $c_n \ne 0$, then $\lim_{k\to\infty} \frac{M^k\mathbf{x}}{||M^k\mathbf{x}||} = \mathbf{v}_n$.

5.4.2. An application: hubs and authorities

Consider a collection V of hyperlinked pages as a directed graph $G = (V, E)$. The vertices correspond to the pages, and a directed edge $(p, q) \in E$ indicates the existence of a link from page p to page q. We informally define "authorities" and "hubs" as follows:

1. a page p is an authority if it is pointed by many pages,
2. a page p is a hub if it points to many pages.

To measure the "authority" and the "hub" of the pages we introduce vectors $\mathbf{a}$ and $\mathbf{h}$ of dimension $|V|$, so that $\mathbf{a}[p]$ and $\mathbf{h}[p]$ are the "authority" and the "hub" of the page p. The following is an iterative process that computes the vectors.

1. set $t = 0$
2. assign initial values $\mathbf{a}^{(t)}$, and $\mathbf{h}^{(t)}$
3. normalize vectors $\mathbf{a}^{(t)}$, and $\mathbf{h}^{(t)}$, so that $\sum_p (\mathbf{a}^{(t)}[p])^2 = \sum_p (\mathbf{h}^{(t)}[p])^2 = 1$
4. set $\mathbf{a}^{(t+1)}[p] = \sum_{(q,p)\in E} \mathbf{h}^{(t)}[q]$, and $\mathbf{h}^{(t+1)}[p] = \sum_{(p,q)\in E} \mathbf{a}^{(t+1)}[q]$
5. if (`stopping criterion fails`)

      increment t by 1

      goto Step 3

  else

      stop.

Let A be the adjacency matrix of the graph G, that is

$$A_{ij} = \begin{cases} 1 & \text{if} \qquad (p_i, p_j) \text{ is an edge of } G \\ 0 & \text{otherwise} \end{cases}$$

Note that

$$\mathbf{a}^{(t+1)} = \frac{A^T \mathbf{h}^{(t)}}{||A^T \mathbf{h}^{(t)}||}, \quad \text{and } \mathbf{h}^{(t+1)} = \frac{A \mathbf{a}^{(t+1)}}{||A \mathbf{a}^{(t+1)}||}.$$

This yields $\mathbf{a}^{(t+1)} = \frac{A^T A \mathbf{a}^{(t)}}{||A^T A \mathbf{a}^{(t)}||}$, and $\mathbf{h}^{(t+1)} = \frac{A A^T \mathbf{h}^{(t)}}{||A A^T \mathbf{h}^{(t)}||}$. Finally

$$\mathbf{a}^{(t)} = \frac{(A^T A)^k \mathbf{a}^{(0)}}{||(A^T A)^k \mathbf{a}^{(0)}||}, \quad \text{and } \mathbf{h}^{(t)} = \frac{(A A^T)^k \mathbf{h}^{(0)}}{||(A A^T)^k \mathbf{h}^{(0)}||}. \qquad (5.4.1)$$

Let $\mathbf{v}$ and $\mathbf{w}$ be a unit eigenvectors corresponding to maximal eigenvalues of the symmetric matrices $A^T A$ and $A A^T$ correspondingly. The above arguments lead to the following result:

$$\lim_{t \to \infty} \mathbf{a}^{(t)} = \mathbf{v}, \quad \lim_{t \to \infty} \mathbf{h}^{(t)} = \mathbf{w}. \qquad (5.4.2)$$

Problem 5.4.1. *Show that* $\mathbf{w} = A\mathbf{v}$, *and* $\mathbf{v} = A^T \mathbf{w}$.

5.5. Bibliographic notes

The Principal Direction Divisive Partitioning algorithm (PDDP) was introduced by Daniel Boley [20]. For best least square approximations of a vector set by an affine subspace consult, for example [11, 55]. A lower bound evaluation for $Q(\Pi)$ through the distance to the affine subspace that provides the best least squares approximation is suggested in [45].

For clustering results generated by PDDP we refer the interested reader, for example, to [18–20] (see also Subsection 2.3.1 that shows only about 10% improvement in the objective function value after an application of the k-means clustering algorithm to a partition generated by PDDP). For clustering data set large enough not to fit into memory consult [99, 100]. For a different approach to cluster very large data sets see, for example [147] (and also Chapter 3 and Section 8.4).

Clustering of the three document collections with the batch spherical k-means algorithm as reported in Table 5.1 is taken from [39]. The Cranfield collection tackled in this paper has two empty documents. In the experiments reported in this chapter the two empty documents have been removed from DC2. The other document collections are identical.

For words stemming we always use Porter stemming (see [113]). The term selection algorithm is due to Salton and McGill [119]. For additional term selection techniques consult, for example, [93, 97, 101, 140], and references therein. For t f n and additional weighting schemes consult, for example [27].

For computations of eigenvectors of $n \times n$ matrices consult, for example, [32, 61, 102, 110]. The concept of "hub" and "authority" along with HITS is introduced by Jon Kleinberg in [77].

6 Information theoretic clustering

This chapter discusses an information theoretic framework for k-means clustering. Let

$$\left(S_1^{n-1}\right)_+ = \left\{\mathbf{a} \; : \; \mathbf{a} \in \mathbf{R}^n, \; \mathbf{a}[j] \geq 0, \; \sum_{j=1}^{n} \mathbf{a}[j] = 1\right\}$$

(when it does not lead to ambiguity, we shall drop the subscript 1 and the superscript $n-1$ and denote the set just by S_+). Although each vector $\mathbf{a} \in S_+$ can be interpreted as a probability distribution in an attempt to keep the exposition of the material as simple as possible we shall turn to probabilistic arguments only when the deterministic approach fails to lead to desired results.

The chapter focuses on k-means clustering of a data set $\mathcal{A} = \{\mathbf{a}_1, \ldots, \mathbf{a}_m\} \subset S_+$ with the Kullback–Leibler divergence.

6.1. Kullback–Leibler divergence

The section provides an additional example of a "distance-like" function and lists a number of its basic properties.

Definition 6.1.1. *The relative entropy, or Kullback–Leibler divergence between two probability distributions* $\mathbf{a}$ *and* $\mathbf{b} \in S_+$ *is defined as* $KL(\mathbf{a}, \mathbf{b}) = \sum_{i=1}^{n} \mathbf{a}[i] \log \frac{\mathbf{a}[i]}{\mathbf{b}[i]}$ *(when $a > 0$ and $b > 0$, motivated by continuity arguments, we use the convention* $a \log \frac{a}{0} = +\infty$ *and* $0 \log \frac{0}{b} = 0$*).*

We first show that when $\mathbf{a} \in \mathcal{S}_+$ is fixed the range of $KL(\mathbf{a}, \mathbf{x}), \mathbf{x} \in \mathcal{S}_+$ is $[0, \infty]$. Since $KL(\mathbf{a}, \mathbf{x}) = \sum_{i=1}^{n} \mathbf{a}[i] \log \mathbf{a}[i] - \sum_{i=1}^{n} \mathbf{a}[i] \log \mathbf{x}[i]$ we shall consider the function $f(\mathbf{x}) = \sum_{i=1}^{n} \mathbf{a}[i] \log \mathbf{x}[i]$. Note that:

1. $f(\mathbf{x}) \leq 0$.
2. Since $\mathbf{a}[j] > 0$ for at least one $j = 1, \ldots, n$ for convenience we may assume that $\mathbf{a}[1] > 0$. Let $0 \leq \epsilon \leq 1$. When $\mathbf{x}_\epsilon$ is defined by $\mathbf{x}_\epsilon[1] = \epsilon$, $\mathbf{x}_\epsilon[i] = \frac{1}{n} - \frac{\epsilon}{n}$ one has $\lim_{\epsilon \to 0} f(\mathbf{x}_\epsilon) = -\infty$, hence $\sup_{\mathbf{x} \in \mathcal{S}_+} KL(\mathbf{a}, \mathbf{x}) = \infty$.
3. To find $\max_{\mathbf{x} \in \mathcal{S}_+} f(\mathbf{x})$ we should focus on the $\mathcal{S}_+$ vectors whose coordinates are strictly positive only when the corresponding coordinates of $\mathbf{a}$ are strictly positive. Indeed, if $\mathbf{a}[1] = 0$ and $\mathbf{x}[1] > 0$, then $f(\mathbf{x}) < f(\mathbf{x}_1)$ where

$$\mathbf{x}_1[1] = 0, \quad \mathbf{x}_1[j] = \mathbf{x}[j] + \frac{\mathbf{x}[1]}{n-1}, \quad j = 2, \ldots, n.$$

To simplify the exposition we assume that $\mathbf{a}[j] > 0$, $j = 1, \ldots, n$. To eliminate the constraint $\sum_{i=1}^{n} \mathbf{x}[i] = 1$ we turn to Lagrange multipliers and reduce the constrained optimization problem to the equation

$$\nabla_\mathbf{x} \left[f(\mathbf{x}) + \lambda \left(1 - \sum_{i=1}^{n} \mathbf{x}[i] \right) \right] = 0.$$

A differentiation with respect to $\mathbf{x}[i]$ leads to $\mathbf{a}[i] = \lambda \mathbf{x}[i]$, $i = 1, \ldots, n$. Keeping in mind that

$$1 = \sum_{i=1}^{n} \mathbf{a}[i] = \sum_{i=1}^{n} \lambda \mathbf{x}[i] = \lambda \text{ we get } \mathbf{a}[i] = \mathbf{x}[i], \; i = 1, \ldots, n.$$

Hence arg min $f(\mathbf{x}) = f(\mathbf{a}) = \sum_{j=1}^{n} \mathbf{a}[j] \log \mathbf{a}[j]$, and

$$KL(\mathbf{a}, \mathbf{x}) = \sum_{i=1}^{n} \mathbf{a}[i] \log \mathbf{a}[i] - \sum_{i=1}^{n} \mathbf{a}[i] \log \mathbf{x}[i] \geq \sum_{i=1}^{n} \mathbf{a}[i] \log \mathbf{a}[i]$$

$$- \sum_{i=1}^{n} \mathbf{a}[i] \log \mathbf{a}[i] = KL(\mathbf{a}, \mathbf{a}) = 0,$$

and for each $\mathbf{a}, \mathbf{b} \in \mathbb{R}_+^n$ with $\|\mathbf{a}\| = \|\mathbf{b}\| = 1$ one has $KL(\mathbf{a}, \mathbf{b}) \geq 0$.

Remark 6.1.1. *Note that $f(t) = -\log t$ is a convex function, and*

$$KL(\mathbf{a}, \mathbf{b}) = \sum_{i=1}^{n} \mathbf{a}[i] f\left(\frac{\mathbf{b}[i]}{\mathbf{a}[i]}\right) \geq f\left(\sum_{i=1}^{n} \mathbf{a}[i] \frac{\mathbf{b}[i]}{\mathbf{a}[i]}\right) = f\left(\sum_{i=1}^{n} \mathbf{b}[i]\right)$$

$$= f(1) = -\log 1 = 0.$$

Let $\mathbf{a}, \mathbf{b}$ be nonzero n-dimensional vectors with nonnegative coordinates. Denote $\sum_{j=1}^{n} \mathbf{a}[j]$ by a and $\sum_{j=1}^{n} \mathbf{b}[j]$ by b. Due to nonnegativity of KL one has

$$0 \leq KL\left(\frac{\mathbf{a}}{a}, \frac{\mathbf{b}}{b}\right) = \frac{1}{a}\left[\sum_{j=1}^{n} \mathbf{a}[j] \log \frac{\mathbf{a}[j]}{\mathbf{b}[j]} + a \log \frac{b}{a}\right],$$

and we obtain the log sum inequality for nonnegative numbers $\mathbf{a}[j] \geq 0$, $\mathbf{b}[j] \geq 0$, $j = 1, \ldots, n$

$$\left(\sum_{j=1}^{n} \mathbf{a}[j]\right) \log \frac{\sum_{j=1}^{n} \mathbf{a}[j]}{\sum_{j=1}^{n} \mathbf{b}[j]} \leq \sum_{j=1}^{n} \mathbf{a}[j] \log \frac{\mathbf{a}[j]}{\mathbf{b}[j]}. \tag{6.1.1}$$

Problem 6.1.1. *Verify that the inequality (6.1.1) becomes equality if and only if $\mathbf{a} = \lambda\mathbf{b}$.*

Problem 6.1.2. *Use the convex function $f(t) = t \log t$ to build a one-line proof of the log sum inequality.*

Problem 6.1.3. *Use the log sum inequality to show that $KL(\mathbf{a}, \mathbf{b})$ is convex with respect to $(\mathbf{a}, \mathbf{b})$ (i.e., $KL(\lambda\mathbf{a}_1 + (1 - \lambda)\mathbf{a}_2, \lambda\mathbf{b}_1 + (1 - \lambda)\mathbf{b}_2) \leq \lambda KL(\mathbf{a}_1, \mathbf{b}_1) + (1 - \lambda)KL(\mathbf{a}_2, \mathbf{b}_2))$.*

Problem 6.1.4. *Let $\mathbf{c}_1, \mathbf{c}_2 \in \mathcal{S}_+$. Consider two subsets $\mathcal{H}_1$ and $\mathcal{H}_2$ of $\mathcal{S}_+$*

$$\mathcal{H}_1 = \{\mathbf{x} : \mathbf{x} \in \mathcal{S}_+, \ KL(\mathbf{x}, \mathbf{c}_1) < KL(\mathbf{x}, \mathbf{c}_2)\}$$

and

$$\mathcal{H}_2 = \{\mathbf{x} : \mathbf{x} \in \mathcal{S}_+, \ KL(\mathbf{x}, \mathbf{c}_1) > KL(\mathbf{x}, \mathbf{c}_2)\}.$$

Show that $\mathcal{H}_1$ and $\mathcal{H}_2$ can be separated by a hyperplane.

6.2. *k*-means with Kullback–Leibler divergence

The implementation of batch *k*-means with Kullback–Leibler divergence follows the familiar scheme already discussed in Chapter 2 and Chapter 4. The fact that $KL(\mathbf{a}, \mathbf{b})$ may become $+\infty$ poses a special challenge and distinguishes the batch *k*-means clustering with Kullback–Leibler divergence from the batch *k*-means algorithms with quadratic or spherical distance-like functions. We shall elaborate on this remark below.

In this chapter we focus on the distance-like function $d(\mathbf{x}, \mathbf{a}) = KL(\mathbf{a}, \mathbf{x})$ (for the treatment of the distance-like function $d(\mathbf{x}, \mathbf{a}) = KL(\mathbf{x}, \mathbf{a})$ see Chapter 8). First, we have to identify centroids, that is, solutions of the minimization problem (2.1.1). That is for a set of vectors $\mathcal{A} = \{\mathbf{a}_1, \ldots, \mathbf{a}_m\} \subset \mathcal{S}_+$ one has to find

$$\mathbf{c} = \mathbf{c}(\mathcal{A}) = \arg\min\left\{\sum_{\mathbf{a}\in\mathcal{A}} KL(\mathbf{a}, \mathbf{x}), \ \mathbf{x} \in \mathcal{S}_+\right\}. \tag{6.2.1}$$

Problem 6.2.1. *Show that* $\mathbf{c} = \frac{\mathbf{a}_1 + \cdots + \mathbf{a}_m}{m}$ *is the unique solution for (6.2.1).*

The following example (see Figure 6.1) furnishes a "standard" reason for combining batch and incremental iterations (see Example 2.1.2 and Example 4.1.1).

Example 6.2.1. *Let* $\mathcal{A} = \{\mathbf{a}_1, \mathbf{a}_2, \mathbf{a}_3\} \subset \mathbf{R}^2$ *with*

$$\mathbf{a}_1 = \begin{bmatrix} 1 \\ 0 \end{bmatrix}, \quad \mathbf{a}_2 = \begin{bmatrix} \frac{1}{3} \\ \frac{2}{3} \end{bmatrix}, \quad \mathbf{a}_3 = \begin{bmatrix} 0 \\ 1 \end{bmatrix}.$$

If the initial partition is $\Pi = \{\pi_1, \pi_2\}$ *with* $\pi_1 = \{\mathbf{a}_1, \mathbf{a}_2\}$, *and* $\pi_2 = \{\mathbf{a}_3\}$, *then*

1. *An iteration of batch k-means with* $d(\mathbf{x}, \mathbf{a}) = KL(\mathbf{a}, \mathbf{x})$ *does not change* Π.
2. $Q(\Pi) = 0.277 > 0.116 = Q(\Pi')$, *where* Π' *is a two-cluster partition* $\{\{\mathbf{a}_1\}, \{\mathbf{a}_2, \mathbf{a}_3\}\}$.
3. *One incremental iteration changes* Π *into* Π'.

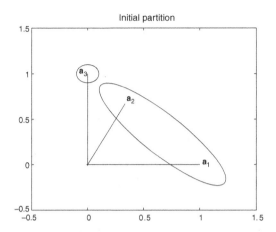

Figure 6.1: Three vector set "bad" initial partition.

Additional reason to augment batch *k*-means by incremental iterations is given below. Consider the following scenario: Let $\{\pi_1, \ldots, \pi_k\}$ be a partition of the data set $\mathcal{A}$. We are about to apply an iteration of the batch version of the clustering algorithm. We focus on two clusters π' and π'' with centroids $\mathbf{c}'$ and $\mathbf{c}''$, and $\mathbf{a} \in \pi'$. Assume for a moment that $d(\mathbf{c}'', \mathbf{a}) = \infty$. In other words, there is an index j such that $\mathbf{a}[j] > 0$ and $\mathbf{c}''[j] = 0$. Since centroid $\mathbf{c}''$ is the arithmetic mean of the cluster the jth coordinate of each vector in cluster π'' is 0 (in the framework of the IR vector space model this means that word j occurs in the document $\mathbf{a}$, and occurs in no document of cluster π'').

On the other hand, if the document $\mathbf{a}$ has no words at all in common with other documents in cluster π', but has, say, five words in common with each document in cluster π'', then reassignment of $\mathbf{a}$ to π'' may improve the partitioning. While batch version of the algorithm will not move $\mathbf{a}$ from π' to π'', the incremental step of the algorithm has the potential to rectify this problem (see also [94] where the same idea is used to compute the distance between a query and a document collection). We, therefore, complement batch iterations by a single incremental step (see Algorithm 2.2.1 for the formal description of the

Table 6.1: KL k-means algorithm generated final "confusion" matrix with **44** "misclassified" documents using best 600 terms.

	DC0	DC1	DC2
cluster 0	1010	6	0
cluster 1	3	4	1387
cluster 2	20	1450	11
"empty" docs cluster 3	0	0	0

procedure) and refer to the resulting scheme as Kullback–Leibler (KL) k-means algorithm.

The logarithmic function sensitivity to low word frequencies has the potential to improve performance of this version of the k-means clustering algorithm. Numerical experiments presented in the next section support this claim.

6.3. Numerical experiments

In what follows we display clustering results for the document collection (DC) described in Section 2.3.1 and Section 5.3.3. The confusion matrix for the three-cluster partition $\Pi = \{\pi_1, \pi_2, \pi_3\}$ of the 600-dimensional data set with 3891 vectors generated by sPDDP is given in Table 5.6 (see Section 5.3.3).

We renormalize the data set (so that L_1 norm of each vector becomes 1) and use Π as the initial partition for the k-means algorithm equipped with Kullback–Leibler distance. The confusion matrix for the three-cluster final partition is given in Table 6.1.

We pause briefly to analyze performance of the k-means algorithm. In the experiment described above the algorithm performs 30 iterations. Figure 6.2 shows the values of $Q(\Pi^{(t)})$, $t = 0, 1, \ldots, 30$. The solid line shows changes in the objective function caused by batch iterations,

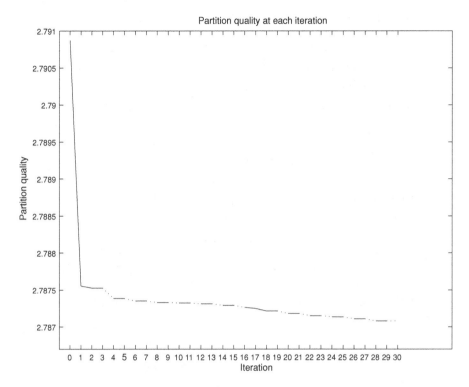

Figure 6.2: Batch and incremental iterations.

and the dotted line does the same for incremental iterations. The figure shows that the lion's share of the work is done by the first three batch iterations. From iteration 4 to iteration 16 values of the objective function drop due to incremental iterations only. At iterations 17, 18, and 19 the batch k-means kicks in. For the rest of the run the objective function changes are due to incremental iterations only.

An inspection reveals that at iteration 4 a vector **a** was moved from cluster π_3 to cluster π_2 by the incremental iteration, and **a** was "missed" by the batch iteration 4 because of the infinite distance between **a** and centroids c_1 and c_2 of clusters π_1 and π_2 respectively (for the very same reason vectors were "missed" by the batch iterations of the algorithm at iterations 5 and 19). The reasons for this behavior are described at the end of Section 6.2.

6.4. Distance between partitions

This section is concerned with a "natural" distance function on pairs of partitions $\Pi_1 = \{\pi_1^1, \ldots, \pi_{k_1}^1\}$ with k_1 clusters and $\Pi_2 = \{\pi_1^2, \ldots, \pi_{k_2}^2\}$ with k_2 clusters of the set $\mathcal{A} = \{\mathbf{a}_1, \ldots, \mathbf{a}_m\}$. First, we need to introduce additional definitions. For a k-clusters partition $\Pi = \{\pi_1, \ldots, \pi_k\}$ define a weight, or random variable, $p(i)$ by

$$p(i) = \frac{|\pi_i|}{m}, \quad i = 1, \ldots, k.$$

Definition 6.4.1. *The entropy of the partition Π is* $H(\Pi) = -\sum_{i=1}^{k} p(i)$ $\log p(i)$.

Let Π_{12} be a product of partitions Π_1 and Π_2 (see Definition 2.3.2) and $p(i, j) = \frac{|\pi_i^1 \cap \pi_j^2|}{m}$ is the random variable associated with Π_{12}.

Definition 6.4.2. *The mutual information $I(\Pi_1, \Pi_2)$ between two partitions Π_1 and Π_2 is*

$$I(\Pi_1, \Pi_2) = \sum_{i,j} p(i, j) \log \frac{p(i, j)}{p_1(i) p_2(j)}$$

where p_i is the random variable associated with Π_i, $i = 1, 2$.

Note that $I(\Pi_1, \Pi_2) = KL(p(i, j), p_1(i)p_2(j))$, in particular $I(\Pi_1, \Pi_2) \geq 0$.

Variation of information between two partitions Π_1 and Π_2 is defined by

$$VI(\Pi_1, \Pi_2) = [H(\Pi_1) - I(\Pi_1, \Pi_2)] + [H(\Pi_2) - I(\Pi_1, \Pi_2)].$$
$$(6.4.1)$$

The function $VI(\cdot, \cdot)$ enjoys distance function properties, that is, for each three partitions Π_1, Π_2, and Π_3 of $\mathcal{A}$ one has:

1. $VI(\Pi_1, \Pi_2) \geq 0$, and $VI(\Pi_1, \Pi_2) = 0$ if and only if $\Pi_1 = \Pi_2$.
2. $VI(\Pi_1, \Pi_2) = VI(\Pi_2, \Pi_1)$.
3. $VI(\Pi_1, \Pi_3) \leq VI(\Pi_1, \Pi_2) + VI(\Pi_2, \Pi_3)$.

Problem 6.4.1. *Prove distance properties 1–3 for $VI(\cdot, \cdot)$.*

6.5. Bibliographic notes

The Kullback–Leibler divergence was introduced by S. Kullback and R.A. Leibler [90]. Applications of information theoretic frameworks to clustering is discussed, for example, in [7] and [123]. Batch k-means clustering with Kullback–Leibler divergence was introduced in [15, 40, 38]. The "merger" of the batch and incremental algorithms is suggested in [80]. The elegant "distance between partitions" idea appears in [104].

7 Clustering with optimization techniques

The classical quadratic k-means clustering algorithm is an iterative procedure that partitions a data set into a prescribed number of clusters. The procedure alternates between the computation of clusters and centroids. In this chapter we exploit the duality between partitions and centroids and focus on searching for a set of centroids that defines an optimal partition. This approach transforms the k-means clustering to minimization of a function of a vector argument and lends itself to application of a wide range of existing optimization tools.

A straightforward translation of the clustering procedure into the optimization problem leads to a nonsmooth objective function F which is difficult to tackle. Instead of dealing with a nonsmooth optimization problem we approximate the nonsmooth function F by a family of smooth functions F_s parametrized by a scalar s (as $s \to 0$ the approximations converge to the original objective). The special form of the smooth objective F_s leads to a very simple iterative algorithm described by an explicit formula. For a given fixed value of the smoothing parameter s this algorithm produces a sequence of centroids $\{(\mathbf{c}_1^i, \ldots, \mathbf{c}_k^i)\}$, $i = 1, \ldots$ so that the corresponding sequence $\{F_s(\mathbf{c}_1^i, \ldots, \mathbf{c}_k^i)\}, i = 1, \ldots$ is monotonically decreasing and bounded below. The computational complexity of one iteration of the proposed method is about the same as that of the classical k-means clustering algorithm.

7.1. Optimization framework

Given a data set $A = \{a_1, \ldots, a_m\} \subset R^n$, and a k-cluster partition $\Pi = \{\pi_1, \ldots, \pi_k\}$ of A one can identify each cluster π_i with its centroid x_i. For each $i = 1, \ldots, m$ let

$$D_i(x_1, \ldots, x_k) = \min_{1 \le l \le k} d(x_l, a_i)$$

be the distance from $a_i \in A$ to the nearest centroid from the set $\{x_1, \ldots, x_k\}$, where $d(\cdot, \cdot)$ is a distance-like function. Then, the objective is to minimize the sum of the distances from the points of the data set A to the nearest centroids. In other words the problem of finding an optimal partition Π° becomes the following: select k vectors $\{x_1^\circ, \ldots, x_k^\circ\} \subset R^n$ that solve the continuous optimization problem

$$\min_{x_1, \ldots, x_k \in R^n} f(x_1, \ldots, x_k) = \sum_{i=1}^{m} D_i(x_1, \ldots, x_k). \qquad (7.1.1)$$

In this chapter we focus on the quadratic function $d(x, y) = \|x - y\|^2$. It will be convenient to introduce the following notations. We denote the $k \times n$-dimensional vector $(x_1^T, \ldots, x_k^T)^T$ by x, the function $f(x_1, \ldots, x_k)$ by $F(x)$, $F : R^N \to R$, with $N = kn$. Then, for all $k > 1$, problem (7.1.1) can be written as the following *nonconvex* and *nonsmooth* optimization problem in R^N:

$$\min_{x \in R^N} F(x) = \sum_{i=1}^{m} \min_{1 \le l \le k} \|x_l - a_i\|^2. \qquad (7.1.2)$$

Therefore, the clustering problem (7.1.1) belongs to the class of continuous optimization problems which combines nonconvexity and nonsmoothness. We shall focus on an approach handling nonsmoothness. We shall use a smooth approximation approach which replaces the nonsmooth objective F by a *family of smooth functions* F_s that depends on the scalar smoothing parameter s (see, for example, Figures 7.1 and 7.2). The special structure of the smoothed objective lends itself to a simple algorithm described by a fixed point explicit iteration

7.2. Smoothing k-means algorithm

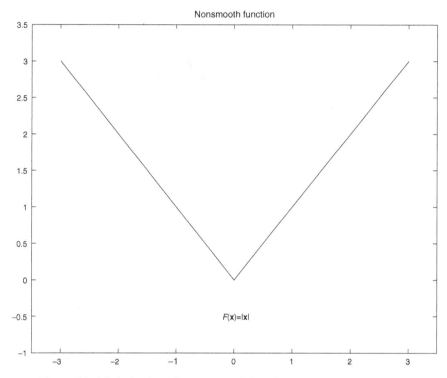

Figure 7.1: Minimization of a nonsmooth function.

formula. The smoothing k-means algorithm (smoka) is introduced in the next section.

7.2. Smoothing k-means algorithm

The algorithm is based on combining smoothing and successive approximation techniques. For any $\mathbf{z} \in \mathbf{R}^N$, one has

$$\max_{1 \le j \le N} \mathbf{z}[j] = \lim_{s \to 0^+} s \log \left(\sum_{j=1}^{N} e^{\frac{\mathbf{z}[j]}{s}} \right)$$

(this is just a reformulation of the definition of the L_∞ norm of a vector in $\mathbf{R}^N$). Thus for small $s > 0$ we can *approximate* the nonsmooth function $f(\mathbf{z}) = \max_{1 \le j \le N} \mathbf{z}[j]$ by the smooth function $f_s(\mathbf{z}) = s \log(\sum_{j=1}^{N} e^{\frac{\mathbf{z}[j]}{s}})$.

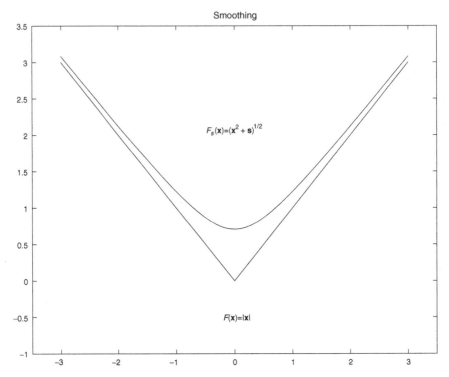

Figure 7.2: Minimization of a nonsmooth function by means of smooth approximation.

Since $\max_{1 \leq l \leq k} \mathbf{y}[l] = -\min_{1 \leq l \leq k}\{-\mathbf{y}[l]\}$, we substitute $F(\mathbf{x})$ by

$$F_s(\mathbf{x}) = \sum_{i=1}^{m} -s \log \left(\sum_{l=1}^{k} e^{-\frac{\|\mathbf{x}_l - \mathbf{a}_i\|^2}{s}} \right)$$

so that $\lim_{s \to 0^+} F_s(\mathbf{x}) = F(\mathbf{x})$. We replace the objective $F(\mathbf{x})$ by a family of smooth functions defined by

$$F_s(\mathbf{x}) = \sum_{i=1}^{m} -s \log \left(\sum_{l=1}^{k} e^{-\frac{\|\mathbf{x}_l - \mathbf{a}_i\|^2}{s}} \right),$$

and replace problem (7.1.2) by the family of smoothed problems parametrized by $s > 0$:

$$\min_{\mathbf{x} \in \mathbf{R}^N} F_s(\mathbf{x}). \tag{7.2.1}$$

For each positive and small enough s the approximation function F_s is a nonnegative infinitely differentiable function of $\mathbf{x}$. The function F_s is not necessarily convex, so finding a global minimum is not guaranteed (the k-means clustering algorithm suffers the same deficiency). However, it turns out that the special "Gaussian-like" form of the function F_s tends to eliminate many potential local minima (see Section 7.4). Furthermore, the proposed smoothed reformulation of (7.1.1) can now be solved by standard smooth optimization techniques. We now fix the smoothing parameter $s > 0$, and use the very special structure of F_s to derive a simple algorithm based on an explicit fixed point iteration formula.

For a fixed $s > 0$ denote a local minimum of F_s by $\bar{\mathbf{x}}(s)$. To simplify the notations, when it does not lead to ambiguity, we shall drop the parameter s and denote $\bar{\mathbf{x}}(s)$ just by $\bar{\mathbf{x}} = (\bar{\mathbf{x}}_1^T, \ldots, \bar{\mathbf{x}}_k^T)^T$. The necessary local optimality condition for problem (7.2.1) is $\nabla F_s(\bar{\mathbf{x}}) = 0$, and thus for each $l = 1, \ldots, k$ we obtain

$$\sum_{i=1}^{m} \frac{(\bar{\mathbf{x}}_l - \mathbf{a}_i) e^{-\frac{\|\bar{\mathbf{x}}_l - \mathbf{a}_i\|^2}{s}}}{\sum_{j=1}^{k} e^{-\frac{\|\bar{\mathbf{x}}_j - \mathbf{a}_i\|^2}{s}}} = 0. \tag{7.2.2}$$

For each $l = 1, \ldots, k$ and $i = 1, \ldots, m$ and $\mathbf{x} = (\mathbf{x}_1^T, \ldots, \mathbf{x}_k^T)^T$ we define the positive numbers

$$\rho^{il}(\mathbf{x}, s) = \frac{e^{-\frac{\|\mathbf{x}_l - \mathbf{a}_i\|^2}{s}}}{\sum_{j=1}^{k} e^{-\frac{\|\mathbf{x}_j - \mathbf{a}_i\|^2}{s}}}. \tag{7.2.3}$$

Equation (7.2.2) now becomes

$$\sum_{i=1}^{m}(\overline{\mathbf{x}}_l - \mathbf{a}_i)\rho^{il}(\overline{\mathbf{x}}, s) = 0, \qquad (7.2.4)$$

and yields

$$\overline{\mathbf{x}}_l = \frac{\sum_{i=1}^{m}\rho^{il}(\overline{\mathbf{x}}, s)\mathbf{a}_i}{\sum_{j=1}^{m}\rho^{jl}(\overline{\mathbf{x}}, s)}. \qquad (7.2.5)$$

To simplify the expression for $\overline{\mathbf{x}}_l$ we define

$$\lambda^{il}(\mathbf{x}, s) = \frac{\rho^{il}(\mathbf{x}, s)}{\sum_{j=1}^{m}\rho^{jl}(\mathbf{x}, s)}, \quad \lambda^{il}(\mathbf{x}, s) > 0, \quad \text{and} \sum_{i=1}^{m}\lambda^{il}(\mathbf{x}, s) = 1. \qquad (7.2.6)$$

Expression for $\overline{\mathbf{x}}_l$ can now be written in a compact form as follows:

$$\overline{\mathbf{x}}_l = \sum_{i=1}^{m}\lambda^{il}(\overline{\mathbf{x}}, s)\mathbf{a}_i, \quad \text{for each } l = 1, \dots, k. \qquad (7.2.7)$$

The fixed point characterization of $\overline{\mathbf{x}}$ suggests to use successive approximations. For each $l = 1, \dots, k$ define the mapping $T^l : \mathbf{R}^N \to \mathbf{R}^n$ by the right-hand side of (7.2.7), that is

$$T^l(\mathbf{x}) = \sum_{i=1}^{m}\lambda^{il}(\mathbf{x}, s)\mathbf{a}_i. \qquad (7.2.8)$$

We use the mappings T^l to generate the sequence $\mathbf{x}(t) = (\mathbf{x}_1^T(t), \dots, \mathbf{x}_k^T(t))^T$ by:

$$\mathbf{x}_l(t + 1) = T^l(\mathbf{x}(t)), \ l = 1, \dots, k. \qquad (7.2.9)$$

The mapping $T : \mathbf{R}^N \to \mathbf{R}^N$ is defined by mappings T^l as follows:

$$T(\mathbf{x}) = (T^1(\mathbf{x}), \dots, T^k(\mathbf{x})). \qquad (7.2.10)$$

The smoka clustering algorithm is given next.

106

7.2. Smoothing k-means algorithm

Algorithm 7.2.1. (smoka). *For a user-defined nonnegative tolerance* tol, *smoothing parameter* $s > 0$, *and initial choice of k distinct centroids* $\mathbf{x}(0) = (\mathbf{x}_1^T(0), \ldots, \mathbf{x}_k^T(0))^T \in \mathbf{R}^N$ *do the following:*

1. *Set* $t = 0$.
2. *For each* $l = 1, \ldots, k$ *compute*

$$\mathbf{x}_l(t+1) = T^l(\mathbf{x}) = \sum_{i=1}^{m} \lambda^{il}(\mathbf{x}(t), s)\mathbf{a}_i.$$

3. *If* $F_s(\mathbf{x}(t)) - F_s(\mathbf{x}(t+1)) >$ tol
        set $t = t + 1$
        goto step 2
   stop

Note that formula (7.2.7) indicates that $\bar{\mathbf{x}}_l$ belongs to the interior of the convex hull of the data set $\mathcal{A}$. In the next section we discuss convergence of the sequence $\{F_s(\mathbf{x}(t))\}_{t=0}^{\infty}$.

Remark 7.2.1. *We note that:*

1. *If for two indices $l \neq l'$ the corresponding "centroid candidates" $\mathbf{x}_l(t)$ and $\mathbf{x}_{l'}(t)$ coincide, then an iteration of* smoka *generates $\mathbf{x}(t+1)$ with* $\mathbf{x}_l(t+1) = \mathbf{x}_{l'}(t+1)$.
2. *A* smoka *iteration applied to k distinct vectors $\mathbf{x}_1(t), \ldots, \mathbf{x}_k(t)$ generates k vectors that should not necessarily be distinct (see Example 7.2.1).*

The above observations indicate that, exactly like k-means, smoka *may generate less than k nonempty clusters from initial k distinct centroids.*

Example 7.2.1. *Consider a two-dimensional two-vector data set $\mathcal{A} = \{\mathbf{a}_1, \mathbf{a}_2\}$ with the initial choice of two distinct centroids $\mathbf{x}_1 = \mathbf{x}_1(0)$ and $\mathbf{x}_2 = \mathbf{x}_2(0)$ (see Figure 7.3):*

$$\mathcal{A} = \left\{ \begin{bmatrix} -1 \\ 0 \end{bmatrix}, \begin{bmatrix} 1 \\ 0 \end{bmatrix} \right\}, \quad \mathbf{x}_1(0) = \begin{bmatrix} 0 \\ 1 \end{bmatrix}, \quad \mathbf{x}_2(0) = \begin{bmatrix} 0 \\ -1 \end{bmatrix}.$$

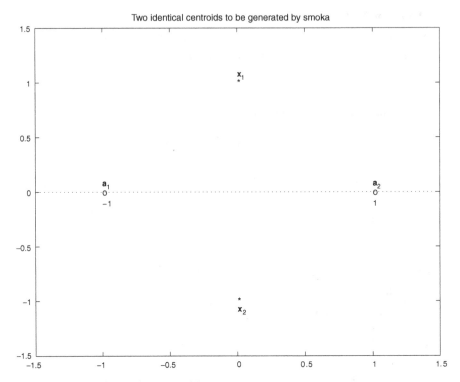

Figure 7.3: Collapsing centroids.

An application of one iteration of smoka *generates centroids* $\mathbf{x}_1(1) = \mathbf{x}_2(1) = \begin{bmatrix} 0 \\ 0 \end{bmatrix}$. *This result is independent of s and holds for any choice of initial centroids* $\mathbf{x}_1(0)$, $\mathbf{x}_2(0)$, *for example, equidistant from elements of the data set. The optimal pair of centroids*

$$\left\{ \begin{bmatrix} -1 \\ 0 \end{bmatrix}, \begin{bmatrix} 1 \\ 0 \end{bmatrix} \right\}$$

is missed by the algorithm. The example illustrates that the final partition generated by smoka *depends on the initial centroids.*

Let $\Pi = \{\pi_1, \pi_2\}$ be an optimal two-cluster partition of the m element vector set $\mathcal{A} = \{\mathbf{a}_1, \ldots, \mathbf{a}_m\} \subset \mathbf{R}^n$ with centroids $\mathbf{c}_1$ and $\mathbf{c}_2$. For small

values of s the function $F_s(\mathbf{x})$ with $\mathbf{x} \in \mathbf{R}^{2n}$ provides good approximation for the quality of partition with "centroids" $\mathbf{x} = (\mathbf{x}_1^T, \mathbf{x}_2^T)^T$. Hence
an iteration of smoka that starts with $\mathbf{x}_1(0) = \mathbf{c}_1, \mathbf{x}_2(0) = \mathbf{c}_2$ most probably will not change $\mathbf{x}_1(0)$ and $\mathbf{x}_2(0)$. Assume now that $\mathbf{x}_i(0)$ is "almost"
equal to $\mathbf{c}_i, i = 1, 2$. We speculate that an iteration of smoka with $\mathbf{x}_1(0)$
and $\mathbf{x}_2(0)$ will not change the initial partition Π and the sequences
$\mathbf{x}_1(t) \to \mathbf{c}_1$ and $\mathbf{x}_2(t) \to \mathbf{c}_2$ as $t \to \infty$. This speculation leads to the following problem.

Problem 7.2.1. *True or False? Let $\Pi = \{\pi_1, \pi_2\}$ be a k-means stable two-
cluster partition of the vector set $\mathcal{A} = \{\mathbf{a}_1, \ldots, \mathbf{a}_m\} \subset \mathbf{R}^n$ with centroids $\mathbf{c}_1$
and $\mathbf{c}_2$. There exists a positive scalar $\bar{s}$ so that for each choice $\mathbf{x}_1(0) \in \mathcal{H}_{12}^-$,
$\mathbf{x}_2(0) \in \mathcal{H}_{12}^+$ (see Subsection 2.1.3)* smoka *with $0 < s < \bar{s}$ generates a
sequence of centroids $(\mathbf{x}_1(t), \mathbf{x}_2(t))$ that converges to $(\mathbf{c}_1, \mathbf{c}_2)$ as $t \to \infty$.*

7.3. Convergence

We begin by stating some properties of the mappings T^l.

Proposition 7.3.1. *For each $l = 1, \ldots, k$ with T^l given by (7.2.8) and the
sequence $\{\mathbf{x}(t)\}_{t=0}^{\infty}$ generated by* smoka *one has:*

1. T^l *is a continuous map.*
2. $\mathbf{x}(t) = \bar{\mathbf{x}}$ *if and only if $T^l(\mathbf{x}(t)) = \mathbf{x}_l(t), l = 1, \ldots, k$ (here $\bar{\mathbf{x}}$ is a stationary point of F_s).*
3. *For each $l = 1, \ldots, k, t = 1, 2, \ldots$ the vector $\mathbf{x}_l(t)$ belongs to the compact convex set $\mathrm{conv}\{\mathbf{a}_1, \ldots, \mathbf{a}_m\}$.*

Proof

1. The functions defining T^l are all in C^{∞} (see (7.2.8)).
2. Follows straightforward from definition of T^l and (7.2.5).
3. Follows from (7.2.6) and (7.2.7).   □

To establish convergence of smoka we need the following technical result.

Lemma 7.3.1. *Let* $\psi : \mathbf{R}^k \to \mathbf{R}$ *be defined by* $\psi(\mathbf{z}) = \log(\sum_{i=1}^{k} e^{-\mathbf{z}[i]})$. *Then:*

1. ψ *is a convex* $C^\infty(\mathbf{R}^k)$ *function.*
2. *For each pair of vectors* $\mathbf{y}, \mathbf{z} \in \mathbf{R}^k$ *one has*

$$\psi(\mathbf{y}) - \psi(\mathbf{z}) \le \sum_{i=1}^{k}(\mathbf{z}[i] - \mathbf{y}[i])\mu_i, \text{ where } \mu_i = \frac{e^{-\mathbf{y}[i]}}{\sum_{j=1}^{k} e^{-\mathbf{y}[j]}}.$$
(7.3.1)

Proof: As a finite sum of C^∞ functions $\psi \in C^\infty(\mathbf{R}^k)$. To prove convexity of ψ we need to show that for each pair of vectors $\mathbf{y}, \mathbf{z} \in \mathbf{R}^k$ and each pair of nonnegative scalars α and β with $\alpha + \beta = 1$ one has

$$\psi(\alpha\mathbf{z} + \beta\mathbf{y}) \le \alpha\psi(\mathbf{z}) + \beta\psi(\mathbf{y}).$$
(7.3.2)

Due to definition of ψ the above inequality is equivalent to

$$\sum_{i=1}^{k}(e^{-\alpha\mathbf{z}[i]})(e^{-\beta\mathbf{y}[i]}) \le \left(\sum_{i=1}^{k} e^{-\mathbf{z}[i]}\right)^{\alpha} \left(\sum_{i=1}^{k} e^{-\mathbf{y}[i]}\right)^{\beta}.$$
(7.3.3)

The substitution $\mathbf{u}[i] = e^{-\alpha\mathbf{z}[i]}$, $\mathbf{v}[i] = e^{-\beta\mathbf{y}[i]}$, $\alpha = \frac{1}{p}$, $\beta = \frac{1}{q}$ reduces (7.3.3) to Hölder's inequality

$$\sum_{i=1}^{k} \mathbf{u}[i]\mathbf{v}[i] \le \left(\sum_{i=1}^{k} \mathbf{u}[i]^p\right)^{\frac{1}{p}} \left(\sum_{i=1}^{k} \mathbf{v}[i]^q\right)^{\frac{1}{q}},$$

and this completes the proof of convexity. Due to convexity of ψ the gradient inequality $\psi(\mathbf{z}) - \psi(\mathbf{y}) \ge (\mathbf{z} - \mathbf{y})^T \nabla\psi(\mathbf{y})$ holds with $\nabla\psi(\mathbf{y})[i] = -\frac{e^{-\mathbf{y}[i]}}{\sum_{j=1}^{k} e^{-\mathbf{y}[j]}}$, and the desired result follows. □

Proposition 7.3.2. *If* $\mathbf{x}(t+1) \ne \mathbf{x}(t)$, *then* $F_s(x(t+1)) < F_s(\mathbf{x}(t))$.

Proof: For a fixed $\mathbf{x}(t)$ define the function $g(\mathbf{y})$, $\mathbf{y} \in \mathbf{R}^N$ by

$$g(\mathbf{y}) = \sum_{l=1}^{k}\sum_{i=1}^{m} \|\mathbf{y}_l - \mathbf{a}_i\|^2 \rho^{il}(\mathbf{x}(t), s). \qquad (7.3.4)$$

We observe that $\mathbf{x}(t+1)$ as computed by the algorithm (see (7.2.4)) is nothing else but

$$\mathbf{x}(t+1) = \arg\min \left\{ g(\mathbf{y}) \ : \ \mathbf{y} \in \mathbf{R}^N \right\}. \qquad (7.3.5)$$

Since $g(\mathbf{y})$ is strictly convex, $\mathbf{x}(t+1)$ is the *unique* minimizer of g, and the assumption $\mathbf{x}(t+1) \neq \mathbf{x}(t)$ implies $g(\mathbf{x}(t+1)) < g(\mathbf{x}(t))$. For convenience we introduce nonnegative scalars

$$w^{il}(\mathbf{x}) = \|\mathbf{x}_l - \mathbf{a}_i\|^2, \quad i = 1, \ldots, m; \quad l = 1, \ldots, k.$$

In the special case when we are interested specifically in $\|\mathbf{x}_l(t) - \mathbf{a}_i\|^2$ we shall abuse notations and denote this quality by w_t^{il} rather than by $w^{il}(\mathbf{x}(t))$. By definition the value $F_s(\mathbf{x}(t))$ can be written as

$$F_s(\mathbf{x}(t)) = \sum_{i=1}^{m} -s \log \left(\sum_{l=1}^{k} e^{\frac{-w_t^{il}}{s}} \right), \qquad (7.3.6)$$

and $\rho^{il}(\mathbf{x}(t), s)$ as defined in (7.2.3) can be written as

$$\rho^{il}(\mathbf{x}(t), s) = \frac{e^{\frac{-w_L^{il}}{s}}}{\sum_{j=1}^{k} e^{\frac{-w_L^{ij}}{s}}} \qquad (7.3.7)$$

so that (see (7.3.4))

$$g(\mathbf{x}) = \sum_{l=1}^{k}\sum_{i=1}^{m} w^{il}(\mathbf{x}) \frac{e^{\frac{-w_L^{il}}{s}}}{\sum_{j=1}^{k} e^{\frac{-w_L^{ij}}{s}}}. \qquad (7.3.8)$$

For a fixed $i \in \{1, \ldots, m\}$ we apply the gradient inequality (7.3.1) of Lemma 7.3.1 at the points $\mathbf{y}$ and $\mathbf{z} \in \mathbf{R}^k$

$$\mathbf{y}[l] = \frac{\|\mathbf{x}_l(t) - \mathbf{a}_i\|^2}{s} = \frac{w_t^{il}}{s}, \quad \mathbf{z}[l] = \frac{\|\mathbf{x}_l(t+1) - \mathbf{a}_i\|^2}{s} = \frac{w_{t+1}^{il}}{s},$$

so that $\mu_l = \rho^{il}(\mathbf{x}(t), s)$. After multiplications by s the gradient inequality becomes

$$s \log \left(\sum_{l=1}^{k} e^{-\frac{w_t^{il}}{s}} \right) - s \log \left(\sum_{l=1}^{k} e^{-\frac{w_{t+1}^{il}}{s}} \right) \le \sum_{l=1}^{k} \left(w_{t+1}^{il} - w_t^{il} \right) \rho^{il}(\mathbf{x}(t), s).$$

Adding the above inequalities for $i = 1, \ldots, m$ and keeping in mind (7.3.6) and (7.3.8) we obtain

$$F_s(\mathbf{x}(t + 1)) - F_s(\mathbf{x}(t)) \le g(\mathbf{x}(t + 1)) - g(\mathbf{x}(t)) < 0.$$

This completes the proof. $\qquad\square$

Theorem 7.3.1. *Let $\{\mathbf{x}(t)\}_{t=0}^{\infty}$ be a sequence generated by* smoka.

1. *The sequence $\{F_s(\mathbf{x}(t))\}_{t=0}^{\infty}$ converges.*
2. *The sequence $\{\mathbf{x}(t)\}_{t=0}^{\infty}$ has a limit point.*
3. *Every limit point $\mathbf{x}$ of $\{\mathbf{x}(t)\}_{t=0}^{\infty}$ is a stationary point of F_s.*
4. *If $\mathbf{x}$, $\mathbf{y}$ are limit points of $\{\mathbf{x}(t)\}_{t=0}^{\infty}$, then $F_s(\mathbf{x}) = F_s(\mathbf{y})$.*

Proof: The first two items above follow from the fact that the sequence $\{\mathbf{x}(t)\}_{t=0}^{\infty}$ belongs to a compact set in $\mathbf{R}^N$, and the monotonicity of the bounded below function F_s is given by Proposition 7.3.2.

Let $\{\mathbf{x}(t_i)\}$ be a convergent subsequence of $\{\mathbf{x}(t)\}_{t=0}^{\infty}$. Denote $\lim_{i \to \infty} \mathbf{x}(t_i)$ by $\bar{\mathbf{x}}$. Since $\lim_{t \to \infty} F_s(\mathbf{x}(t))$ exists one has

$$\lim_{t \to \infty} [F_s(\mathbf{x}(t) - F_s(\mathbf{x}(t + 1))] = 0. \qquad (7.3.9)$$

Due to continuity of T one has $\lim_{i \to \infty} T(\mathbf{x}(t_i)) = T(\bar{\mathbf{x}})$. Due to (7.3.9) one has $F_s(\bar{\mathbf{x}}) = F_s(T(\bar{\mathbf{x}}))$, this implies $\bar{\mathbf{x}} = T(\bar{\mathbf{x}})$, and due to Proposition 7.3.1 the point $\bar{\mathbf{x}}$ is a stationary point of T. This shows that every limit point of $\{\mathbf{x}(t)\}_{t=0}^{\infty}$ is a stationary point of F_s.

If $\mathbf{x}$ and $\mathbf{y}$ are two distinct limit point of $\{\mathbf{x}(t)\}_{t=0}^{\infty}$, then due to the decreasing property of $F_s(\mathbf{x}(t))$ one has $F_s(\mathbf{x}) = F_s(\mathbf{y})$. $\qquad\square$

7.3. Convergence

The next statement shows uniform convergence of F_s to F.

Proposition 7.3.3. *For each $\mathbf{x} \in \mathbf{R}^N$ and $s > 0$ one has*

$$0 \le F(\mathbf{x}) - F_s(\mathbf{x}) \le sm \log k. \qquad (7.3.10)$$

Proof: By definition of F_s and F one has

$$F_s(\mathbf{x}) - F(\mathbf{x}) = \sum_{i=1}^{m} \left[-s \log \left(\sum_{l=1}^{k} e^{-\frac{\|\mathbf{x}_l - \mathbf{a}_i\|^2}{s}} \right) - s \min_{1 \le l \le k} \frac{\|\mathbf{x}_l - \mathbf{a}_i\|^2}{s} \right]$$

$$= -s \sum_{i=1}^{m} \left[\log \left(\sum_{l=1}^{k} e^{-\frac{\|\mathbf{x}_l - \mathbf{a}_i\|^2}{s}} \right) - \log \max_{1 \le l \le k} e^{-\frac{\|\mathbf{x}_l - \mathbf{a}_i\|^2}{s}} \right]$$

$$= -s \sum_{i=1}^{m} \log \left[\frac{\sum_{l=1}^{k} e^{-\frac{\|\mathbf{x}_l - \mathbf{a}_i\|^2}{s}}}{\max_{1 \le l \le k} e^{-\frac{\|\mathbf{x}_l - \mathbf{a}_i\|^2}{s}}} \right].$$

Keeping in mind that $\sum_{l=1}^{k} e^{-\frac{\|\mathbf{x}_l - \mathbf{a}_i\|^2}{s}} \le k[\max_{1 \le l \le k} e^{-\frac{\|\mathbf{x}_l - \mathbf{a}_i\|^2}{s}}]$ one has

$$\log \left[\frac{\sum_{l=1}^{k} e^{-\frac{\|\mathbf{x}_l - \mathbf{a}_i\|^2}{s}}}{\max_{1 \le l \le k} e^{-\frac{\|\mathbf{x}_l - \mathbf{a}_i\|^2}{s}}} \right] \le \log k.$$

Finally, we obtain

$$|F_s(\mathbf{x}) - F(\mathbf{x})| = \left| -s \sum_{i=1}^{m} \log \frac{\sum_{l=1}^{k} e^{-\frac{\|\mathbf{x}_l - \mathbf{a}_i\|^2}{s}}}{\max_{1 \le l \le k} e^{-\frac{\|\mathbf{x}_l - \mathbf{a}_i\|^2}{s}}} \right| \le sm \log k \quad (7.3.11)$$

as requested. $\qquad \square$

We now focus on the upper bound $sm \log k$ for the nonnegative expression $F(\mathbf{x}) - F_s(\mathbf{x})$ and pick $i \in \{1, \ldots, m\}$. To simplify the exposition we assume that

$$\|\mathbf{x}_1 - \mathbf{a}_i\|^2 \le \|\mathbf{x}_2 - \mathbf{a}_i\|^2 \cdots \le \|\mathbf{x}_k - \mathbf{a}_i\|^2 \qquad (7.3.12)$$

and denote $\|\mathbf{x}_l - \mathbf{a}_i\|^2$ by $\Delta_l, l = 1, \ldots, k$. Then

$$-s \log \left(\sum_{l=1}^{k} e^{-\frac{\|\mathbf{x}_l - \mathbf{a}_i\|^2}{s}} \right) = -s \log \left(\sum_{l=1}^{k} e^{\frac{-\Delta_l}{s}} \right)$$

$$= -s \log \left[e^{\frac{-\Delta_1}{s}} \left(1 + e^{\frac{\Delta_1 - \Delta_2}{s}} + \cdots + e^{\frac{\Delta_1 - \Delta_k}{s}} \right) \right]$$

$$= \Delta_1 - s \log \left(1 + e^{\frac{\Delta_1 - \Delta_2}{s}} + \cdots + e^{\frac{\Delta_1 - \Delta_k}{s}} \right)$$

$$\leq \min_{1 \leq l \leq k} \|\mathbf{x}_l - \mathbf{a}_i\|^2 - s \log \left(1 + e^{\frac{\Delta_1 - \Delta_2}{s}} + \cdots \right.$$

$$\left. + e^{\frac{\Delta_1 - \Delta_k}{s}} \right).$$

We remark that in many cases the first inequality in (7.3.12) is strict (i.e. $\|\mathbf{x}_1 - \mathbf{a}_i\|^2 < \|\mathbf{x}_2 - \mathbf{a}_i\|^2$), and as $s \to 0$ the expression $\epsilon_i(s) = \log(1 + e^{\frac{\Delta_1 - \Delta_2}{s}} + \cdots + e^{\frac{\Delta_1 - \Delta_k}{s}})$ is much smaller than $\log k$. Since

$$-s \log \left(\sum_{l=1}^{k} e^{-\frac{\|\mathbf{x}_l - \mathbf{a}_i\|^2}{s}} \right) = \min_{1 \leq l \leq k} \|\mathbf{x}_l - \mathbf{a}_i\|^2 - s\epsilon_i(s), \qquad (7.3.13)$$

one has

$$F_s(\mathbf{x}) = -s \sum_{i=1}^{m} \log \left(\sum_{l=1}^{k} e^{-\frac{\|\mathbf{x}_l - \mathbf{a}_i\|^2}{s}} \right) = \sum_{i=1}^{m} \min_{1 \leq l \leq k} \|\mathbf{x}_l - \mathbf{a}_i\|^2 - s \sum_{i=1}^{m} \epsilon_i(s)$$

$$= F(\mathbf{x}) - s \sum_{i=1}^{m} \epsilon_i(s).$$

Hence, as $s \to 0$ the nonnegative expression $F(\mathbf{x}) - F_s(\mathbf{x}) = s \sum_{i=1}^{m} \epsilon_i(s)$ has the potential to be much smaller than $sm \log k$. In the next section we report numerical experiments with classical k-means clustering algorithms and smoka.

7.4. Numerical experiments

First, we go back to Example 2.1.2 and recall that while an iteration of the batch k-means algorithm applied to $\Pi^{(0)} = \{\{0, 2\}, \{3\}\}$ does not change the partition, a single iteration of the k-means algorithm changes $\Pi^{(0)}$ into the optimal partition $\Pi^{(1)} = \{\{0\}, \{2, 3\}\}$. An application of smoka with parameters $s = 0.1$ and tol $= 0.001$ to the partition $\Pi^{(0)}$ produces centroids $x_1 = 0$ and $x_2 = 2.5$, thus recovering $\Pi^{(1)}$.

Next we report final partitions-related results for the three clustering algorithms (quadratic batch k-means, quadratic k-means, and smoka) and the following document collections:

1. A merger of the three document collections classic3 (see Subsection 5.3.3).
2. The 20 newsgroups data set available at http://kdd.ics.uci.edu/ databases/20newsgroups/20newsgroups.html.
   - The "mini" data set is a subset of the "full" data set with 100 documents from each of the 20 Usenet newsgroups.
   - The "full" data set of 19,997 messages from 20 Usenet newsgroups.

We remove stop-words (see ftp://ftp.cs.cornell.edu/pub/smart/english. stop), and stem the texts with Porter stemming. We select n "best" terms as described in Section 5.3.3 with slice(0), that is, we rate all collection terms. We then apply IDFB normalization scheme and build vectors of dimension n for each document collection. The principal direction divisive partitioning algorithm is applied to the vector set to generate the initial partition $\Pi^{(0)}$. We then apply the batch k-means, k-means, and smoka to the partition $\Pi^{(0)}$ and report qualities of the obtained final partitions along with the number of iterations performed by each algorithm. Since the first three collections (classic3) are known to be well separated we also provide confusion matrices corresponding to partitions of these collections.

Since k-means generates a sequence of partition $\Pi^{(t)}$ with $Q(\Pi^{(t)}) \geq Q(\Pi^{(t+1)}) \geq 0, t = 1, 2, \ldots$ it is clear that $Q(\Pi^{(t)}) = Q(\Pi^{(t+1)})$ for some t, and one can select the stopping criterion $Q(\Pi^{(t)}) - Q(\Pi^{(t+1)}) >$ tol with tol $= 0$. On the other hand, smoka minimizes a function of a

Table 7.1: Collection: **classic3**. PDDP generated initial "confusion" matrix with **250** "misclassified" documents using 600 best terms, $Q = 3612.61$

	DC0	DC1	DC2
cluster 0	907	91	13
cluster 1	120	7	1372
cluster 2	6	1362	13
"empty" documents			
cluster 3	0	0	0

Table 7.2: Collection: **classic3**. Batch k-means generated "confusion" matrix with **131** "misclassified" documents using 600 best terms, $Q = 3608.06$

	DC0	DC1	DC2
cluster 0	984	50	12
cluster 1	42	2	1368
cluster 2	7	1408	18
"empty" documents			
cluster 3	0	0	0

vector argument and, to be on the safe side, it would be wise to pick `tol` > 0 for this algorithm stopping criterion. In the experiments reported below batch k-means, and k-means run with `tol` $= 0$, smoka runs with $s = 0.0001$ and `tol` $= 0.0001$.

We conduct the first experiment with classic3 collection. The confusion matrix for the partition $\Pi^{(0)}$ is given in Table 7.1. Application of the batch k-means clustering algorithm to the partition $\Pi^{(0)}$ iterates three times only and generates a partition with confusion matrix given in Table 7.2. Application of the k-means clustering algorithm to the partition $\Pi^{(0)}$ produces 87 batch iterations and 72 incremental iterations. The confusions matrix corresponding to the generated final partition is given in Table 7.3. Finally, smoka applied to $\Pi^{(0)}$ after only seven

Table 7.3: Collection: **classic3**. k-means generated "confusion" matrix with **79** "misclassified" documents using 600 best terms, $Q = 3605.5$

	DC0	DC1	DC2
cluster 0	1018	21	19
cluster 1	5	1	1356
cluster 2	10	1438	23
"empty" documents			
cluster 3	0	0	0

Table 7.4: Collection: **classic3**. smoka generated "confusion" matrix with **73** "misclassified" documents using 600 best terms, $Q = 3605.5$

	DC0	DC1	DC2
cluster 0	1019	22	15
cluster 1	5	1	1362
cluster 2	9	1437	21
"empty" documents			
cluster 3	0	0	0

Table 7.5: Collection: **classic3**. Number of iterations per clustering algorithm applied to the initial partition generated by PDDP, the vector space dimension is 600

Algorithm	PDDP	Batch k-means	k-means	smoka
iterations		3	87	7
Q	3612.61	3608.06	3605.5	3605.5

iterations builds a partition with the confusion matrix given in Table 7.4. While the quality of final partitions generated by k-means and smoka are almost identical the number of iterations performed by smoka is significantly smaller. This information is collected in Table 7.5. To highlight smoka's performance, Figure 7.4 compares quality of first

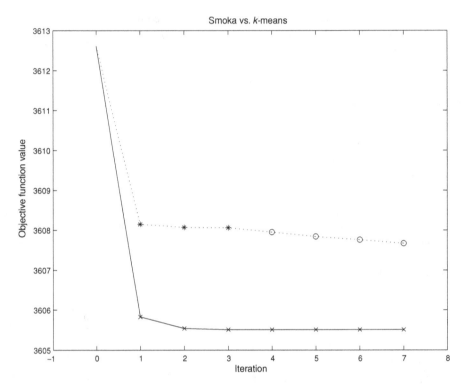

Figure 7.4: Quality Q of the first 7 partitions generated by smoka (marked by "x") and k-means (marked by "*" for batch iterations, and "o" for incremental iterations) for **classic3** document collection with vector space model of dimension 600.

seven partitions generated by smoka and k-means. The top dotted line passing through stars and circles indicates k-means performance. Each "*" indicates result of a batch iteration, and "o" points to quality of a partition generated by an incremental iterations. The bottom solid line presents smoka values, the quality Q of partitions generated at iterations $i = 1, \ldots, 7$ are marked by "x".

While the first iteration of batch k-means moves around 122 vectors (about 3% of the population), and leads to a significant drop in the objective function, first iteration of smoka does better. Batch k-means does not change partitions at iterations 4, 5, 6, and 7, and incremental

118

Table 7.6: Collection: **classic3**. PDDP generated initial "confusion" matrix with **880** "misclassified" documents using 100 best terms, $Q = 3379.17$

	DC0	DC1	DC2
cluster 0	384	35	1364
cluster 1	3	999	5
cluster 2	642	425	28
"empty" documents			
cluster 3	4	1	1

iterations move a single vector at each of these iterations leading to a mild decrease in the objective function Q.

While smoka stops at iteration 7, Figure 7.4 indicates that the objective function stabilizes already at iteration 3. The decrease of the objective function at iterations 4, 5, 6, and 7 is exceeding the 0.0001 threshold, but remains almost flat and can hardly be recognized on the graph. To reach the smoka 7 (in fact only 3!) iterations result takes k-means additional 80 iterations.

Final partitions generated by smoka are not always superior to those generated by k-means (see e.g. Table 7.10, Table 7.11, and Section 8.7), however the rapid reduction of the objective function due to first few smoka iterations appears in all smoka–k-means related experiments observed by this author. This suggests to apply the sequence of clustering algorithms PDDP$\longrightarrow$smoka$\longrightarrow$$k$-means so that the output of each "left" algorithm is the input of the corresponding "right" algorithm.

We reduce the vector space dimension to 100 and repeat the experiment with the same data set. The confusion matrix for the three-cluster partition $\Pi^{(0)}$ generated by PDDP is given in Table 7.6.

Tables 7.7, 7.8, and 7.9 present confusion matrices generated from $\Pi^{(0)}$ by batch k-means, k-means, and smoka respectively. Table 7.10 reports quality of partition generated and number of iterations performed by the algorithms applied to $\Pi^{(0)}$.

Table 7.7: Collection: **classic3**. batch k-means generated initial "confusion" matrix with **643** "misclassified" documents using 100 best terms, $Q = 3365.3$

	DC0	DC1	DC2
cluster 0	193	34	1354
cluster 1	11	1063	7
cluster 2	825	362	36
"empty" documents			
cluster 3	4	1	1

Table 7.8: Collection: **classic3**. k-means generated "confusion" matrix with **346** "misclassified" documents using 100 best terms, $Q = 3341.06$

	DC0	DC1	DC2
cluster 0	154	19	1360
cluster 1	116	1420	29
cluster 2	759	20	8
"empty" documents			
cluster 3	4	1	1

We now cluster the "mini" subset of the 20 newsgroups data set (total of 2000 documents). We first apply PDDP to 2000 vectors of dimension 600 and generate the initial partition $\Pi^{(0)}$ with $Q = 1758.39$. Applications of batch k-means, k-means, and smoka are reported in Table 7.11. While smoka appears to generate partitions of quality comparable with k-means it performs few iterations only. As Table 7.11 shows an application of smoka to $\Pi^{(0)}$ leads to the partition $\Pi^{(1)}$ with $Q = 1726.29$ after only 15 iterations. A subsequent application of k-means to $\Pi^{(1)}$ stops after 226 batch and 194 incremental iterations that result in the final partition with $Q = 1721.95$.

Finally, we cluster the full set of 19,997 documents. We build the vector space model of dimension 1000, generate the initial 20-cluster

Table 7.9: Collection: **classic3**. smoka generated "confusion" matrix with **341** "misclassified" documents using 100 best terms, $Q = 3341.07$

	DC0	DC1	DC2
cluster 0	150	19	1361
cluster 1	115	1419	28
cluster 2	764	21	8
"empty" documents			
cluster 3	4	1	1

Table 7.10: Collection: **classic3**. Number of iterations per clustering algorithm applied to the initial partition $\Pi^{(0)}$ generated by PDDP, the vector space dimension is 100

Algorithm	PDDP	Batch k-means	k-means	smoka
iterations		9	550	31
Q	3379.17	3365.3	3341.06	3341.07

Table 7.11: Collection: **the "mini" subset of the 20 newsgroups data set**. Number of iterations per clustering algorithm applied to the initial partition generated by PDDP, 2000 vectors of dimension 600

Algorithm	PDDP	Batch k-means	k-means	smoka
iterations		11	473	15
Q	1758.39	1737.73	1721.9	1726.29

partition $\Pi^{(0)}$ with PDDP, and apply batch k-means, k-means, and smoka to $\Pi^{(0)}$. The clustering results are reported in Table 7.12. Time and time again smoka performs about the same number of iterations as batch k-means does, and generates partitions of about the same quality as k-means does.

Table 7.12: Collection: **the "full" 20 newsgroups data set**. Number of iterations per clustering algorithm applied to the initial partition generated by PDDP, 19,997 vectors of dimension 1000 from the "full" 20 newsgroups data set

Algorithm	PDDP	Batch k-means	k-means	smoka
iterations		47	5862	51
Q	18156.5	17956.1	17808	17808

Note that Proposition 7.3.2 holds for $d(\mathbf{x}, \mathbf{a})$ `strictly` convex with respect to $\mathbf{x}$. Generalization of smoka with distance-like functions other than the squared Euclidean distance is described in Chapter 8.

7.5. Bibliographic notes

In 1990, Rose, Gurewitz, and Fox introduced a statistical mechanics formulation for clustering and derived a remarkable algorithm called the deterministic annealing (DA). DA focuses on centroids and attempts to minimize a nonconvex objective function. The algorithm was devised in order to avoid local minima of the nonconvex objective [116–118]. This approach is reviewed and numerous applications are provided in [115]. Algorithm 7.2.1 coincides with the one provided in [116] with constant s.

Optimization with respect to centroids rather than optimization with respect to partitions for a special case of harmonic means objective function is considered in [144]. This approach transforms clustering to optimization of a *smooth* function of a vector variable. Approximations L_∞ norm by the limit of L_p norms and reduction the nonsmooth k-means objective to a sequence of smooth objective functions is suggested in [109]. The approximations provide, as the authors put it, "the amount of crispness or equivalently fuzziness in the resulting partition."

In 2005, motivated by optimization arguments, Teboulle and Kogan introduced smoka [134]. Optimization techniques provide a natural extension of smoka to distance-like functions other than the quadratic Euclidean distance (see Chapter 8). Most of the relevant material of this chapter is taken from [133].

For the gradient inequality and optimization-related results see for example [112]. Porter stemming is described, for example, by Martin Porter in [113]. For IDFB and many other normalization schemes consult [27].

8 k-means clustering with divergences

The chapter focuses on two families of distance-like functions based on φ-divergences and Bregman distances. The approach presented below recovers many results attributed to clustering with squared Euclidean distance. Centroids computation is the basic problem associated with applications k-means clustering with various distance-like functions. Surprisingly, it turns out that in many cases optimization Problem 2.1.1 with divergences admits simple solutions.

To generate the families of distance-like functions we shall need convex, proper functions with nonempty effective domain. In addition often the functions will be required to be lower semicontinuous (see Chapter 10.3 for appropriate definitions).

8.1. Bregman distance

Let $\psi : \mathbf{R}^n \to (-\infty, +\infty]$ be a closed proper convex function. Suppose that ψ is continuously differentiable on int(dom ψ) $\neq \emptyset$. The Bregman distance (also called "Bregman divergence") D_ψ : dom $\psi \times$ int(dom ψ) $\to \mathbf{R}_+$ is defined by

$$D_\psi(\mathbf{x}, \mathbf{y}) = \psi(\mathbf{x}) - \psi(\mathbf{y}) - \nabla\psi(\mathbf{y})(\mathbf{x} - \mathbf{y}), \qquad (8.1.1)$$

where $\nabla\psi$ is the gradient of ψ.

This function measures the convexity of ψ, i.e. $D_\psi(\mathbf{x}, \mathbf{y}) \geq 0$ if and only if the gradient inequality for ψ holds, that is, if and only if ψ is

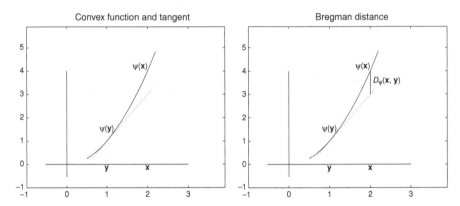

Figure 8.1: Bregman divergence.

convex. With ψ strictly convex one has $D_\psi(\mathbf{x}, \mathbf{y}) \geq 0$ and $D_\psi(\mathbf{x}, \mathbf{y}) = 0$ iff $\mathbf{x} = \mathbf{y}$ (See Figure 8.1).

Note that $D_\psi(\mathbf{x}, \mathbf{y})$ is not a distance (it is, in general, not symmetric and does not satisfy the triangle inequality). We now consider some examples of Bregman distances.

Example 8.1.1. *With $\psi(\mathbf{x}) = ||\mathbf{x}||^2$ (dom $\psi = \mathbf{R}^n$) one has $D_\psi(\mathbf{x}, \mathbf{y}) = ||\mathbf{x} - \mathbf{y}||^2$.*

Example 8.1.2. *With $\psi(\mathbf{x}) = \sum_{j=1}^{n} \mathbf{x}[j] \log \mathbf{x}[j] - \mathbf{x}[j]$ (dom $\psi = \mathbf{R}^n_+$ with the convention $0 \log 0 = 0$), we obtain the Kullback–Leibler relative entropy distance*

$$D_\psi(\mathbf{x}, \mathbf{y}) = \sum_{j=1}^{n} \mathbf{x}[j] \log \frac{\mathbf{x}[j]}{\mathbf{y}[j]} + \mathbf{y}[j] - \mathbf{x}[j] \ \forall \ (\mathbf{x}, \mathbf{y}) \in \mathbf{R}^n_+ \times \mathbf{R}^n_{++}.$$

(8.1.2)

Note that under the additional assumption $\sum_{j=1}^{n} \mathbf{x}[j] = \sum_{j=1}^{n} \mathbf{y}[j] = 1$ the Bregman divergence $D_\psi(\mathbf{x}, \mathbf{y})$ reduces to $\sum_{j=1}^{n} \mathbf{x}[j] \log \frac{\mathbf{x}[j]}{\mathbf{y}[j]}$.

Problem 8.1.1. *Show that $D_\psi(\mathbf{x}, \mathbf{y})$ is convex with respect to $\mathbf{x}$ variable. Give examples of functions $D_\psi(\mathbf{x}, \mathbf{y})$ convex also with respect to $\mathbf{y}$.*

8.1. Bregman distance

Problem 8.1.2. *Show that*

1. If $\psi(x) = e^x$, then $D_\psi(x, y) = e^y - e^x - e^y(x - y)$.

2. If $x \in [0, 1]$, and $\psi(x) = x \log x + (1 - x) \log(1 - x)$, then

$$D_\psi(x, y) = x \log\left(\frac{x}{y}\right) + (1 - x)\left(\frac{1 - x}{1 - y}\right).$$

3. If $x > 0$ and $\psi(x) = -\log x$, then $D_\psi(x, y) = \dfrac{x}{y} - \log\left(\dfrac{x}{y}\right) - 1$.

4. If $\psi(\mathbf{x}) = \mathbf{x}^T A\mathbf{x}$ (where A is a positive definite and symmetric matrix of an appropriate size), then $D_\psi(\mathbf{x}, \mathbf{y}) = (\mathbf{x} - \mathbf{y})A^T(\mathbf{x} - \mathbf{y})$.

Example 8.1.3. *By reversing the order of variables in D_ψ, that is,*

$$\overleftarrow{D_\psi}(\mathbf{x}, \mathbf{y}) = D_\psi(\mathbf{y}, \mathbf{x}) = \psi(\mathbf{y}) - \psi(\mathbf{x}) - \nabla\psi(\mathbf{x})(\mathbf{y} - \mathbf{x}) \qquad (8.1.3)$$

(compare with (8.1.1)) and using the kernel

$$\psi(\mathbf{x}) = \frac{v}{2}\|\mathbf{x}\|^2 + \mu\left[\sum_{j=1}^{n} \mathbf{x}[j] \log \mathbf{x}[j] - \mathbf{x}[j]\right], \qquad (8.1.4)$$

we obtain

$$\overleftarrow{D_\psi}(\mathbf{x}, \mathbf{y}) = D_\psi(\mathbf{y}, \mathbf{x}) = \frac{v}{2}\|\mathbf{y} - \mathbf{x}\|^2 + \mu\sum_{j=1}^{n}\left[\mathbf{y}[j] \log \frac{\mathbf{y}[j]}{\mathbf{x}[j]} + \mathbf{x}[j] - \mathbf{y}[j]\right].$$
$$(8.1.5)$$

While in general $\overleftarrow{D_\psi}(\mathbf{x}, \mathbf{y})$ given by (8.1.3) is not necessarily convex in $\mathbf{x}$, when $\psi(\mathbf{x})$ is given either by $\|\mathbf{x}\|^2$ or by $\sum_{j=1}^{n} \mathbf{x}[j] \log \mathbf{x}[j] - \mathbf{x}[j]$ the resulting functions $\overleftarrow{D_\psi}(\mathbf{x}, \mathbf{y})$ are strictly convex with respect to the first variable.

We display a simple identity satisfied by the Bregman distance. This identity (called the *three points identity*) is a natural generalization of the quadratic identity valid for the Euclidean norm, that is, of the Pythagoras theorem (or the law of cosines).

127

Lemma 8.1.1. *For any three points* $\mathbf{a}, \mathbf{b} \in \text{int}\,(\text{dom}\;\psi)$ *and* $\mathbf{c} \in \text{dom}\;\psi$ *the following identity holds true:*

$$D_\psi(\mathbf{c}, \mathbf{b}) - D_\psi(\mathbf{c}, \mathbf{a}) = D_\psi(\mathbf{a}, \mathbf{b}) + [\nabla\psi(\mathbf{a}) - \nabla\psi(\mathbf{b})]\,(\mathbf{c} - \mathbf{a})\,. \quad (8.1.6)$$

While in many cases centroids can be computed for Bregman divergences provided a convenient expression for ψ^*, the conjugate of ψ, is available the following surprising result[1] holds for Bregman divergences with reversed order of variables

$$d(\mathbf{x}, \mathbf{a}) = D_\psi(\mathbf{a}, \mathbf{x}) = \overleftarrow{D}_\psi(\mathbf{x}, \mathbf{a})$$

given by (8.1.3):

Theorem 8.1.1. *If* $\mathbf{z} = \frac{\mathbf{a}_1 + \cdots + \mathbf{a}_m}{m}$, *then* $\sum_{i=1}^{m} D_\psi(\mathbf{a}_i, \mathbf{z}) \le \sum_{i=1}^{m} D_\psi(\mathbf{a}_i, \mathbf{x})$.

Proof: Due to Lemma 8.1.1

$$D_\psi(\mathbf{a}_i, \mathbf{x}) - D_\psi(\mathbf{a}_i, \mathbf{z}) = D_\psi(\mathbf{z}, \mathbf{x}) + [\nabla\psi(\mathbf{z}) - \nabla\psi(\mathbf{x})]\,(\mathbf{a}_i - \mathbf{z})$$
$$\ge [\nabla\psi(\mathbf{z}) - \nabla\psi(\mathbf{x})]\,(\mathbf{a}_i - \mathbf{z}),$$

hence $\sum_{i=1}^{m} D_\psi(\mathbf{a}_i, \mathbf{x}) - \sum_{i=1}^{m} D_\psi(\mathbf{a}_i, \mathbf{z}) \ge [\nabla\psi(\mathbf{z}) - \nabla\psi(\mathbf{x})](\sum_{i=1}^{m} \mathbf{a}_i - m\mathbf{z}) = 0$. This completes the proof. $\qquad\square$

Problem 8.1.3. *Investigate convexity of batch k-means and k-means stable partitions generated with*

1. *Bregman distances,*
2. *Bregman distances with reversed order of variables.*

8.2. φ-divergences

Consider a collection of vectors $\{\mathbf{a}_1, \ldots, \mathbf{a}_m\}$ in the n-dimensional non-negative octant $\mathbf{R}_+^n$. A "distance" between vectors is provided by the class of φ-divergence (or Csiszar divergence) measures. This class is

---

[1] Note that this distance-like function is not necessarily convex with respect to $\mathbf{x}$.

a generalized measure of information on the set of probability distributions that gauges the proximity between two probability measures (hence Csiszar divergences generalize the concept of relative entropy). Csiszar divergences allow to overcome the restrictions to the probability setting and to consider the more general case of arbitrary vectors in the nonnegative octant (as it is often the case in Information Retrieval).

We denote by $\Phi = \{\varphi : \mathbf{R} \to (-\infty, +\infty]\}$ the class of functions satisfying (1)–(4) given below. We assume that for each $\varphi \in \Phi$ one has dom $\varphi \subseteq [0, +\infty)$, $\varphi(t) = +\infty$ when $t < 0$ and φ satisfies the following:

1. φ is twice continuously differentiable on int(dom φ) = $(0, +\infty)$.
2. φ is strictly convex on its domain.
3. $\lim\limits_{t \to 0^+} \varphi'(t) = -\infty.$
4. $\varphi(1) = \varphi'(1) = 0$ and $\varphi''(1) > 0$.

Given $\varphi \in \Phi$, for $\mathbf{x}, \mathbf{y} \in \mathbf{R}^n$ we define $d_\varphi(\mathbf{x}, \mathbf{y})$ by

$$d_\varphi(\mathbf{x}, \mathbf{y}) = \sum_{j=1}^{n} \mathbf{y}[j]\varphi\left(\frac{\mathbf{x}[j]}{\mathbf{y}[j]}\right). \tag{8.2.1}$$

Problem 8.2.1. *Show that $d_\varphi(\mathbf{x}, \mathbf{y})$ is convex with respect to $\mathbf{x}$ and with respect to $\mathbf{y}$.*[2]

Problem 8.2.2. *Show that $d_\varphi(\mathbf{x}, \mathbf{y})$ is convex with respect to $(\mathbf{x}, \mathbf{y})$.*

Recall that centroid computations require to solve a minimization problem involving d_φ (see (2.1.1)). Assumptions (1)–(2) ensure existence of global minimizers, assumption (3) enforces the minimizer to stay in the positive octant. Condition (4) is just a normalization that allows us to handle vectors in $\mathbf{R}^n_+$ (rather than probabilities).

---

[2] In [115, 136] the function $d(\mathbf{x}, \mathbf{y})$ is *required* to be convex with respect to $\mathbf{x}$. Csiszar divergences are natural candidates for distance-like functions satisfying this requirement.

The functional d_φ enjoys basic properties of a distance-like function, namely one has

$$\forall (\mathbf{x}, \mathbf{y}) \in \mathbf{R}^n \times \mathbf{R}^n \quad d_\varphi(\mathbf{x}, \mathbf{y}) \geq 0 \quad \text{and} \quad d_\varphi(\mathbf{x}, \mathbf{y}) = 0 \quad \text{iff} \quad \mathbf{x} = \mathbf{y}.$$

Indeed, the strict convexity of φ and (4) imply

$$\varphi(t) \geq 0, \quad \text{and} \quad \varphi(t) = 0 \quad \text{iff } t = 1.$$

Example 8.2.1. *Some examples of φ include*

$$\varphi_1(t) = t \log t - t + 1, \qquad \text{dom}\, \varphi = [0, +\infty).$$
$$\varphi_2(t) = - \log t + t - 1, \qquad \text{dom}\, \varphi = (0, +\infty).$$
$$\varphi_3(t) = 2(\sqrt{t} - 1)^2, \qquad \text{dom}\, \varphi = [0, +\infty).$$

The first example leads to the Kullback–Leibler divergence (KL) defined on $\mathbf{R}_+^n \times \mathbf{R}_{++}^n$ by

$$d_{\varphi_1}(\mathbf{x}, \mathbf{y}) \equiv KL(\mathbf{x}, \mathbf{y}) = \sum_{j=1}^{n} \mathbf{x}[j] \log \frac{\mathbf{x}[j]}{\mathbf{y}[j]} + \mathbf{y}[j] - \mathbf{x}[j]. \qquad (8.2.2)$$

The centroid $\mathbf{c} = \mathbf{c}(\pi)$ of a p element set π is given by the geometric mean, i.e.,

$$\mathbf{c}[j] = \begin{cases} \prod_{\mathbf{a} \in \pi} (\mathbf{a}[j])^{\frac{1}{p}} & \text{if } \mathbf{a}[j] > 0 \ \forall \ \mathbf{a} \in \pi \\ \\ 0 & \text{otherwise} \end{cases} \qquad j = 1, \ldots, n.$$

$$(8.2.3)$$

Note that for unit L_1 norm vectors $\mathbf{x}$ and $\mathbf{y}$ with nonnegative coordinates one has $\sum_{j=1}^{n} \mathbf{x}[j] = \sum_{j=1}^{n} \mathbf{y}[j] = 1$, and $d_{\varphi_1}(\mathbf{x}, \mathbf{y})$ becomes the standard Kullback–Leibler divergence. The function $d_{\varphi_1}(\mathbf{x}, \mathbf{y})$ allows us to apply the relative entropy distance to the text data (which is usually L_2 normalized). By adopting the convention $0 \log 0 \equiv 0$, the KL functional has been continuously extended on $\mathbf{R}_+^n \times \mathbf{R}_{++}^n$, that is, it admits vectors with zero entries in its first argument (in text mining applications $\mathbf{x}[j] = \mathbf{y}[j] = 0$ corresponds to the case when a word/term does not occur in both documents and motivates the convention $0 \log 0/0 \equiv 0$). The Kullback–Leibler divergence is one of the most popular distances used in data mining research.

The second example φ_2 also yields the KL distance but with reversed order of variables, i.e.,

$$d_{\varphi_2}(\mathbf{x}, \mathbf{y}) \equiv KL(\mathbf{y}, \mathbf{x}) = \sum_{j=1}^{n} \mathbf{y}[j] \log \frac{\mathbf{y}[j]}{\mathbf{x}[j]} + \mathbf{x}[j] - \mathbf{y}[j] \qquad (8.2.4)$$

(compare this formula with (8.1.5) with $\nu = 0$, and $\mu = 1$). The centroid $\mathbf{c} = \mathbf{c}(\pi)$ of a p element set π is given by the arithmetic mean, that is $\mathbf{c} = \frac{1}{p} \sum_{\mathbf{a} \in \pi} \mathbf{a}$.

The third choice gives the Hellinger distance

$$d_{\varphi_3}(\mathbf{x}, \mathbf{y}) = 2 \sum_{j=1}^{n} \left(\sqrt{\mathbf{x}[j]} - \sqrt{\mathbf{y}[j]} \right)^2.$$

As an additional example consider a "distance-like" function defined through the squared Euclidean distance, the kernel φ_2, and nonnegative scalars ν and μ:

$$d(\mathbf{x}, \mathbf{y}) = \frac{\nu}{2} \|\mathbf{x} - \mathbf{y}\|^2 + \mu d_{\varphi_2}(\mathbf{x}, \mathbf{y}) = \frac{\nu}{2} \|\mathbf{x} - \mathbf{y}\|^2 + \mu \sum_{j=1}^{n} \mathbf{y}[j] \varphi_2 \left(\frac{\mathbf{x}[j]}{\mathbf{y}[j]} \right)$$

$$= \frac{\nu}{2} \|\mathbf{x} - \mathbf{y}\|^2 + \mu \sum_{j=1}^{n} \left[\mathbf{y}[j] \log \frac{\mathbf{y}[j]}{\mathbf{x}[j]} + \mathbf{x}[j] - \mathbf{y}[j] \right]. \qquad (8.2.5)$$

Note that the obtained distance is identical to the one given by (8.1.5).

Problem 8.2.3. *Let $\phi : \mathbf{R}_{++} \to \mathbf{R}$ be a twice differentiable convex function. If for each $x, \ y \in \mathbf{R}_{++}$ one has*

$$\phi(x) - \phi(y) - \phi'(y)(x - y) = y\phi \left(\frac{x}{y} \right), \qquad (8.2.6)$$

then $\phi(t) = c\left[t \log t - t + 1\right], \ c > 0$.

Problem 8.2.4. *Consider a separable Bregman divergence*

$$D_{\psi}(\mathbf{x}, \mathbf{y}) = \sum_{j=1}^{n} [\psi_j(\mathbf{x}[j]) - \psi_j(\mathbf{y}[j]) - \psi_j'(\mathbf{y}[j])(\mathbf{x}[j] - \mathbf{y}[j])]$$

and a separable Csiszar divergence

$$d_\varphi(\mathbf{x}, \mathbf{y}) = \sum_{j=1}^{n} \mathbf{y}[j] \varphi_j \left(\frac{\mathbf{x}[j]}{\mathbf{y}[j]} \right).$$

Show that the only kernel that generates identical separable Bregman and Csiszar divergences is the entropy kernel $c[t \log t - t + 1]$, $c > 0$.

Problem 8.2.5. *Let $n = 1$, that is, $d_\varphi(x, y) = y\varphi(\frac{x}{y})$. If $\pi = \{a_1, \ldots, a_p\}$ (a set of scalars), then $c(\pi) = \sum_{i=1}^{P} \omega_i a_i$ where $\sum_{i=1}^{P} \omega_i = 1$ and $\omega_i > 0$, $i = 1, \ldots, p$.*

8.3. Clustering with entropy-like distances

As soon as an efficient computational procedure for building centroids with a distance-like function $d(\mathbf{x}, \mathbf{y})$ is available the two step batch k-means scheme (2.1.4)–(2.1.5) can be applied.

The discussion in Subsection 2.2.2 holds true for a general distance-like function $d(\mathbf{x}, \mathbf{y})$. Indeed, given a partition Π the decision whether a vector $\mathbf{a} \in \pi_i$ should be moved from cluster π_i to cluster π_j is made by the batch k-means algorithm based on examination of the expression

$$\Delta_k = d(\mathbf{c}_i, \mathbf{a}) - d(\mathbf{c}_j, \mathbf{a}). \tag{8.3.1}$$

We denote centroids $\mathbf{c}(\pi_i^-)$ and $\mathbf{c}(\pi_j^+)$ by $\mathbf{c}_i^-$ and $\mathbf{c}_j^+$, respectively. The exact change in the value of the objective function caused by the move is

$$\Delta = [Q(\pi_i) - Q(\pi_i^-)] + [Q(\pi_j) - Q(\pi_j^+)]$$

$$= \left[\sum_{\mathbf{a}' \in \pi_i^-} d(\mathbf{c}_i, \mathbf{a}') - \sum_{\mathbf{a}' \in \pi_i^-} d(\mathbf{c}_i^-, \mathbf{a}') \right] + d(\mathbf{c}_i, \mathbf{a})$$

$$+ \left[\sum_{\mathbf{a}' \in \pi_j^+} d(\mathbf{c}_j, \mathbf{a}') - \sum_{\mathbf{a}' \in \pi_j^+} d(\mathbf{c}_j^+, \mathbf{a}') \right] - d(\mathbf{c}_j, \mathbf{a}).$$

Hence $\Delta - \Delta_k$ is given by

$$\left[\sum_{\mathbf{a}' \in \pi_i^-} d(\mathbf{c}_i, \mathbf{a}') - \sum_{\mathbf{a}' \in \pi_i^-} d(\mathbf{c}_i^-, \mathbf{a}')\right] + \left[\sum_{\mathbf{a}' \in \pi_j^+} d(\mathbf{c}_j, \mathbf{a}') - \sum_{\mathbf{a}' \in \pi_j^+} d(\mathbf{c}_j^+, \mathbf{a}')\right].$$
(8.3.2)

Due to definition of $\mathbf{c}(\pi)$ both differences in (8.3.2) are nonnegative, hence

$$\Delta - \Delta_k \geq 0. \qquad (8.3.3)$$

If $d(\mathbf{x}, \mathbf{a})$ is strictly convex with respect to $\mathbf{x}$, then the inequality in (8.3.3) is strict provided at least one new centroid is different from the corresponding old centroid. This observation justifies application of an incremental iteration following a series of batch iterations for general distance-like functions $d(\mathbf{x}, \mathbf{y})$ as suggested in Algorithm 2.2.1 for $d(\mathbf{x}, \mathbf{y}) = \|\mathbf{x} - \mathbf{y}\|^2$.

Note that removal/assignment of a vector from/to a cluster changes cluster centroids and all distances from the vectors in the two clusters involved to the "new" centroids. Often the actual computations needed to evaluate the change in the objective function use the distances between the "old" centroid and the vector changing its cluster affiliation only.

Example 8.3.1. *Incremental step with a Bregman distance with reversed order of arguments, that is, $d(\mathbf{x}, \mathbf{y}) = \overleftarrow{D_\psi}(\mathbf{x}, \mathbf{y}) = D_\psi(\mathbf{y}, \mathbf{x})$.*

Let π be a set with p vectors, and $\mathbf{a} \in \pi$. We denote the set $\pi - \{\mathbf{a}\}$ by π^-, and centroids of the sets π and π^- (which are given by the arithmetic mean) by $\mathbf{c}$ and $\mathbf{c}^-$, respectively. We now provide a formula for $Q(\pi) - Q(\pi^-)$. Note that

$$Q(\pi) - Q(\pi^-) = \sum_{\mathbf{a}' \in \pi^-} d(\mathbf{c}, \mathbf{a}') + d(\mathbf{c}, \mathbf{a}) - \sum_{\mathbf{a}' \in \pi^-} d(\mathbf{c}^-, \mathbf{a}')$$

$$= \sum_{\mathbf{a}' \in \pi^-} [\psi(\mathbf{a}') - \psi(\mathbf{c}) - \nabla\psi(\mathbf{c})(\mathbf{a}' - \mathbf{c})]$$

133

$$-\sum_{\mathbf{a}'\in\pi^-}[\psi(\mathbf{a}')-\psi(\mathbf{c}^-)-\nabla\psi(\mathbf{c}^-)(\mathbf{a}'-\mathbf{c}^-)]+d(\mathbf{c},\mathbf{a})$$

$$=(p-1)[\psi(\mathbf{c}^-)-\psi(\mathbf{c})]-\nabla\psi(\mathbf{c})\left[\sum_{\mathbf{a}'\in\pi^-}\mathbf{a}'-(p-1)\mathbf{c}\right]$$

$$+d(\mathbf{c},\mathbf{a}).$$

Keeping in mind that

$$\sum_{\mathbf{a}'\in\pi^-}\mathbf{a}'=\sum_{\mathbf{a}'\in\pi}\mathbf{a}'-\mathbf{a}=p\mathbf{c}-\mathbf{a},$$

we get

$$Q(\pi)-Q(\pi^-)=(p-1)[\psi(\mathbf{c}^-)-\psi(\mathbf{c})]-\nabla\psi(\mathbf{c})(\mathbf{c}-\mathbf{a})+d(\mathbf{c},\mathbf{a}).$$

(8.3.4)

Next we derive a convenient formula for $Q(\pi)-Q(\pi^+)$, where π is a set with p vectors, $\mathbf{a}\notin\pi$, $\pi^+=\pi\cup\{\mathbf{a}\}$, $\mathbf{c}=\mathbf{c}(\pi)$, and $\mathbf{c}^+=\mathbf{c}(\pi^+)$.

$$Q(\pi)-Q(\pi^+)=\sum_{\mathbf{a}'\in\pi^+}d(\mathbf{c},\mathbf{a}')-d(\mathbf{c},\mathbf{a})-\sum_{\mathbf{a}'\in\pi^+}d(\mathbf{c}^+,\mathbf{a}')$$

$$=\sum_{\mathbf{a}'\in\pi^+}[\psi(\mathbf{a}')-\psi(\mathbf{c})-\nabla\psi(\mathbf{c})(\mathbf{a}'-\mathbf{c})]$$

$$-\sum_{\mathbf{a}'\in\pi^+}[\psi(\mathbf{a}')-\psi(\mathbf{c}^+)-\nabla\psi(\mathbf{c}^+)(\mathbf{a}'-\mathbf{c}^+)]-d(\mathbf{c},\mathbf{a})$$

$$=(p+1)[\psi(\mathbf{c}^+)-\psi(\mathbf{c})]-\nabla\psi(\mathbf{c})\left[\sum_{\mathbf{a}'\in\pi^+}\mathbf{a}'-(p+1)\mathbf{c}\right]$$

$$-d(\mathbf{c},\mathbf{a}).$$

Keeping in mind that

$$\sum_{\mathbf{a}'\in\pi^+}\mathbf{a}'=\sum_{\mathbf{a}'\in\pi}\mathbf{a}'+\mathbf{a}=p\mathbf{c}+\mathbf{a},$$

we obtain

$$Q(\pi)-Q(\pi^+)=(p+1)[\psi(\mathbf{c}^+)-\psi(\mathbf{c})]-\nabla\psi(\mathbf{c})(\mathbf{a}-\mathbf{c})-d(\mathbf{c},\mathbf{a}).$$

(8.3.5)

Finally we select two clusters π_i and π_j from a partition Π, and a vector $\mathbf{a} \in \pi_i$. *We denote the number of vectors in each cluster by m_i and m_j,* *respectively. The formula for*

$$[Q(\pi_i) - Q(\pi_i^-)] + [Q(\pi_j) - Q(\pi_j^+)]$$

follows from (8.3.4) and (8.3.5) and is given by

$$
\begin{aligned}
[Q(\pi_i) - Q(\pi_i^-)] &+ [Q(\pi_j) - Q(\pi_j^+)] \\
&= (m_i - 1)d(\mathbf{c}_i, \mathbf{c}_i^-) + d(\mathbf{c}_i, \mathbf{a}) + (m_j + 1)d(\mathbf{c}_j, \mathbf{c}_j^+) \\
&\quad + d(\mathbf{c}_j, \mathbf{a}) \\
&= (m_i - 1)[\psi(\mathbf{c}_i^-) - \psi(\mathbf{c}_i)] - \psi(\mathbf{c}_i) \\
&\quad + (m_j + 1)[\psi(\mathbf{c}_j^+) - \psi(\mathbf{c}_j)] + \psi(\mathbf{c}_j). \qquad (8.3.6)
\end{aligned}
$$

In text mining applications, due to sparsity of the data vector $\mathbf{a}$, most *coordinates of centroids $\mathbf{c}^-$, $\mathbf{c}^+$ and $\mathbf{c}$ coincide. Hence, when the function* *ψ is separable, computations of $\psi(\mathbf{c}_i^-)$ and $\psi(\mathbf{c}_j^+)$ are relatively cheap.*

While the computational cost of an incremental iteration following a batch iteration remains negligible for distance-like functions generated by Bregman distances with reversed order of variables, it may be as expensive as the cost of a batch iteration for distance-like functions generated by Csiszar divergences.

8.4. BIRCH-type clustering with entropy-like distances

In this section we extend the "data squashing" approach described in Chapter 3 for a quadratic Euclidean distance-like function to a more general class of functions. To implement the "squashing" strategy one has to address the following question: "What information is needed for clustering "cluster-points?" In other words given a set of clusters $\pi_1, \ldots, \pi_k$ what one needs to know in order to compute $Q(\pi_1 \cup \cdots \cup \pi_k)$? This Chapter provides answers to these questions for some special choices of distance-like functions. It turns out that for these special cases one needs to know clusters' centroids $\mathbf{c}(\pi_i)$, and only two additional scalars for each cluster. Hence, an application of "BIRCH" type approach to k-means may lead to significant memory savings.

We note that if $\pi = \{\mathbf{a}_1, \ldots, \mathbf{a}_p\}$, $\mathbf{c}(\pi)$ is the centroid, and $\mathbf{x}$ is a vector, then

$$\sum_{i=1}^{p} d(\mathbf{x}, \mathbf{a}_i) = \sum_{i=1}^{p} d(\mathbf{c}(\pi), \mathbf{a}_i) + \left[\sum_{i=1}^{p} d(\mathbf{x}, \mathbf{a}_i) - \sum_{i=1}^{p} d(\mathbf{c}(\pi), \mathbf{a}_i) \right]$$

$$= Q(\pi) + \left[\sum_{i=1}^{p} d(\mathbf{x}, \mathbf{a}_i) - \sum_{i=1}^{p} d(\mathbf{c}(\pi), \mathbf{a}_i) \right]. \qquad (8.4.1)$$

Possible simplifications of this formula are distance dependent. We first focus on a Bregman distance with reversed order of variables

$$d(\mathbf{x}, \mathbf{y}) = \overleftarrow{D_\psi}(\mathbf{x}, \mathbf{y}) = D_\psi(\mathbf{y}, \mathbf{x}) = \psi(\mathbf{y}) - \psi(\mathbf{x}) - \nabla\psi(\mathbf{x})(\mathbf{y} - \mathbf{x}).$$

Due to (8.4.1), one has

$$\sum_{i=1}^{p} d(\mathbf{x}, \mathbf{a}_i) = Q(\pi) + p\left[\psi(\mathbf{c}(\pi)) - \psi(\mathbf{x}) - \nabla\psi(\mathbf{x})(\mathbf{c}(\pi) - \mathbf{x})\right]$$

$$= Q(\pi) + pd(\mathbf{x}, \mathbf{c}(\pi)). \qquad (8.4.2)$$

The above expression is a generalization of (2.2.2). The result stated next follows straightforward from (8.4.2).

Theorem 8.4.1. *If* $\mathcal{A} = \pi_1 \cup \pi_2 \cup \cdots \cup \pi_k$ *with* $m_i = |\pi_i|$, $\mathbf{c}_i = \mathbf{c}(\pi_i)$, $i = 1, \ldots, k$;

$$\mathbf{c} = \mathbf{c}(\mathcal{A}) = \frac{m_1}{m}\mathbf{c}_1 + \cdots + \frac{m_k}{m}\mathbf{c}_k, \text{ where } m = m_1 + \cdots + m_k,$$

and $\Pi = \{\pi_1 \pi_2, \ldots, \pi_k\}$, *then*

$$Q(\Pi) = \sum_{i=1}^{k} Q(\pi_i) + \sum_{i=1}^{k} m_i d(\mathbf{c}, \mathbf{c}_i) = \sum_{i=1}^{k} Q(\pi_i) + \sum_{i=1}^{k} m_i \left[\psi(\mathbf{c}_i) - \psi(\mathbf{c})\right].$$

$$(8.4.3)$$

Proof:

$$Q(\Pi) = \sum_{i=1}^{k} \left\{ \sum_{\mathbf{a} \in \pi_i} d(\mathbf{c}, \mathbf{a}) \right\} = \sum_{i=1}^{k} \left\{ Q(\pi_i) + m_i d(\mathbf{c}, \mathbf{c}_i) \right\}$$

$$= \sum_{i=1}^{k} Q(\pi_i) + \sum_{i=1}^{k} m_i \left[\psi(\mathbf{c}_i) - \psi(\mathbf{c}) - \nabla\psi(\mathbf{c})(\mathbf{c}_i - \mathbf{c}) \right]$$

$$= \sum_{i=1}^{k} \left\{ Q(\pi_i) + m_i \left[\psi(\mathbf{c}_i) - \psi(\mathbf{c}) \right] \right\} - \nabla\psi(\mathbf{c}) \left(\sum_{i=1}^{k} m_i \mathbf{c}_i - \mathbf{c} \sum_{i=1}^{k} m_i \right)$$

$$= \sum_{i=1}^{k} \left\{ Q(\pi_i) + m_i [\psi(\mathbf{c}_i) - \psi(\mathbf{c})] \right\}.$$

This completes the proof. □

Note that the above result is a straightforward generalization of Theorem 2.2.1. Equation 8.4.3 shows that clustering of "cluster-points" requires centroids (given by the arithmetic mean in this case), as well as two additional scalars per "cluster-point" ("cluster-point" size and quality).

Going back to Chapter 3 we focus on a k cluster partition $\Pi_B = \{\pi_1^B, \ldots, \pi_k^B\}$ of the set $B = \{\mathbf{b}_1, \ldots, \mathbf{b}_M\}$. To be able to run an incremental iteration of birch k-means one has to be able to compute the change of the partition quality due to removal of a vector $\mathbf{b}$ from cluster π_i^B with centroid $\mathbf{c}_i = \mathbf{c}(\pi_i^B)$ and assignment of $\mathbf{b}$ to π_j^B with centroid $\mathbf{c}_j = \mathbf{c}(\pi_j^B)$. A starightforward computation leads to the formula

$$\left[Q_B(\pi_i^B) - Q_B(\pi_i^{B-}) \right] + \left[Q_B(\pi_j^B) - Q_B(\pi_j^{B+}) \right]$$
$$= [M_i - m(\mathbf{b})] d(\mathbf{c}_i, \mathbf{c}_i^-) + m(\mathbf{b})d(\mathbf{c}_i, \mathbf{b})$$
$$+ [M_j + m(\mathbf{b})] d(\mathbf{c}_j, \mathbf{c}_j^+) - m(\mathbf{b})d(\mathbf{c}_j, \mathbf{b})$$
$$= [M_i - m(\mathbf{b})] [\psi(\mathbf{c}_i^-) - \psi(\mathbf{c}_i)] - m(\mathbf{b})\psi(\mathbf{c}_i)$$
$$+ [M_j + m(\mathbf{b})] [\psi(\mathbf{c}_j^+) - \psi(\mathbf{c}_j)] + m(\mathbf{b})\psi(\mathbf{c}_j).$$

$$(8.4.4)$$

The left-hand side is a generalization of both (3.2.7) and (8.3.6).

Problem 8.4.1. *Let* $\pi^B = \{\mathbf{b}_1, \ldots, \mathbf{b}_{p-1}, \mathbf{b}\}$, $\pi^{B^-} = \{\mathbf{b}_1, \ldots, \mathbf{b}_{p-1}\}$, *and* $m_- = \sum_{i=1}^{p-1} m(\mathbf{b}_i)$. *Show that*

$$Q(\pi^B) - Q(\pi^{B^-}) = q(\mathbf{b}) + m_- d(\mathbf{c}, \mathbf{c}^-) - m(\mathbf{b})d(\mathbf{c}, \mathbf{b}),$$

where $\mathbf{c} = \mathbf{c}(\pi^B)$, *and* $\mathbf{c}^- = \mathbf{c}(\pi^{B^-})$.

Problem 8.4.2. *Let* $\pi^B = \{\mathbf{b}_1, \ldots, \mathbf{b}_p\}$, $\pi^{B^+} = \{\mathbf{b}_1, \ldots, \mathbf{b}_p, \mathbf{b}\}$, *and* $m_+ = \sum_{i=1}^{p} m(\mathbf{b}_i) + m(\mathbf{b})$. *Show that*

$$Q(\pi^B) - Q(\pi^{B^+}) = -q(\mathbf{b}) + m_+ d(\mathbf{c}, \mathbf{c}^+) + m(\mathbf{b})d(\mathbf{c}, \mathbf{b}),$$

where $\mathbf{c} = \mathbf{c}(\pi^B)$, *and* $\mathbf{c}^+ = \mathbf{c}(\pi^{B^+})$.

We now turn to a special distance-like function generated by Csiszar divergence. Let $\varphi_1(t) = t \log t - t + 1$. The corresponding distance-like function is

$$d(\mathbf{x}, \mathbf{a}) = \sum_{j=1}^{n} \left[\mathbf{x}[j] \log \frac{\mathbf{x}[j]}{\mathbf{a}[j]} - \mathbf{x}[j] + \mathbf{a}[j] \right].$$

For a vector set $\pi = \{\mathbf{a}_1, \ldots, \mathbf{a}_p\}$ with p elements, centroid $\mathbf{c}(\pi)$ and a vector $\mathbf{x}$ formula (8.4.1) becomes

$$\sum_{i=1}^{p} d(\mathbf{x}, \mathbf{a}_i) = \sum_{i=1}^{p} d(\mathbf{c}, \mathbf{a}_i) + p \sum_{j=1}^{n} \left(\mathbf{x}[j] \log \frac{\mathbf{x}[j]}{\mathbf{c}[j]} - \mathbf{x}[j] + \mathbf{c}[j] \right)$$
$$= Q(\pi) + p d(\mathbf{x}, \mathbf{c}). \tag{8.4.5}$$

The centroid $\mathbf{c} = \mathbf{c}(\pi)$ of the set π is given by the geometric mean (see (8.2.3)).

Theorem 8.4.2. *If* $\mathcal{A} = \pi_1 \cup \pi_2 \cup \ldots \cup \pi_k$ *with* $m_i = |\pi_i|$, $\mathbf{c}_i = \mathbf{c}(\pi_i)$, $i = 1, \ldots, k$, *and* $\mathbf{c} = \mathbf{c}(\mathcal{A})$ *so that*

$$(\mathbf{c}[j])^m = (\mathbf{c}_1[j])^{m_1} \times \cdots \times (\mathbf{c}_k[j])^{m_k} \text{ where } m = m_1 + \cdots + m_k$$
$$\text{and } j = 1, \cdots, n,$$

then

$$Q(\mathcal{A}) = \sum_{i=1}^{k} \{Q(\pi_i) + m_i d(\mathbf{c}, \mathbf{c}_i)\} = \sum_{i=1}^{k} Q(\pi_i) + \sum_{i=1}^{k} m_i \mathbf{e}^T \mathbf{c}_i - m \mathbf{e}^T \mathbf{c}$$

(8.4.6)

where $\mathbf{e}$ is the vector of ones.

Proof:

$$Q(\mathcal{A}) = \sum_{\mathbf{a} \in \mathcal{A}} d(\mathbf{c}, \mathbf{a}) = \sum_{i=1}^{k} \left\{ \sum_{\mathbf{a} \in \pi_i} d(\mathbf{c}, \mathbf{a}) \right\} = \sum_{i=1}^{k} \left\{ \sum_{\mathbf{a} \in \pi_i} d(\mathbf{c}_i, \mathbf{a}) + m_i d(\mathbf{c}, \mathbf{c}_i) \right\}$$

$$= \sum_{i=1}^{k} \{Q(\pi_i) + m_i d(\mathbf{c}, \mathbf{c}_i)\}.$$

(8.4.7)

Further

$$\sum_{i=1}^{k} m_i d(\mathbf{c}, \mathbf{c}_i) = \sum_{i=1}^{k} m_i \left[\sum_{j=1}^{n} \left(\mathbf{c}[j] \log \frac{\mathbf{c}[j]}{\mathbf{c}_i[j]} - \mathbf{c}[j] + \mathbf{c}_i[j] \right) \right]$$

$$= \sum_{j=1}^{n} \sum_{i=1}^{k} m_i \left(\mathbf{c}[j] \log \frac{\mathbf{c}[j]}{\mathbf{c}_i[j]} - \mathbf{c}[j] + \mathbf{c}_i[j] \right)$$

$$= \sum_{j=1}^{n} \mathbf{c}[j] \log \frac{(\mathbf{c}[j])^m}{\prod_{i=1}^{k} (\mathbf{c}_i[j])^{m_i}} - \left(\sum_{i=1}^{k} m_i \right) \sum_{j=1}^{n} \mathbf{c}[j]$$

$$+ \sum_{i=1}^{k} \left(m_i \sum_{j=1}^{n} \mathbf{c}_i[j] \right)$$

$$= \sum_{i=1}^{k} m_i \mathbf{e}^T \mathbf{c}_i - m \mathbf{e}^T \mathbf{c}.$$

Substitution of the right-hand side into (8.4.7) completes the proof.

□

The formula shows that in order to employ the "BIRCH type" clustering procedure one needs to have the following information concerning each cluster π:

1. centroid $\mathbf{c}(\pi)$,
2. cluster size $|\pi|$,

Table 8.1: $\nu = 0$, $\mu = 1$ generated final "confusion" matrix with 44 "misclassified" documents

	DC0	DC1	DC2
Cluster 0	1010	6	0
Cluster 1	2	4	1387
Cluster 2	21	1450	11
"Empty" documents			
Cluster 3	0	0	0

3. $\mathbf{e}^T \mathbf{c}(\pi)$.

Generalizations of Algorithm 3.2.1 to Bregman distances with reversed order of variables or by the Csiszar divergence $d(\mathbf{x}, \mathbf{a}) = \sum_{j=1}^n [\mathbf{x}[j] \log \frac{\mathbf{x}[j]}{\mathbf{a}[j]} - \mathbf{x}[j] + \mathbf{a}[j]]$ are starightforward.

8.5. Numerical experiments with (ν, μ) *k*-means

In this Section we provide clustering results for the document collection DC (classic3) described in Section 5.3.3. We use the distance-like function (8.2.5) that combines weighted squared Euclidean distance and Kullback–Leibler divergence. To distinguish between *k*-means algorithms with different distance-like function we shall call the clustering procedure considered in this section the (ν, μ) *k*-means clustering algorithm.

We use the final partition Π generated by sPDDP as an input for the (ν, μ) *k*-means. When Π is available (see Table 5.6) the document vectors are renormalized in L_1 norm, and the (ν, μ) *k*-means algorithm is applied to Π (clustering L_2 unit norm vectors with (ν, μ) *k*-means is reported in Section 8.6). The final partitions for three selected values of the (ν, μ) pair are reported in Tables 8.1, 8.2, and 8.3, respectively. We display results for the "extreme" values $(0, 1)$, $(1, 0)$, and an intermediate value of (ν, μ). In this experiment we have decided to choose

8.5. Numerical experiments with (ν, μ) k-means

Table 8.2: $\nu = 100$, $\mu = 1$ generated final "confusion" matrix with 48 "misclassified" documents using best 600 terms

	DC0	DC1	DC2
Cluster 0	1010	5	1
Cluster 1	3	6	1384
Cluster 2	20	1449	13
"Empty" documents			
Cluster 3	0	0	0

Table 8.3: $\nu = 1$, $\mu = 0$ generated final "confusion" matrix with 52 "misclassified" documents using best 600 terms

	DC0	DC1	DC2
Cluster 0	1011	6	2
Cluster 1	8	12	1386
Cluster 2	14	1442	10
"Empty" documents			
Cluster 3	0	0	0

the intermediate value $(100, 1)$ to balance the "extreme" values of the objective functions.

A subsequent application of (ν, μ) k-means to the partition Π generated by sPDDP further reduces misclassification (see Tables 8.1, 8.2 8.3).

We pause briefly to discuss some properties of the algorithm.

1. Unlike the algorithm presented in Chapter 6 the dataset $\mathcal{A}$ for the algorithm is not restricted to L_1 unit norm vectors in $\mathbf{R}_+^n$ (and, in fact, the algorithm does not require any normalization of the non negative data).

2. In the extreme case $\nu = 1$, $\mu = 0$ the classical quadratic k-means algorithm is recovered, and the data is no longer required to be restricted to $\mathbf{R}_+^n$.

Table 8.4: Number of documents "misclassified" by sPDDP, and "sPDDP $+ (v, \mu)$ *k*-means" algorithms.

# of terms	Zero vectors	Documents misclassified by sPDDP			
		Alone	$+(1, 0)$	$+(100, 1)$	$+(0, 1)$
100	12	383	499	269	166
200	3	277	223	129	112
300	0	228	124	80	68
400	0	88	68	58	56
500	0	76	63	40	41
600	0	68	52	48	44

3. When $v = 0, \mu = 1$ and the document vectors are normalized in L_1 norm the algorithm coincides with KL *k*-means.

Table 8.4 summarizes clustering results for the sPDDP algorithm and the combinations of "sPDDP+(v, μ) *k*-means" algorithm for the three selected values for (v, μ) and different choices of index terms. Note that zero document vectors are created when the number of selected terms is less than 300. Table 8.4 indicates consistent superiority of the "sPDDP $+ (0, 1)$ *k*-means" algorithm. We next show by an example that this indication is not necessarily always correct. Figure 8.2 shows the number of misclassified documents for 600 selected terms and 25 values of the (v, μ) pair. While μ is kept 1, v varies from 100 to 2500 with step 100. The graph indicates the best performance for $\frac{v}{\mu} = 500$, 600, 700, 1000, and 1100.

We complete the section with clustering results generated by the "sPDDP + quadratic *k*-means" and "sPDDP + spherical *k*-means". The algorithms are applied to the three document collections DC0, DC1, and DC2. We use the same vector space construction as for the "sPDDP+(v, μ) *k*-means" procedure, but do not change the document vectors unit L_2 norm at the second stage of the clustering scheme. The results of the experiment are summarized in Table 8.5 for different choices of index terms.

Table 8.5: Number of unit L_2 document vectors "misclassified" by "sPDDP + k-means", and "sPDDP + spherical k-means".

		Documents misclassified by	
# of terms	Zero vectors	sPDDP + quadratic k-means	sPDDP + spherical k-means
100	12	258	229
200	3	133	143
300	0	100	104
400	0	80	78
500	0	62	57
600	0	62	54

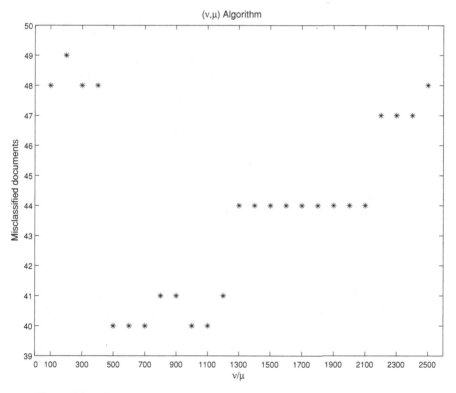

Figure 8.2: Misclassification vs. $\frac{\nu}{\mu}$ ratio.

Project 8.5.1. *This book deals with clustering of a vector set $\mathcal{A} = \{\mathbf{a}_1, \ldots, \mathbf{a}_m\}$ with m distinct elements. Extend results of the book to the case when the dataset $\mathcal{A}$ contains multiple copies of vectors. Note, that due to Problem 2.2.3, the quadratic k-means clustering algorithm assigns identical vectors to the same cluster.*

8.6. Smoothing with entropy-like distances

The "smoothing" approach of Chapter 7 can be applied to a variety of kernels in a number of different ways. In this section we focus on the special distance-like function (8.2.5)

$$d(\mathbf{x}, \mathbf{y}) = \frac{v}{2}\|\mathbf{x} - \mathbf{y}\|^2 + \mu \sum_{j=1}^{n} \left[\mathbf{y}[j] \log \frac{\mathbf{y}[j]}{\mathbf{x}[j]} + \mathbf{x}[j] - \mathbf{y}[j] \right],$$

where v and μ are nonnegative constants. Since the special case $\mu = 0$ has been discussed in detail in Chapter 7, in this section we shall assume throughout that $\mu > 0$. Our goal is to substitute the following nonconvex and *nonsmooth* objective function:

$$F(\mathbf{x}) = \sum_{i=1}^{m} \min_{1 \leq l \leq k} d(\mathbf{x}_l, \mathbf{a}_i),$$

$$\mathbf{x} = \left(\mathbf{x}_1^T, \ldots, \mathbf{x}_k^T\right)^T \in \underbrace{\mathcal{C} \times \cdots \times \mathcal{C}}_{k} = \mathcal{C}^k \subseteq \mathbf{R}^{nk} = \mathbf{R}^N \quad (8.6.1)$$

by the family of *smooth* objective functions

$$F_s(\mathbf{x}) = \sum_{i=1}^{m} -s \log \left(\sum_{l=1}^{k} e^{-\frac{d(\mathbf{x}_l, \mathbf{a}_i)}{s}} \right).$$

The set $\mathcal{C}$ housing centroids is $\mathbf{R}^n$ when $\mu = 0$, and $\mathbf{R}^n_{++}$ otherwise. In what follows we focus on the case $\mu > 0$ (for the special case $\mu = 0$ see Chapter 7).

We fix $s > 0$ and attempt to solve the optimization problem with a *smooth* objective

$$\min_{\mathbf{x} \in \mathbf{R}^N_{++}} F_s(\mathbf{x}). \quad (8.6.2)$$

8.6. Smoothing with entropy-like distances

Motivated by *IR* applications we shall assume that for each $j = 1, \ldots, n$ there exists $\mathbf{a}_i$ such that $\mathbf{a}_i[j] > 0$. This assumption along with the positivity of μ guarantees the existence of the minimizer $\bar{\mathbf{x}} \in \mathbf{R}_{++}^N$. Hence the necessary optimality condition the solution of (8.6.2) satisfies is

$$\nabla F_s(\mathbf{x}) = 0, \tag{8.6.3}$$

and for each $l = 1, \ldots, k$, we obtain

$$\sum_{i=1}^{m} \frac{\nabla_{\mathbf{x}} d(\bar{\mathbf{x}}_l, \mathbf{a}_i) e^{-\frac{d(\bar{\mathbf{x}}_l, \mathbf{a}_i)}{s}}}{\sum_{j=1}^{k} e^{-\frac{d(\bar{\mathbf{x}}_j, \mathbf{a}_i)}{s}}} = 0. \tag{8.6.4}$$

For each $l = 1, \ldots, k$ and $i = 1, \ldots, m$ and $\mathbf{x} = (\mathbf{x}_1^T, \ldots, \mathbf{x}_k^T)^T$ we define the positive numbers

$$\rho^{il}(\mathbf{x}, s) = \frac{e^{-\frac{d(\bar{\mathbf{x}}_l, \mathbf{a}_i)}{s}}}{\sum_{j=1}^{k} e^{-\frac{d(\bar{\mathbf{x}}_j, \mathbf{a}_i)}{s}}}. \tag{8.6.5}$$

Equation (8.6.4) now becomes

$$\sum_{i=1}^{m} \nabla_{\mathbf{x}} d(\bar{\mathbf{x}}_l, \mathbf{a}_i) \rho^{il}(\bar{\mathbf{x}}, s) = 0. \tag{8.6.6}$$

We now compute the partial derivative $\sum_{i=1}^{m} \left[\frac{\partial}{\partial \mathbf{x}[j]} d(\bar{\mathbf{x}}_l, \mathbf{a}_i) \right] \rho^{il}(\bar{\mathbf{x}}, s)$ and obtain the following quadratic equation for $\bar{\mathbf{x}}_l[j]$:

$$\left(\nu \sum_{i=1}^{m} \rho^{il}(\bar{\mathbf{x}}, s) \right) (\bar{\mathbf{x}}_l[j])^2 + \left(\mu \sum_{i=1}^{m} \rho^{il}(\bar{\mathbf{x}}, s) - \nu \sum_{i=1}^{m} \mathbf{a}_i[j] \rho^{il}(\bar{\mathbf{x}}, s) \right) \bar{\mathbf{x}}_l[j]$$
$$- \mu \left(\sum_{i=1}^{m} \mathbf{a}_i[j] \rho^{il}(\bar{\mathbf{x}}, s) \right) = 0.$$

The positive solution for this equation is given by

$$\overline{\mathbf{x}}_l[j] = \frac{\sum\limits_{i=1}^{m} \mathbf{a}_i[j] \rho^{il}(\overline{\mathbf{x}}, s)}{\sum\limits_{i=1}^{m} \rho^{il}(\overline{\mathbf{x}}, s)} = \sum\limits_{i=1}^{m} \frac{\rho^{il}(\overline{\mathbf{x}}, s)}{\sum\limits_{p=1}^{m} \rho^{pl}(\overline{\mathbf{x}}, s)} \mathbf{a}_i[j].$$

We denote $\frac{\rho^{il}(\overline{\mathbf{x}}, s)}{\sum_{p=1}^{m} \rho^{pl}(\overline{\mathbf{x}}, s)}$ by $\lambda^{il}(\overline{\mathbf{x}}, s)$ and obtain the following equation for $\overline{\mathbf{x}}_l$:

$$\overline{\mathbf{x}}_l = \sum\limits_{i=1}^{m} \lambda^{il}(\overline{\mathbf{x}}, s) \mathbf{a}_i, \quad \lambda^{il}(\overline{\mathbf{x}}, s) > 0, \quad \sum\limits_{i=1}^{m} \lambda^{il}(\overline{\mathbf{x}}, s) = 1. \qquad (8.6.7)$$

This formula is identical to equation (7.2.7) of Chapter 7.

Project 8.6.2. *Show that for the mapping* $T : \mathbf{R}_{++}^N \to \mathbf{R}^N$ *defined by* (7.2.8) *and* (7.2.10) *with* λ^{il} *defined in this chapter:*

1. *For each* $\mathbf{x} \in \mathbf{R}_{++}^N$ *one has* $T(\mathbf{x}) \in \mathbf{R}_{++}^N$.
2. *Theorem* 7.3.1 *holds.*
3. *Proposition* 7.3.3 *holds.*

8.7. Numerical experiments with (ν, μ) smoka

In this section we report some numerical results on data sets arising in text mining for the following document collections:

1. A merger of the three document collections classic3 (see Subsection 5.3.3).
2. The "full" data set of 19,997 messages from 20 Usenet newsgroups (see Section 7.4).

We remove stop words (see ftp://ftp.cs.cornell.edu/pub/smart/english.stop) and stem the words with Porter stemmer. We then select n "best" terms and build vectors of dimension n for each document collection (see [37] for selection procedure details, unlike [37] in this experiment we rate all collection terms).

Table 8.6: Collection: classic3. PDDP generated initial "confusion" matrix with 227 "misclassified" documents using 600 best terms, $Q = 3612.61$

	DC0	DC1	DC2
Cluster 0	7	1379	14
Cluster 1	113	7	1372
Cluster 2	913	74	12
"Empty" documents			
Cluster 3	0	0	0

We focus on the family of distance-like functions (8.2.5) and call smoka with this distance-like function (v, μ) smoka. In this section we run the (v, μ) k-means and (v, μ) smoka algorithms for two extreme values (i.e. $(v, \mu) = (2, 0)$ and $(v, \mu) = (0, 1)$) and an intermediate value of (v, μ).

The principal direction divisive partitioning is applied to a vector set to generate the initial partition $\Pi^{(0)}$, needed to initialize the algorithm. We then apply the (v, μ) k-means and (v, μ) smoka clustering algorithms to the partition $\Pi^{(0)}$ and report quality of the obtained final partitions along with the number of iterations performed by each algorithm. Since the first three collections (classic3) are known to be well separated we also provide confusion matrices corresponding to partitions of these collections with the squared Euclidean distance only. In the experiments reported below unless indicated otherwise the (v, μ) k-means algorithm is run with $\text{tol} = 0$, and (v, μ) smoka is run with $s = 0.0001$ and $\text{tol} = 0.0001$ (the different choice for tol is explained in Section 7.4).

We conduct the first experiment with classic3 collection. The confusion matrix for the partition $\Pi^{(0)}$ is given in Table 8.6.

Application of the (v, μ) k-means clustering algorithm with $v = 2$, $\mu = 0$ to the partition $\Pi^{(0)}$ iterates 87 times and generates a partition with confusion matrix given in Table 8.7. Application of smoka with $v = 2$, $\mu = 0$ to the partition $\Pi^{(0)}$ produces seven iterations only.

Table 8.7: Collection: classic3. $2 - 0$ clustering
generated "confusion" matrix with 79 "misclassified"
documents using 600 best terms, $Q = 3605.5$

	DC0	DC1	DC2
Cluster 0	1018	21	19
Cluster 1	5	1	1356
Cluster 2	10	1438	23
"Empty" documents			
Cluster 3	0	0	0

Table 8.8: Collection: classic3. $2 - 0$ smoka
generated "confusion" matrix with **73** "misclassified"
documents using 600 best terms, $Q = 3605.5$

	DC0	DC1	DC2
Cluster 0	1019	22	15
Cluster 1	5	1	1362
Cluster 2	9	1437	21
"Empty" documents			
Cluster 3	0	0	0

The confusions matrix corresponding to the generated final partition
is given in Table 8.8. While the quality of final partitions generated by
(v, μ) *k*-means and (v, μ) smoka are almost identical, the number of
iterations performed by the algorithms is very different (see Table 8.9).
We repeat this experiment with (v, μ) *k*-means and (v, μ) smoka clustering algorithms for $v = 0, \mu = 1$ (pure logarithmic distance-like function) and $v = 20, \mu = 1$ (a combination of the squared Euclidean and
the logarithmic distance) and report the results below. Note that due to
different distances the quality of partition generated by PDDP is different in Table 8.9, Table 8.10, and Table 8.11. The choice $v = 20, \mu = 1$
is motivated by the desire to "balance out" the different scales generated by the combination of two distances. The final experiment deals
with the set of 19,997 documents. We build the vector space model of

Table 8.9: Collection: classic3. Number of iterations per clustering algorithm applied to the initial partition generated by PDDP, the vector space dimension is 600

Algorithm	PDDP	(2, 0) batch k-means	(2, 0) k-means	(2, 0) smoka
Iterations		3	87	7
Misclassifications	250	131	79	73
Q	3612.61	3608.1	3605.5	3605.5

Table 8.10: Collection: **classic3**. Number of iterations per clustering algorithm applied to the initial partition generated by PDDP, the vector space dimension is 600

Algorithm	PDDP	(0, 1) batch k-means	(0, 1) k-means	(0, 1) smoka
Iterations		4	100	4
Misclassifications	250	117	43	66
Q	44 138.9	43 759.1	43 463.8	43 496.5

dimension 1000, generate the initial 20 cluster partition $\Pi^{(0)}$ with PDDP, and apply $(2, 0)$ and $(2, 0)$ smoka to $\Pi^{(0)}$. The clustering results are reported in Table 8.12. The corresponding results for $(0, 1)$ k-means and $(0, 1)$ smoka, and $(20, 1)$ k-means and $20 - 1$ smoka are reported in Tables 8.13 and 8.14, respectively.

The numerical experiments for the two data sets and the three choices of distance functions indicate that smoka generates clustering results of the quality comparable with those generated by k-means. The number of iterations performed by smoka is a *fraction* (less than 10% for classic3, and less than 1% for the larger data set "20 newsgroups") of the number of iterations performed by k-means. These experiments indicate that the fraction $\dfrac{\text{\# of smoka iterations}}{\text{\# of } k\text{–means iterations}}$ decreases sharply with the growing size of the dataset.

149

Table 8.11: Collection: classic3. Number of iterations per clustering algorithm applied to the initial partition generated by PDDP, the vector space dimension is 600

Algorithm	PDDP	(20, 1) batch *k*-means	(20, 1) *k*-means	(20, 1) smoka
Iterations		0	246	5
Misclassifications	250	250	39	66
Q		80 265.1	80 265.1	79 520.4	79 561.3

Table 8.12: Collection: the "full" 20 newsgroups data set. Number of iterations per clustering algorithm applied to the initial partition generated by PDDP, 19,997 vectors of dimension 1000 from the "full" 20 newsgroups data set

Algorithm	PDDP	(2, 0) batch *k*-means	(2, 0) *k*-means	(2, 0) smoka
Iterations		47	5862	51
Q	18 156.5	17 956	17 808	17 810

Table 8.13: Collection: the "full" 20 newsgroups dataset. Number of iterations per clustering algorithm applied to the initial partition generated by PDDP, 19,997 vectors of dimension 1000 from the "full" 20 newsgroups data set

Algorithm	PDDP	(0, 1) batch *k*-means	(0, 1) *k*-means	(0, 1) smoka
Iterations		18	7737	23
Q	261 907	256 472	250 356	252 708

To convince a skeptical reader we appear to visual intuition. Figure 8.3 illustrates performance of the first 23 iterations of $(0, 1)$ *k*-means and $(0, 1)$ smoka. The plot is an immediate sibling of the one presented in Section 7.4 (see Figure 7.4). While, for example, the first five iterations of $(0, 1)$ *k*-means move $4275 (= 3171 + 645 + 267 + 118 + 74)$ vectors, the first five $(0, 1)$ smoka iterations lead to an even

Table 8.14: Collection: the "full" 20 newsgroups data set. Number of iterations per clustering algorithm applied to the initial partition generated by PDDP, 19 997 vectors of dimension 1000 from the "full" 20 newsgroups data set

Algorithm	PDDP	(20, 1) batch k-means	(20, 1) k-means	(20, 1) smoka
Iterations		1	9988	25
Q	443 472	443 427	429 921	432 781

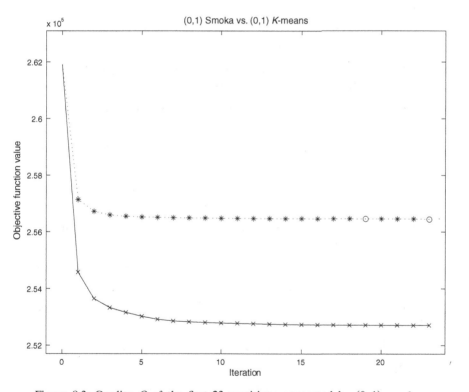

Figure 8.3: Quality Q of the first 23 partitions generated by $(0, 1)$ smoka (marked by "x") and $(0, 1)$ k-means (marked by "*" for batch iterations, and "o" for incremental iterations) for the "full" 20 newsgroups data set with the vector space model of dimension 1000.

sharper decrease of the objective function. The nineteenth batch iteration of $(0, 1)$ *k*-means fails to change a partition, and from now on a sequence of 7719 batch and incremental iterations slowly lead to a $(0, 1)$ *k*-means stable partition.

Time and again smoka demonstrates the remarkable ability to generate partitions of quality comparable with that generated by *k*-means while running only a fraction of iterations performed by *k*-means.

8.8. Bibliographic notes

The distance-like measure (8.1.1) was introduced by Bregman [24]. Some examples of Bregman distances and their relevance specifically to clustering are provided, for example, in [9, 132] . The *"three points identity"* was first reported in [26]. For useful inequalities concerning φ-divergences consult [6, 131]. Theorem 8.1.1 was discovered by Banerjee, Merugu, Dhillon, and Ghosh and first reported in [8].

The class of φ-divergences was introduced by Csiszar [29] as a generalized measure of information on the set of probability distributions (for additional results on convex statistical distances see, for instance, the monograph [98] and references therein). Our presentation of the relevant material follows [129–131]. Clustering with geometric means is reported in [83].

For a detailed discussion concerning applications of divergences to clustering consult, for example, [8, 9, 83, 84]. Additional examples, and formulas for centroid evaluation through conjugate functions are given in [132]. Convexity of batch *k*-means stable partitions generated with a Bregman distance with reversed order of arguments is reported in [8].

An axiomatic approach to clustering is reported in [74]. A framework for partitional clustering based on "general mean" is proposed in [141]. The "general mean", as well as "generalized reformulation functions" introduced in [74], reminds very much the nonlinear means of

Hardy, Littlewood, and Polya [67] (means as optimal solutions of a minimization problem are presented by Ben-Tal, Charnes, and Teboulle [13]).

An approach to k-means clustering based on optimization arguments involving asymptotic functions of convex analysis and the nonlinear means is suggested by Teboulle in [128]. This approach provides a general unified framework for k-means clustering and recovers as special particular cases many known techniques such as the expectation maximization algorithm, fuzzy k-means, and deterministic annealing.

BIRCH clustering algorithm with the squared Euclidean distance was introduced in [146, 147]. Implementation of "BIRCH like" clustering with entropy-like distance functions is discussed in [132]. Three step clustering procedures combining BIRCH, PDDP, and k-means or smoka equipped with divergences are reported in [81, 82].

9 Assessment of clustering results

This chapter is concerned with quality assessment of results generated by various clustering algorithms. There are two basic ways to evaluate results generated by a clustering algorithm. *Internal* criteria formulate quality as a function of the given data and/or the distance-like function. When using internal criteria, clustering becomes an optimization problem. *External* criteria evaluate quality by using additional, external information not available to the algorithm, such as class labels (confusion matrix is a good example of external criteria), one has to keep in mind that in reality clustering results are often evaluated externally by humans.

9.1. Internal criteria

When a number of clustering algorithms attempt to optimize the same objective function Q, a natural way to evaluate the results is just to compare the objective function values for final partitions generated by different algorithms. Given two k-cluster partitions Π' and Π'' such that $Q(\Pi') < Q(\Pi'')$, it seems reasonable to claim that Π' is "better" than Π''. Analogously one can compare two clusters π' and π'' (of the same or different partitions) by comparing, for example, their "average cohesion" $\frac{Q(\pi')}{|\pi'|}$ and $\frac{Q(\pi'')}{|\pi''|}$.

The trouble is, however, that neither Π^{min} nor $Q(\Pi^{min})$ is available and the inequality $Q(\Pi') < Q(\Pi'')$ by itself provides no indication of "how much better" is one partitioning than the other. Furthermore, estimates of $Q(\Pi^{min})$ available in the literature are far from being accurate. The fact that in many applications there exists no consensus on the objective function, Q only complicates the evaluation problem.

A method of *silhouette coefficient* associates a scalar $s(\mathbf{a})$ with an element $\mathbf{a}$ of the data set $\mathcal{A}$. If $\Pi = \{\pi_1, \ldots, \pi_k\}$, and $\mathbf{a} \in \pi_i$, then

1. Compute $I(\mathbf{a}) = \frac{1}{|\pi_i|} \sum_{\mathbf{x} \in \pi_i} d(\mathbf{x}, \mathbf{a})$, the average distance from $\mathbf{a}$ to other vectors in the same cluster.
2. For $j \neq i$ compute $O_j(\mathbf{a}) = \frac{1}{|\pi_j|} \sum_{\mathbf{x} \in \pi_j} d(\mathbf{x}, \mathbf{a})$, the average distance from $\mathbf{a}$ to other vectors in a different cluster and let $O(\mathbf{a}) = \min\{O_1(\mathbf{a}), \ldots, O_{i-1}(\mathbf{a}), O_{i+1}(\mathbf{a}), \ldots, O_k(\mathbf{a})\}$ ($O_i(\mathbf{a})$ is omitted).
3. Compute the silhouette coefficient $s(\mathbf{a}) = \frac{O(\mathbf{a}) - I(\mathbf{a})}{\max\{O(\mathbf{a}), I(\mathbf{a})\}}$.

The value of the silhouette coefficient $s(\mathbf{a})$ is between -1 and 1. A negative value of $s(\mathbf{a})$ indicates that $O(\mathbf{a}) < I(\mathbf{a})$, and, perhaps, a better clustering can be achieved by placing $\mathbf{a}$ in a cluster other than π_i. When $s(\mathbf{a})$ is about 1, one has $O(\mathbf{a}) > I(\mathbf{a})$ and $I(\mathbf{a})$ is "small" (i.e. the cluster π_i is "dense"). The silhouette coefficient for a cluster $\pi \in \Pi$ can be computed by averaging the silhouette coefficients $s(\mathbf{a})$ for $\mathbf{a} \in \pi$. The silhouette coefficient for the partition Π can be computed by averaging the silhouette coefficients for all $\mathbf{a} \in \mathcal{A}$.

9.2. External criteria

The best way to evaluate clustering results is to compare them with a given standard. However, when golden standards and perfect partitions are available, there is no need of new clustering algorithms and evaluation of clustering results. The external criteria are, therefore, useful for learning purposes only. One also has to keep in mind that the "golden standards" are often hand-built by humans and objectivity is not among the strongest human features. In what follows we assume that the "optimal" k_m-cluster partitioning $\Pi^{\min} = \{\pi_1^{\min}, \ldots, \pi_{k_m}^{\min}\}$ of the m element data set $\mathcal{A} = \{\mathbf{a}_1, \ldots, \mathbf{a}_m\}$ is available, and the k-cluster partitioning $\Pi = \{\pi_1, \ldots, \pi_k\}$ is generated by a clustering algorithm. Let $c_{ij} = |\pi_i \cap \pi_j^{\min}|$, that is c_{ij} is the number of elements of cluster π_i contained in cluster $\pi_j^{\min}$ that belongs to the "optimal" partition $\Pi^{\min}$ (and (c_{ij}) is the $k \times k_m$ confusion matrix with $\sum_{i=1}^{k} \sum_{j=1}^{k_m} c_{ij} = m$). A number of ways to evaluate "goodness" of Π (or degree of agreement between Π and $\Pi^{\min}$) are listed below.

1. *Confusion matrix*

   We assume now that $k_m = k$. If, for example, $c_{1r_1} = \max\{c_{11}, \ldots, c_{1k}\}$, then most of the elements of π_1 belong to $\pi_{r_1}^{\min}$ and one could claim that the other elements of π_1 are "misclassified". Repetition of this argument for clusters π_i, $i = 2, \ldots, k$ leads to the numbers $c_{2r_2}, \ldots, c_{kr_k}$. The total number of "misclassifications" is, therefore, $\sum_{i,j=1}^{k} c_{ij} - \sum_{i=1}^{k} c_{ir_i} = m - \sum_{i=1}^{k} c_{ir_i}$. The fraction $0 \le \frac{m - \sum_{i=1}^{k} c_{ir_i}}{m} < 1$ indicates a measure of "disagreement" between Π and the optimal partition $\Pi^{\min}$. We shall call the fraction $\mathrm{cm}(\Pi)$. When the partitions coincide, $\mathrm{cm}(\Pi)$ vanishes. Values of $\mathrm{cm}(\Pi)$ near 1 indicate a high degree of disagreement between the partitions.

2. *Entropy*

   The entropy $e_i = e(\pi_i)$ of cluster π_i is computed as $e_i = -\sum_{j=1}^{k_m} (\frac{c_{ij}}{|\pi_i|}) \log(\frac{c_{ij}}{|\pi_i|})$. The entropy $e = e(\Pi)$ of the partition Π is given by $e = \sum_{i=1}^{k} \frac{|\pi_i|}{m} e_i$.

   Problem 9.2.1. *Show that $e(\pi_i)$ is*

   (a) *Minimized when there is an index j_0 so that $c_{ij_0} = |\pi_i|$, and $c_{ij} = 0$, $j \ne j_0$. The minimal value of $e(\pi_i)$ is 0.*

   (b) *Maximized when $c_{i1} = c_{i2} = \cdots = c_{ik_m} = \frac{|\pi_i|}{k_m}$, and $e(\pi_i) = \log k_m$.*

   Hence $0 \le e(\Pi) \le \log k_m$ and when $e(\Pi) = 0$ the partitions Π and $\Pi^{\min}$ are identical.

3. *Purity*

   The purity $p_i = p(\pi_i)$ of cluster π_i is given by $p_i = \max\{\frac{c_{i1}}{|\pi_i|}, \ldots, \frac{c_{ik_m}}{|\pi_i|}\}$, so that $0 \le p_i \le 1$ and high values for p_i indicate that most of the vectors in π_i come from the same cluster of the optimal partition. The overall purity $p = p(\Pi)$ of the partition Π is $p = \sum_{i=1}^{k} \frac{|\pi_i|}{m} p_i$, and $p = 1$ corresponds to the optimal partition. When $k_m = k$ one has $p(\Pi) = \frac{1}{m} \sum_{i=1}^{k} c_{ir_i} = 1 - \text{cm}(\Pi)$, in other words $p(\Pi) + \text{cm}(\Pi) = 1$.

4. *Precision, recall and F-measure*

   Precision and recall are standard IR measures. Suppose a document set $\mathcal{D}$ is retrieved from a set $\mathcal{A}$ in response to a query. Suppose that only a subset $\mathcal{D}_r \subseteq \mathcal{D}$ contains documents relevant to the query, while the subset $\mathcal{A}_r \subseteq \mathcal{A}$ contains documents relevant to the query. Precision is a fraction of correctly retrieved objects in the retrieved set, that is

   $$\text{precision} = \frac{|\mathcal{D}_r|}{|\mathcal{D}|}.$$

   Recall is the fraction of correctly retrieved objects out of all documents relevant to the query

   $$\text{recall} = \frac{|\mathcal{D}_r|}{|\mathcal{A}_r|}.$$

   If cluster π_i is considered as a result of query for a particular "label" j, then

   $$\text{precision}(i, j) = \frac{c_{ij}}{|\pi_i|}, \text{ and recall}(i, j) = \frac{c_{ij}}{|\pi_j^{\min}|}.$$

   F-measure combines both precision and recall. The *F*-measure of cluster π_i with respect to "label" j is

   $$F(i, j) = 2\frac{\text{precision}(i, j) \times \text{recall}(i, j)}{\text{precision}(i, j) + \text{recall}(i, j)} = 2\frac{c_{ij}}{|\pi_i| + |\pi_j^{\min}|}.$$

5. *Mutual information*

   Mutual information $I(\Pi_1, \Pi_2)$ between two partitions is given by Definition 6.4.2. Application of mutual information formula to the partitions Π and $\Pi^{\min}$ leads to the following quality measure

$$\text{mi}\,(\Pi) = \sum_{i=1}^{k} \sum_{j=1}^{k_m} \frac{c_{ij}}{m} \log\left(\frac{mc_{ij}}{|\pi_i||\pi_j^{\min}|}\right)$$

$$= \frac{1}{m^2} \sum_{i=1}^{k} \sum_{j=1}^{k_m} mc_{ij} \log \frac{mc_{ij}}{|\pi_i||\pi_j^{\min}|}. \qquad (9.2.1)$$

6. *Variation of Information*

Variation of Information as defined by (6.4.1) is a distance function on the set of partitions and can be used to evaluate the proximity between Π and $\Pi^{\min}$.

7. *Rand statistic and Jaccard coefficient*

Consider a pair $(\mathbf{a}_i, \mathbf{a}_j)$ so that $\mathbf{a}_i \in \pi \in \Pi$, and $\mathbf{a}_i \in \pi^{\min} \in \Pi^{\min}$. The vector $\mathbf{a}_j$ may or may not belong to π and/or $\pi^{\min}$. The set $\mathcal{A} \times \mathcal{A}$ can, therefore, be divided into four subsets which we denote by $(\mathcal{A} \times \mathcal{A})_{ij}$:

$$(\mathcal{A} \times \mathcal{A})_{00} \quad : \quad \mathbf{a}_j \notin \pi \text{ and } \mathbf{a}_j \notin \pi^{\min},$$
$$(\mathcal{A} \times \mathcal{A})_{01} \quad : \quad \mathbf{a}_j \in \pi \text{ and } \mathbf{a}_j \notin \pi^{\min},$$
$$(\mathcal{A} \times \mathcal{A})_{10} \quad : \quad \mathbf{a}_j \notin \pi \text{ and } \mathbf{a}_j \in \pi^{\min},$$
$$(\mathcal{A} \times \mathcal{A})_{11} \quad : \quad \mathbf{a}_j \in \pi \text{ and } \mathbf{a}_j \in \pi^{\min},$$

where, for example, "$(\mathcal{A} \times \mathcal{A})_{00} : \mathbf{a}_j \notin \pi$ and $\mathbf{a}_j \notin \pi^{\min}$" defines the set $(\mathcal{A} \times \mathcal{A})_{00}$ as

$$(\mathcal{A} \times \mathcal{A})_{00} = \big\{(\mathbf{a}_i, \mathbf{a}_j) \; : \; (\mathbf{a}_i \in \pi \text{ and } \mathbf{a}_i \in \pi^{\min})$$

and

$$(\mathbf{a}_j \notin \pi \text{ and } \mathbf{a}_j \notin \pi^{\min})\big\}$$

or

$(\mathcal{A} \times \mathcal{A})_{00}$ consists of all pairs $(\mathbf{a}_i, \mathbf{a}_j)$ so that
$\mathbf{a}_i$ and $\mathbf{a}_j$ belong to different clusters of partition Π
and
$\mathbf{a}_i$ and $\mathbf{a}_j$ belong to different clusters of partition $\Pi^{\min}$).

We denote the cardinality of $(\mathcal{A} \times \mathcal{A})_{ij}$ by m_{ij}. Rand statistic and Jaccard coefficient are defined next:

$$\text{Rand statistic} = \frac{m_{00} + m_{11}}{m_{00} + m_{01} + m_{10} + m_{11}}. \qquad (9.2.2)$$

$$\text{Jaccard coefficient} = \frac{m_{11}}{m_{01} + m_{10} + m_{11}}. \qquad (9.2.3)$$

9.3. Bibliographic notes

An approximation algorithm for k-means that generates a solution "that is at most a factor c larger than the optimal solution" is discussed and solutions with $c = 25 + \epsilon$ and $c = 9 + \epsilon$ are generated in [73]. For additional internal cluster quality measures we refer the reader, for example, to Dunn's index [51], Davis–Bouldin index [31], and Bolshakova–Azuaje family of the cluster quality indices [21]. A variety of *internal, external,* and *relative* tests are provided in [71] and [46].

Evaluation of text clustering motivated by the "cluster hypothesis" [135] is provided in [96]. For a variety of evaluation criteria consult [44, 59, 60, 69, 126, 127, 148]. For Xie–Beni index for fuzzy clustering and additional cluster validity criteria see, for example, [139] and references therein. An elegant evaluation of a lower bound for quadratic k-means is suggested by Drineas, Frieze, Kannan, Vempala, and Vinay in [45].

10 Appendix: Optimization and linear algebra background

This Chapter collects some basic optimization and linear algebra results.

10.1. Eigenvalues of a symmetric matrix

In this section we collect a number of well-known facts concerning a symmetric n by n matrix M with real entries.

Proposition 10.1.1. *Let $\mathbf{v}_1$ and $\mathbf{v}_2$ be eigenvectors of M with the corresponding real eigenvalues λ_1 and λ_2. If $\lambda_1 \neq \lambda_2$, then $\mathbf{v}_1^T \mathbf{v}_2 = 0$.*

Proof

$$\mathbf{v}_1^T M \mathbf{v}_2 = \mathbf{v}_1^T (\lambda_2 \mathbf{v}_2) = \lambda_2 \mathbf{v}_1^T \mathbf{v}_2, \quad \text{and} \quad \mathbf{v}_2^T M \mathbf{v}_1 = \mathbf{v}_2^T (\lambda_1 \mathbf{v}_1) = \lambda_1 \mathbf{v}_2^T \mathbf{v}_1.$$

Since $(\mathbf{v}_1^T M \mathbf{v}_2)^T = \mathbf{v}_2^T M \mathbf{v}_1$ one has $\lambda_2 \mathbf{v}_1^T \mathbf{v}_2 = \lambda_1 \mathbf{v}_2^T \mathbf{v}_1$, and $(\lambda_1 - \lambda_2)$ $\mathbf{v}_1^T \mathbf{v}_2 = 0$. Due to the assumption $\lambda_1 - \lambda_2 \neq 0$, this yields $\mathbf{v}_1^T \mathbf{v}_2 = 0$, and completes the proof. $\square$

Proposition 10.1.2. *If λ be an eigenvalue of M, then λ is real.*

Proof: Suppose that $\lambda = \alpha + i\beta$, and $\mathbf{x}$ is an eigenvector corresponding to λ, i.e.

$$M\mathbf{x} = \lambda \mathbf{x}, \quad \mathbf{x} \neq 0. \tag{10.1.1}$$

161

Since $\lambda = \alpha + i\beta$ is a complex number the vector $\mathbf{x} = \mathbf{v} + i\mathbf{w}$, where $\mathbf{v}$ and $\mathbf{w}$ are real vectors of dimension n. The condition $\mathbf{x} \neq 0$ implies $\|\mathbf{x}\|^2 = \|\mathbf{v}\|^2 + \|\mathbf{w}\|^2 > 0$. Separating the real and imaginary parts in (10.1.1) we get

$$M\mathbf{v} = \alpha\mathbf{v} - \beta\mathbf{w}, \quad \text{and} \quad M\mathbf{w} = \beta\mathbf{v} + \alpha\mathbf{w},$$

and the left multiplication of the first equation by $\mathbf{w}^T$ and the left multiplication of the second equation by $\mathbf{v}^T$ yield

$$\mathbf{w}^T M\mathbf{v} = \alpha\mathbf{w}^T\mathbf{v} - \beta\mathbf{w}^T\mathbf{w}, \quad \text{and} \quad \mathbf{v}^T M\mathbf{w} = \beta\mathbf{v}^T\mathbf{v} + \alpha\mathbf{v}^T\mathbf{w}.$$

Since $\mathbf{v}^T M\mathbf{w} - \mathbf{w}^T M\mathbf{v} = 0$ one has $\beta[\mathbf{v}^T\mathbf{v} + \mathbf{w}^T\mathbf{w}] = \beta\|\mathbf{x}\|^2 = 0$. This implies $\beta = 0$, shows that λ is real, and completes the proof. $\square$

Problem 10.1.1. *Let M be a real symmetric matrix. Show that there are n real eigenvalues*

$$\lambda_n \geq \cdots \geq \lambda_1 \text{ with the corresponding eigenvectors } \mathbf{v}_n, \ldots, \mathbf{v}_1, \ \mathbf{v}_i^T\mathbf{v}_j = \delta_{ij}.$$
(10.1.2)

Proposition 10.1.3. *If* $\quad Q = [\mathbf{v}_n, \mathbf{v}_{n-1}, \ldots, \mathbf{v}_1], \quad$ *then* $\quad Q^T M Q = \text{diag}\{\lambda_n, \ldots, \lambda_1\}$.

Proof: A straightforward substitution. $\square$

Problem 10.1.2. *For a (not necessarily symmetric) $n \times n$ matrix B the sum of the diagonal elements, $\sum_{i=1}^{n} b_{ii}$, is denoted by $\text{tr}(B)$. Show that the following is true.*

1. *If C is a $n \times m$ matrix, then $\text{tr}(CC^T) = \text{tr}(C^TC) = \sum_{i,j} |c_{ij}|^2$.*
2. *If B and C are $n \times n$ matrices, then $\text{tr}(BC) = \text{tr}(CB)$.*
3. *If B and C are $n \times n$ matrices, and C is nonsingular, then $\text{tr}(C^{-1}BC) = \text{tr}(B)$.*

10.2. Lagrange multipliers

This section is concerned with a simple constrained optimization problem. For given smooth functions f and g mapping $\mathbf{R}^n$ into $\mathbf{R}$ we would like to solve the problem

$$\min_{\mathbf{x}}\{f(\mathbf{x}) \text{ subject to } g(\mathbf{x}) = 0\}. \tag{10.2.1}$$

First we fix a vector $\mathbf{x}_0 \in \mathbf{R}^n$ and observe that for each $\mathbf{h} \in \mathbf{R}^n$ the difference

$$f(\mathbf{x}_0 + \mathbf{h}) - f(\mathbf{x}_0) \approx \nabla f(\mathbf{x}_0)\mathbf{h}, \tag{10.2.2}$$

when $\|\mathbf{h}\|$ is small. Equation (10.2.2) shows that when $\nabla f(\mathbf{x}_0) \neq 0$ the space $\mathbf{R}^n$ is partitioned into two half spaces

$$\mathcal{H}_+ = \{\mathbf{h} : \mathbf{h} \in \mathbf{R}^n, \ \nabla f(\mathbf{x}_0)\mathbf{h} > 0\} \quad \text{and} \quad \mathcal{H}_- = \{\mathbf{h} : \mathbf{h} \in \mathbf{R}^n,$$
$$\nabla f(\mathbf{x}_0)\mathbf{h} < 0\}$$

so that

$$f(\mathbf{x}_0 + \mathbf{h}) > f(\mathbf{x}_0) \text{ when } \mathbf{h} \in \mathcal{H}_+ \text{ and } f(\mathbf{x}_0 + \mathbf{h}) < f(\mathbf{x}_0) \text{ when } \mathbf{h} \in \mathcal{H}_-$$

(see Figure 10.1). Let now $\mathbf{x}_0$ be the point of the level set $g(\mathbf{x}) = 0$ where the minimum of $f(\mathbf{x})$ is attained (see Figure 10.2). We assume that the gradients $\nabla g(\mathbf{x}_0)$ and $\nabla f(\mathbf{x}_0)$ are two nonzero and *nonproportional* vectors (see Figure 10.3). We now focus on vectors $\mathbf{x}_0 + \mathbf{h}$ that belong to the level set $g(\mathbf{x}) = 0$ with $\|\mathbf{h}\|$ "small." Note that $\nabla g(\mathbf{x}_0)\mathbf{h} \approx 0$, and, due to the assumption about $\nabla g(\mathbf{x}_0)$ and $\nabla f(\mathbf{x}_0)$, $\nabla f(\mathbf{x}_0)\mathbf{h} \neq 0$. Hence there is a "small" $\mathbf{h} \neq 0$ such that $\nabla f(\mathbf{x}_0)\mathbf{h} < 0$, $\mathbf{h} \in \mathcal{H}_-$, and $f(\mathbf{x}_0 + \mathbf{h}) < f(\mathbf{x}_0)$. The assumption $\nabla g(\mathbf{x}_0)$ and $\nabla f(\mathbf{x}_0)$ are linearly independent leads to a contradiction. We, therefore, conclude that the vectors $\nabla g(\mathbf{x}_0)$ and $\nabla f(\mathbf{x}_0)$ are proportional, i.e. there is a scalar λ such that

$$\nabla f(\mathbf{x}_0) = \lambda \nabla g(\mathbf{x}_0) \tag{10.2.3}$$

(see Figure 10.4). We now consider the mapping $F : \mathbf{R}^{n+1} \to \mathbf{R}$ defined by $F(\mathbf{x}, \lambda) = f(\mathbf{x}) - \lambda g(\mathbf{x})$ and substitute the constrained minimization

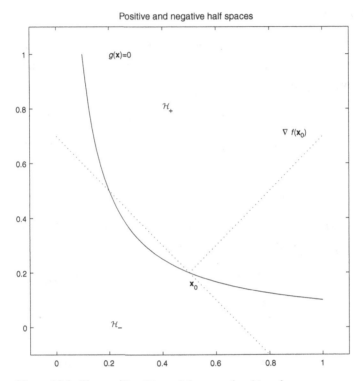

Figure 10.1: The positive $\mathcal{H}_+$ and the negative $\mathcal{H}_-$ subspaces.

problem (10.2.1) with n variables by the gradient equation

$$\nabla F(\mathbf{x}, \lambda) = 0. \tag{10.2.4}$$

Problem 10.2.1. *Give a rigorous proof of existence* $\mathbf{h} \neq 0$ *so that* $\nabla f(\mathbf{x}_0)\mathbf{h} < 0$.

10.3. Elements of convex analysis

We shall consider functions $f : \mathbf{R}^n \to \overline{\mathbf{R}} = [+\infty, -\infty]$, and will tacitly assume throughout that the functions are proper, i.e.,

$$\exists \mathbf{x} \text{ such that } f(\mathbf{x}) < +\infty, \text{ and } \forall \mathbf{x} \text{ one has } f(\mathbf{x}) > -\infty.$$

164

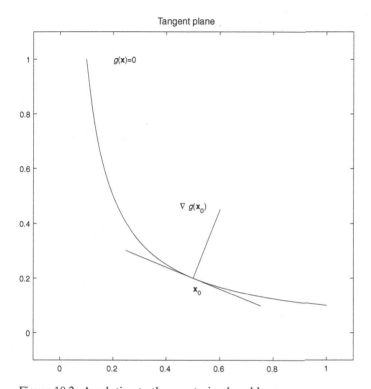

Figure 10.2: A solution to the constrained problem.

Definition 10.3.1. *The effective domain* dom f *of* f *is defined by*

$$\text{dom} f = \{\mathbf{x} \in \mathbf{R}^n : f(\mathbf{x}) < +\infty\}.$$

We shall frequently associate a function f with epi f, a subset of $\mathbf{R}^{n+1}$ defined next.

Definition 10.3.2. *The epigraph of the function* f *is defined by*

$$\text{epi} f = \{(\mathbf{x}, \mu) : \mathbf{x} \in \mathbf{R}^n, \ \mu \in \mathbf{R}, \ f(\mathbf{x}) \le \mu\}. \tag{10.3.1}$$

Definition 10.3.3. *A function* $f : \mathbf{R}^n \to \overline{\mathbf{R}} = [+\infty, -\infty]$ *is lower semi-continuous (l.s.c.) or closed if* $\liminf_{\mathbf{x} \to \mathbf{y}} f(\mathbf{x}) = f(\mathbf{y})$ *(i.e., the epigraph of* f *is a closed set).*

165

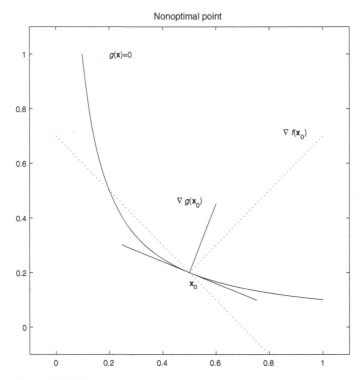

Figure 10.3: Nonoptimal point.

Analogously for a set $\mathcal{F} \subseteq \mathbf{R}^{n+1}$ one can define the function $f_{\mathcal{F}} : \mathbf{R}^n \to \overline{\mathbf{R}}$ by

$$f_{\mathcal{F}}(\mathbf{x}) = \inf\{\mu : (\mathbf{x}, \mu) \in \mathcal{F}\}. \tag{10.3.2}$$

10.3.1. Conjugate functions

Definition 10.3.4. *For a function f the lower closure of f is defined as a function $\mathrm{cl}\, f$ so that $\mathrm{epi}\,(\mathrm{cl}\, f) = \overline{(\mathrm{epi}\, f)}$, that is,*

$$(\mathrm{cl}\, f)(\mathbf{x}) = \liminf\{f(\mathbf{y}), \ \mathbf{y} \to \mathbf{x}\}.$$

The function f is closed if $f = \mathrm{cl}\, f$.

10.3. Elements of convex analysis

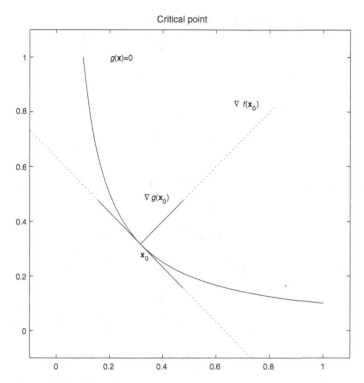

Figure 10.4: Critical point.

Definition 10.3.5. *A function h is less than or equal to a function f (h ≤ f) if*

$$\forall \mathbf{x} \in \mathbf{R}^n \text{ one has } h(\mathbf{x}) \le f(\mathbf{x}).$$

Theorem 10.3.1. (*see Rockafellar [114]*). *A closed convex function f is the pointwise supremum of the collection of all affine functions $h(\mathbf{x}) = \mathbf{x}^T \mathbf{y} - \mu$ such that $h \le f$.*

Consider an affine function $h(\mathbf{x}) = \mathbf{x}^T \mathbf{y} - \mu$ so that $h \le f$, i.e., $\mathbf{x}^T \mathbf{y} - \mu \le f(\mathbf{x})$ for each $\mathbf{x}$, or, equivalently, $\mathbf{x}^T \mathbf{y} - f(\mathbf{x}) \le \mu$ for each $\mathbf{x} \in \mathbf{R}^n$. That is

$$\sup_{\mathbf{x}} \{\mathbf{x}^T \mathbf{y} - f(\mathbf{x})\} \le \mu. \tag{10.3.3}$$

167

On the other hand if a vector $\mathbf{y}$ and a scalar μ satisfy (10.3.3), then $h(\mathbf{x}) = \mathbf{x}^T\mathbf{y} - \mu \leq f(\mathbf{x})$ for each $\mathbf{x} \in \mathbf{R}^n$. The equation leads to a dual way to describe a closed convex function f. Consider the set $\mathcal{F}^* \subseteq \mathbf{R}^{n+1}$ defined by

$$\mathcal{F}^* = \{(\mathbf{y}, \mu) : \mu \geq \mathbf{y}^T\mathbf{x} - f(\mathbf{x}) \text{ for each } \mathbf{x} \in \mathbf{R}^n\}.$$

The definition implies that $\mathcal{F}^*$ is the epigraph of the function f^* defined next.

Definition 10.3.6. *For a function* $f : \mathbf{R}^n \to \mathbf{R} \cup \{+\infty\}$ *the conjugate function* $f^* : \mathbf{R}^n \to \mathbf{R} \cup \{+\infty\}$ *is defined by*

$$f^*(\mathbf{y}) = \sup_{\mathbf{x} \in \mathbf{R}^n}\{\mathbf{x}^T\mathbf{y} - f(\mathbf{x})\}. \tag{10.3.4}$$

The function f^* is always convex, indeed for $0 \leq t \leq 1$ one has

$$f^*(t\mathbf{y}_1 + (1-t)\mathbf{y}_2) = \sup_{\mathbf{x}} \left\{\mathbf{x}^T(t\mathbf{y}_1 + (1-t)\mathbf{y}_2) - f(\mathbf{x})\right\}$$

$$\leq t \sup_{\mathbf{x}} \left\{\mathbf{x}^T\mathbf{y}_1 - f(\mathbf{x})\right\} + (1-t)\sup_{\mathbf{x}} \left\{\mathbf{x}^T\mathbf{y}_2 - f(\mathbf{x})\right\}$$

$$= tf^*(\mathbf{y}_1) + (1-t)f^*(\mathbf{y}_2).$$

A simple continuity argument shows that f^* is closed. Arguments preceding (10.3.3) show that $h(\mathbf{x}) = \mathbf{x}^T\mathbf{y} - \mu$ is majorized by $f(\mathbf{x})$ if and only if $(\mathbf{y}, \mu) \in \text{epi } f^*$.

The conjugate function is the pointwise supremum of the affine functions $g(\mathbf{y}) = \mathbf{x}^T\mathbf{y} - \lambda$ where $(\mathbf{x}, \lambda) \in \text{epi } f$. Since a closed convex function f is the pointwise supremum of the affine functions $h(\mathbf{x}) = \mathbf{y}^T\mathbf{x} - \mu$, where $(\mathbf{y}, \mu) \in \text{epi } f^*$ one has

$$f(\mathbf{x}) = \sup_{\mathbf{y}}\{\mathbf{y}^T\mathbf{x} - f^*(\mathbf{y})\} = f^{**}(\mathbf{x}), \tag{10.3.5}$$

where f^{**} is the conjugate of the conjugate function f^* (which is called the biconjugate function). In particular

$$f(0) = f^{**}(0) = \sup_{\mathbf{y}}\{0^T\mathbf{y} - f^*(\mathbf{y})\} = \sup_{\mathbf{y}} -f^*(\mathbf{y}). \tag{10.3.6}$$

For a proof of the next result consult [114].

10.3. Elements of convex analysis

Theorem 10.3.2. *Let f be a convex function. The conjugate function f^* is a closed convex function, proper if and only if f is proper. Moreover $(\mathrm{cl}\, f)^* = f^*$, and $f^{**} = \mathrm{cl}\, f$.*

Problem 10.3.1.

$$\mathrm{Let} f(\mathbf{x}) = \begin{cases} \sum_{i=1}^{n} \mathbf{x}[i] \log \mathbf{x}[i] & \text{if } \mathbf{x} \in R_+^n, \\ +\infty & \text{otherwise.} \end{cases}$$

Compute $f^*(\mathbf{y})$ and prove that $g(\mathbf{y}) = \log(\sum_{i=i}^{n} e^{\mathbf{y}[i]})$ is convex.

10.3.2. Asymptotic cones

We start with an elementary auxiliary result.

Lemma 10.3.1. *(Three points lemma). Let $\mathbf{a}, \mathbf{b}, \mathbf{d}$ be vectors in $\mathbf{R}^n$, $\beta \geq \alpha > 0$, and $\epsilon > 0$ such that*

$$\left\| \frac{\mathbf{a}}{\alpha} - \mathbf{d} \right\| < \epsilon \quad and \quad \left\| \frac{\mathbf{b}}{\beta} - \mathbf{d} \right\| < \epsilon.$$

If $0 \leq t \leq 1$, $\gamma = t\alpha + (1-t)\beta$ and $\mathbf{c} = t\mathbf{a} + (1-t)\mathbf{b}$, then $\| \frac{\mathbf{c}}{\gamma} - \mathbf{d} \| < \epsilon$ see (Figure 10.5).

Proof

$$\| t\mathbf{a} + (1-t)\mathbf{b} - \gamma\mathbf{d} \| = \| t(\mathbf{a} - \alpha\mathbf{d}) + (1-t)(\mathbf{b} - \beta\mathbf{d}) \|$$
$$\leq t\| \mathbf{a} - \alpha\mathbf{d} \| + (1-t)\| \mathbf{b} - \beta\mathbf{d} \|$$
$$\leq t\alpha\epsilon + (1-t)\beta\epsilon = \epsilon\gamma. \qquad \square$$

Definition 10.3.7. *The asymptotic cone of a nonempty set $\mathcal{C} \subset \mathbf{R}^n$ is the set*

$$\mathcal{C}_\infty = \left\{ \mathbf{d} : \mathbf{d} = \lim_{i \to \infty} \frac{\mathbf{c}_i}{t_i} \text{ where } \mathbf{c}_i \in \mathcal{C}, \text{ and } t_i \to +\infty \right\}.$$

The definition immediately implies that $\mathcal{C}_\infty$ is a closed cone. When $\mathcal{C}$ is a closed convex set the asymptotic cone is also called the recession

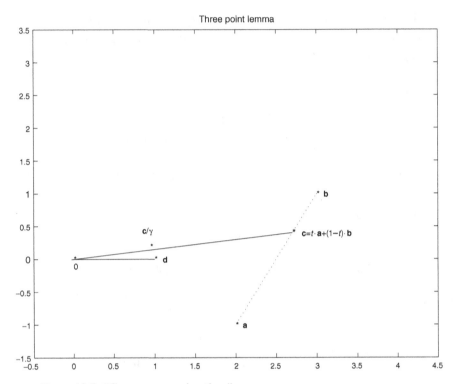

Figure 10.5: "Convex approximation."

cone. The next technical result leads to convexity of the recession cone.

Lemma 10.3.2. *If C is a nonempty convex subset of $\mathbf{R}^n$ and $\mathbf{d} \in C_\infty$, then for each $\epsilon > 0$ there is a positive scalar T such that for each $\gamma \geq T$ there is $\mathbf{c}(\gamma) \in C$ and*

$$\left\| \frac{\mathbf{c}(\gamma)}{\gamma} - \mathbf{d} \right\| < \epsilon. \tag{10.3.7}$$

Proof: Due to Definition 10.3.7 there is N so that for each $i \geq N$ one has $\|\frac{\mathbf{c}_i}{t_i} - \mathbf{d}\| < \epsilon$. If $\gamma = t \cdot t_1 + (1 - t) \cdot t_{i+1}$ for $0 \leq t \leq 1$, then, due to Lemma 10.3.1, Inequality (10.3.7) holds with $\mathbf{c}(\gamma) = t\mathbf{c}_i + (1 - t)\mathbf{c}_{i+1}$.

This shows that (10.3.7) holds for each $\gamma \geq T = \min_{i \geq N} t_i$, and completes the proof. $\qquad\square$

The lemma yields convexity of $\mathcal{C}_\infty$ when $\mathcal{C}$ is a nonempty convex set. Indeed, let $\mathbf{d}_1, \mathbf{d}_2 \in \mathcal{C}_\infty$, and $\mathbf{d} = t\mathbf{d}_1 + (1-t)\mathbf{d}_2$ for some $0 \leq t \leq 1$. Fix $\epsilon > 0$, and $T = \max\{T_1, T_2\}$, where T_i are the positive scalars corresponding to $\mathbf{d}_i$, $i = 1, 2$ and guaranteed by Lemma 10.3.7 so that

$$\left\|\frac{\mathbf{c}_1}{T} - \mathbf{d}_1\right\| < \epsilon \quad \text{and} \quad \left\|\frac{\mathbf{c}_2}{T} - \mathbf{d}_2\right\| < \epsilon \text{ for some } \mathbf{c}_1, \mathbf{c}_2 \in \mathcal{C}.$$

For $\mathbf{c} = t\mathbf{c}_1 + (1-t)\mathbf{c}_2 \in \mathcal{C}$ one has

$$\left\|\frac{\mathbf{c}}{T} - \mathbf{d}\right\| \leq \left\|\frac{t\mathbf{c}_1}{T} - t\mathbf{d}_1\right\| + \left\|\frac{(1-t)\mathbf{c}_2}{T} - (1-t)\mathbf{d}_2\right\| < \epsilon.$$

Since $T_1, T_2 \to +\infty$ as $\epsilon \to 0$ this shows that $\mathbf{d} \in \mathcal{C}_\infty$.

With a vector $\mathbf{c} \in \mathcal{C}$ we associate the set

$$\mathcal{D}(\mathbf{c}) = \{\mathbf{d} : \mathbf{c} + t\mathbf{d} \in \mathrm{cl}\mathcal{C} \text{ for each } t \geq 0\}. \tag{10.3.8}$$

Lemma 10.3.3. *If $\mathcal{C}$ is a convex set, then $\mathcal{D}(\mathbf{c})$ is independent of $\mathbf{c}$.*

Proof: Let $\mathbf{c}_1$ and $\mathbf{c}_2$ be two distinct vectors in $\mathcal{C}$. In what follows we shall show that $\mathcal{D}(\mathbf{c}_1) = \mathcal{D}(\mathbf{c}_2)$. First we show that $\mathcal{D}(\mathbf{c}_1) \subseteq \mathcal{D}(\mathbf{c}_2)$. Let $\mathbf{d} \in \mathcal{D}(\mathbf{c}_1)$, consider the vector $\mathbf{c}_2 + s\mathbf{d}$, $s \geq 0$. Our goal is to show that $\mathbf{c}_2 + s\mathbf{d} \in \mathrm{cl}\mathcal{C}$. Fix $\epsilon > 0$. For each $t \geq 0$ the vector $\mathbf{c}_1 + t\mathbf{d}$ belongs to $\mathrm{cl}\mathcal{C}$, in particular there is a vector $\mathbf{v}_t$ so that

$$\mathbf{c} = \mathbf{c}_1 + t\mathbf{d} + \mathbf{v}_t \in \mathcal{C} \text{ and } \|\mathbf{v}_t\| < \epsilon.$$

We now consider the convex combination $\lambda\mathbf{c} + (1-\lambda)\mathbf{c}_2 \in \mathcal{C}$ and will pick λ and t so that the distance between the convex combination and $\mathbf{c}_2 + s\mathbf{d}$ does not exceed ϵ. Note that

$$\|\lambda\mathbf{c} + (1-\lambda)\mathbf{c}_2 - \mathbf{c}_2 - s\mathbf{d}\| \leq \lambda\|\mathbf{c}_1 - \mathbf{c}_2\| + \lambda\|\mathbf{v}_t\| + |\lambda t - s|\|\mathbf{d}\|.$$

To eliminate the last term we set $t = \frac{s}{\lambda}$, to make the distance smaller than ϵ we just have to pick $\lambda < \frac{\epsilon}{\|\mathbf{c}_1 - \mathbf{c}_2\| + \epsilon}$. This shows that $\mathcal{D}(\mathbf{c}_1) \subseteq \mathcal{D}(\mathbf{c}_2)$

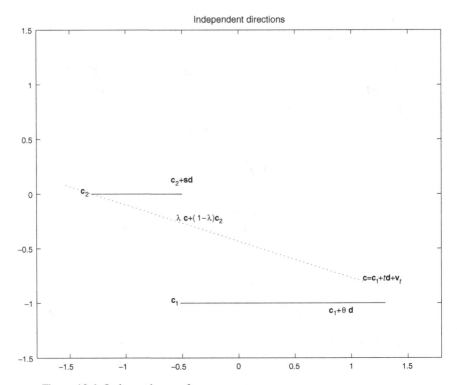

Figure 10.6: Independence of **c**.

(see Figure 10.6). Analogously one can show that $\mathcal{D}(\mathbf{c}_2) \subseteq \mathcal{D}(\mathbf{c}_1)$. This completes the proof. □

From now on we shall denote $\mathcal{D}(\mathbf{c})$ just by $\mathcal{D}$. Due to the lemma one has $\mathbf{d} + \mathcal{C} \subseteq \mathrm{cl}\mathcal{C}$ for each $\mathbf{d} \in \mathcal{D}$. Simple continuity arguments show that

$$\mathbf{d} + \mathrm{cl}\mathcal{C} \subseteq \mathrm{cl}\mathcal{C} \text{ for each } \mathbf{d} \in \mathcal{D}. \tag{10.3.9}$$

On the other hand a vector **d** that satisfies (10.3.9) belongs to $\mathcal{D}$. Furthermore, due to Definition 10.3.7 and Lemma 10.3.3 one has $\mathcal{D} = \mathcal{C}_\infty$.

Problem 10.3.1. *Let f be a closed proper function. If*

$$\mathcal{C}_1 = \{\mathbf{x} : f(\mathbf{x}) \le \alpha_1\} \quad and \quad \mathcal{C}_2 = \{\mathbf{x} : f(\mathbf{x}) \le \alpha_2\}$$

are two nonempty levels sets of f, then the recession cones $(C_1)_\infty$ and $(C_2)_\infty$ are equal.

10.3.3. Asymptotic functions

The connection between a function f and the set epi f suggests to define f_∞ through the asymptotic cone of epi f. Indeed, let $\mathcal{F} = (\text{epi} f)_\infty$. If $(\mathbf{x}, \mu) \in \mathcal{F}$, then there is a sequence

$$(\mathbf{x}_i, \mu_i) \in \text{epi} f \text{ and } t_i \to +\infty \text{ so that } \lim_{i \to \infty} \frac{(\mathbf{x}_i, \mu_i)}{t_i} = (\mathbf{x}, \mu).$$

If $\mu^+ > \mu$, then

$$(\mathbf{x}_i, \mu_i + t_i(\mu^+ - \mu)) \in \text{epi} f \text{ and } \lim_{i \to \infty} \frac{(\mathbf{x}_i, \mu_i + t_i(\mu^+ - \mu))}{t_i} = (\mathbf{x}, \mu^+).$$

This shows that $(\mathbf{x}, \mu^+) \in \mathcal{F}$ and $\mathcal{F}$ is an epigraph of a certain function. This function is called the asymptotic function of f.

Definition 10.3.8. *The asymptotic function of f is denoted by f_∞ and defined by (10.3.2) with $\mathcal{F} = (\text{epi} f)_\infty$.*

Since $(\text{epi} f)_\infty$ is a closed cone the following two properties of f_∞ are immediate:

1. f_∞ is positively homogeneous,
2. f_∞ is lower semicontinuous.

If $(\text{epi} f)_\infty$ is a convex set, then f_∞ is a convex function.

We now focus on computation f_∞ for a given proper function f.

Theorem 10.3.3. *The asymptotic function f_∞ of a proper function f is given by*

$$f_\infty(\mathbf{x}) = \liminf \left\{ s f\left(\frac{\mathbf{y}}{s}\right) : s \to 0, \ \mathbf{y} \to \mathbf{x} \right\}. \tag{10.3.10}$$

173

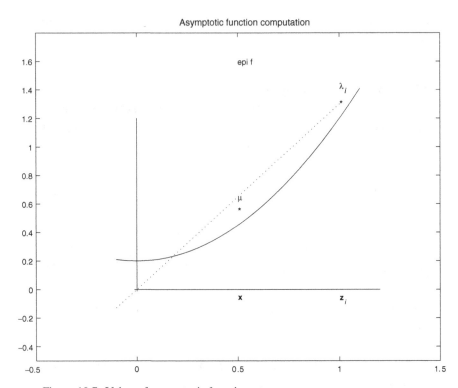

Figure 10.7: Value of asymptotic function at **x**.

Proof: Let $(\mathbf{x}, \mu) \in (\text{epi} f)_\infty$ as shown at Figure 10.7. There are $(\mathbf{z}_i, \lambda_i) \in \text{epi} f$ and t_i so that

$$\mathbf{t}_i \to +\infty, \quad \text{and} \quad \frac{(\mathbf{z}_i, \lambda_i)}{t_i} \to (\mathbf{x}, \mu) \text{ as } i \to \infty. \qquad (10.3.11)$$

Denote $\frac{\mathbf{z}_i}{t_i}$ by $\mathbf{y}_i$, $\frac{1}{t_i}$ by s_i and observe that

1. $\mathbf{y}_i \to \mathbf{x}, s_i \to 0$;
2. $f(\frac{\mathbf{y}_i}{s_i}) = f(\mathbf{z}_i) \leq \lambda_i$
3. $\liminf s_i f(\frac{\mathbf{y}_i}{s_i}) = \liminf \frac{f(\mathbf{z}_i)}{t_i} \leq \frac{\lambda_i}{t_i}$ and $\frac{\lambda_i}{t_i} \to \mu$.

This shows that $\liminf s f(\frac{\mathbf{y}}{s}) \leq f_\infty(\mathbf{x})$. To complete the proof we have to show that the strict inequality is not possible. Assume the contrary,

174

that is there are sequences $\mathbf{y}_i \to \mathbf{x}$ and $s_i \to 0$ so that

$$\alpha = \lim_{i \to \infty} s_i f\left(\frac{\mathbf{y}_i}{s_i}\right) < f_\infty(\mathbf{x}).$$

The sequence $(\frac{\mathbf{y}_i}{s_i}, f(\frac{\mathbf{y}_i}{s_i})) \in \text{epi} f$, and the vector $\lim_{i \to \infty}(\mathbf{y}_i, s_i f(\frac{\mathbf{y}_i}{s_i})) = (\mathbf{x}, \alpha) \in (\text{epi} f)_\infty$. This contradicts definition of $f_\infty(\mathbf{x})$ (see Definition 10.3.8), and completes the proof. □

We now apply Theorem 10.3.3 and compute two asymptotic functions important for applications.

Example 10.3.1. *If* $f(\mathbf{x}) = \sum_{j=1}^{n} \sqrt{1 + \mathbf{x}[j]^2}$, *then*

$$f_\infty(\mathbf{x}) = \liminf\left\{ s \sum_{j=1}^{n} \sqrt{1 + \left(\frac{\mathbf{y}[j]}{s}\right)^2} : s \to 0, \ \mathbf{y} \to \mathbf{x} \right\}$$

$$= \sum_{j=1}^{n} \|\mathbf{x}[j]\| = \|\mathbf{x}\|_1.$$

Example 10.3.2. *If* $f(\mathbf{x}) = \log \sum_{j=1}^{n} e^{\mathbf{x}[j]}$, *then*

$$f_\infty(\mathbf{x}) = \liminf\left\{ s \log \left(\sum_{j=1}^{n} e^{\frac{\mathbf{y}[j]}{s}}\right) : s \to 0, \ \mathbf{y} \to \mathbf{x} \right\} = \max_j \mathbf{x}[j].$$

The next statement helps establish uniform approximation of a nonsmooth function ψ by a family of smooth approximations ψ_s (see Theorem 10.3.5).

Theorem 10.3.4. *Let* f *be a proper convex closed function. Then*

$$f_\infty(\mathbf{x}) = \sup_{\mathbf{y} \in \text{dom} f^*} \mathbf{x}^T \mathbf{y}. \tag{10.3.12}$$

Proof: Consult [114]. □

Problem 10.3.2. *The set* $\{\mathbf{x} : f_\infty(\mathbf{x}) \leq 0\}$ *is called the recession cone of* f. *Let* $C = \{\mathbf{x}^* : f(\mathbf{x}^*) \leq \alpha\}$. *If* $C \neq \emptyset$, *then* C_∞ *is the recession cone of* f.

Table 10.1: Smooth approximations.

$f(0)$	$f(\mathbf{y})$	$sf\left(\frac{\mathbf{y}}{s}\right)$	$f_\infty(\mathbf{y})$	$\psi(\mathbf{x})$	$\psi_s(\mathbf{x})$
m	$\displaystyle\sum_{j=1}^{m}\sqrt{1+\mathbf{y}[j]^2}$	$\displaystyle\sum_{j=1}^{m}\sqrt{s^2+\mathbf{y}[j]^2}$	$\displaystyle\sum_{j=1}^{m}\|\mathbf{y}[j]\|$	$\displaystyle\sum_{i=1}^{m}\|f_i(\mathbf{x})\|$	$\displaystyle\sum_{i=1}^{m}\sqrt{s^2+[f_i(\mathbf{x})]^2}$
$\log m$	$\displaystyle\log\sum_{j=1}^{m}e^{\mathbf{y}[j]}$	$\displaystyle s\log\sum_{j=1}^{m}e^{\frac{\mathbf{y}[j]}{s}}$	$\displaystyle\max_j \mathbf{y}[j]$	$\displaystyle\max_i f_i(\mathbf{x})$	$\displaystyle s\log\sum_{i=1}^{m}e^{\frac{f_i(\mathbf{x})}{s}}$

10.3.4. Smoothing

Let $f_1,\ldots,f_m$ be real functions defined in $\mathbf{R}^n$, and f be a convex function in $\mathbf{R}^m$. We shall be concerned with the function $\psi(\mathbf{x}) = f_\infty(f_1(\mathbf{x}),\ldots,f_m(\mathbf{x}))$ and the optimization problem

$$\inf_{\mathbf{x}\in\mathbf{R}^n}\psi(\mathbf{x}). \tag{10.3.13}$$

Motivated by Theorem 10.3.10 we would like to approximate $f_\infty(\mathbf{y})$ by $sf(\frac{\mathbf{y}}{s})$, and $\psi(\mathbf{x})$ by $\psi_s(\mathbf{x}) = sf(\frac{f_1(\mathbf{x})}{s},\ldots,\frac{f_m(\mathbf{x})}{s})$, so that instead of the original optimization problem (10.3.13) we focus on the family of approximated problems parametrized by s

$$\inf_{\mathbf{x}\in\mathbf{R}^n}\psi_s(\mathbf{x}). \tag{10.3.14}$$

Table 10.1 indicates that for the functions given in Example 10.3.1 and Example 10.3.2 the smooth function ψ_s approximates the nondifferentiable function ψ and $sf(\frac{\mathbf{y}}{s}) \geq f_\infty(\mathbf{y})$. Denote by $\bar{\mathbf{x}}$ and $\bar{\mathbf{x}}_s$ minimizers of $\psi(\mathbf{x})$ and $\psi_s(\mathbf{x})$, respectively. The following result describes approximation of ψ by ψ_s.

Theorem 10.3.5. *Let f be a closed convex function so that for each* $\mathbf{y} \in \mathbf{R}^m$ *and each $s > 0$ the following inequality holds*

$$sf\left(\frac{\mathbf{y}}{s}\right) \geq f_\infty(\mathbf{y}). \tag{10.3.15}$$

If $\bar{\mathbf{x}} = \arg\min\psi(\mathbf{x})$ *and* $\bar{\mathbf{x}}_s = \arg\min\psi_s(\mathbf{x})$, *then for each $s > 0$ one has*

$$0 \leq \psi_s(\mathbf{x}) - \psi(\mathbf{x}) \leq s \cdot f(0) \text{ for each } \mathbf{x} \in \mathbf{R}^n \tag{10.3.16}$$

10.3. Elements of convex analysis

and

$$0 \leq \psi(\bar{\mathbf{x}}_s) - \psi(\bar{\mathbf{x}}) \leq s \cdot f(0). \qquad (10.3.17)$$

Proof: Note that the left side of (10.3.16) follows from (10.3.15). Due to Theorem 10.3.2

$$f(\mathbf{y}) = f^{**}(\mathbf{y}) = \sup_{\mathbf{z} \in \text{dom} f^*} \{\mathbf{z}^T \mathbf{y} - f^*(\mathbf{z})\}$$
$$\leq \sup_{\mathbf{z} \in \text{dom} f^*} \mathbf{z}^T \mathbf{y} + \sup_{\mathbf{z} \in \text{dom} f^*} (-f^*(\mathbf{z})).$$

Due to (10.3.12) $\sup_{\mathbf{z} \in \text{dom} f^*} \mathbf{z}^T \mathbf{y} = f_\infty(\mathbf{y})$, and due to (10.3.6) $\sup_{\mathbf{z} \in \text{dom} f^*} (-f^*(\mathbf{z})) = f(0)$. Hence for each $\mathbf{y} \in \mathbf{R}^m$ one has

$$f(\mathbf{y}) - f_\infty(\mathbf{y}) \leq f(0).$$

We apply the inequality at $\mathbf{y} = (\frac{f_1(\mathbf{x})}{s}, \ldots, \frac{f_m(\mathbf{x})}{s})^T$ and, keeping in mind that f_∞ is positively homogeneous, obtain the following

$$f\left(\frac{f_1(\mathbf{x})}{s}, \ldots, \frac{f_m(\mathbf{x})}{s}\right) - \frac{1}{s} f_\infty(f_1(\mathbf{x}), \ldots, f_m(\mathbf{x})) \leq f(0).$$

In other words

$$\psi_s(\mathbf{x}) - \psi(\mathbf{x}) \leq s \cdot f(0) \text{ for each } \mathbf{x} \in \mathbf{R}^n. \qquad (10.3.18)$$

This proves the right side of (10.3.16). To prove (10.3.17) we consider the following inequalities

$$\psi(\bar{\mathbf{x}}_s) - \psi(\bar{\mathbf{x}}) \leq \psi_s(\bar{\mathbf{x}}_s) - \psi(\bar{\mathbf{x}}) \leq \psi_s(\bar{\mathbf{x}}) - \psi(\bar{\mathbf{x}}) \leq s \cdot f(0),$$

and observe that

1. Due to (10.3.15) one has $\psi(\bar{\mathbf{x}}_s) \leq \psi_s(\bar{\mathbf{x}}_s)$, this implies the left inequality.

177

2. Since $\bar{\mathbf{x}}_s$ is a minimizer of ψ_s one has $\psi_s(\bar{\mathbf{x}}_s) \leq \psi_s(\bar{\mathbf{x}})$. This yields the middle inequality.

3. The right inequality holds due to (10.3.18).

This completes the proof. $\qquad\qquad\qquad\qquad\qquad\qquad\qquad\qquad$ $\square$

10.4. Bibliographic notes

The exposition of the linear algebra results follows [103, 110]. The discussion of Lagrange multipliers follows [112]. For recession and asymptotic cones one can consult [114]. In this chapter we closely follow exposition of relevant material given in [5]. Smoothing results are reported in [12].

11 Solutions to selected problems

Problem 2.1.6. True or False? If $\left\{\pi_1^l, \pi_2^l\right\}$ is the optimal partition, then $x_l \leq c(\mathcal{A}) \leq x_{l+1}$.

Solution to Problem 2.1.6

Consider a four scalar set $\mathcal{A} = \{0, 1/9, 4/9, 1\}$. While the arithmetic mean of the set is $7/18$ the optimal 2 cluster partition is $\Pi^{\min} = \{\pi_1^{\min}, \pi_2^{\min}\}$, where $\pi_1^{\min} = \{0, 1/9, 4/9\}$ and $\pi_2^{\min} = \{1\}$. In this case the mean fails to separate the optimal clusters.

Problem 2.2.2. Show that the k-means clustering algorithm does not necessarily lead to the optimal partition.

Solution to Problem 2.2.2

Consider the one dimensional data set $\mathcal{A} = \{0, 1, 1 + \epsilon, 3\}$. Since the optimal partition should be "convex" (see Lemma 2.1.1 and Theorem 2.3.1) the three candidates for an optimal 2 cluster partition are

1. $\Pi^{(0)} = \{\{0, 1, 1 + \epsilon\}, \{3\}\}$ with $Q(\Pi^{(0)}) = \dfrac{12 + 8\epsilon + 18\epsilon^2}{18}$.

2. $\Pi^{(1)} = \{\{0, 1\}, \{1 + \epsilon, 3\}\}$ with $Q(\Pi^{(1)}) = \dfrac{18 - 18\epsilon + 9\epsilon^2}{18}$.

3. $\Pi^{(2)} = \{\{0\}, \{1, 1 + \epsilon, 3\}\}$ with $Q(\Pi^{(2)}) = \dfrac{12 - 12\epsilon + 18\epsilon^2}{18}$.

Hence, when ϵ is a small positive number (for example $0 < \epsilon < 0.05$), one has

$$Q(\Pi^{(2)}) < Q(\Pi^{(0)}) < Q(\Pi^{(1)}).$$

An application of a batch k-means iteration to $\Pi^{(0)}$ does not change the partition. The first variation of $\Pi^{(0)}$ is $\Pi^{(0)}$ itself. An application of k-means to $\Pi^{(0)}$ does not change the partition, and the algorithm misses the optimal partition $\Pi^{(2)}$.

Problem 2.2.3. Assume that the data set $\mathcal{A}$ contains two identical vectors $\mathbf{a}' = \mathbf{a}''$.

1. If $\Pi = \{\pi_1, \ldots, \pi_k\}$ is a k-means stable partition, $\mathbf{a}' \in \pi'$, $\mathbf{a}'' \in \pi''$, and at least one of the clusters π', π'' is not a singleton, then $\pi' = \pi''$.
2. Show that the above result does not necessarily hold when k-means is substituted by *batch* k-means. In other words give an example of a data set $\mathcal{A}$ with identical vectors and an initial partition $\Pi^{(0)}$ so that application of the *batch* k-means to $\Pi^{(0)}$ generates a final partition in which identical vectors are assigned to different clusters.

Solution to Problem 2.2.3

1. Assume the contrary, i.e. $\mathbf{a}' \in \pi'$, $\mathbf{a}'' \in \pi''$, and $\pi' \neq \pi''$. Let $\mathbf{c}' = \mathbf{c}(\pi')$ and $\mathbf{c}'' = \mathbf{c}(\pi'')$. Due to Theorem 2.3.1 one has $\mathbf{c}' \neq \mathbf{c}''$, hence the vectors $\mathbf{a}' = \mathbf{a}''$ are different from at least one of the centroids. Assume that $\mathbf{a}' \neq \mathbf{c}'$, this implies, in particular, that π' may not be a singleton, i.e. $|\pi'| > 1$.

   Consider a first variation Π' of Π that removes $\mathbf{a}'$ from π' and assigns it to π''. Due to (2.2.9)

   $$Q(\pi'') - Q((\pi'')^+) + Q(\pi') - Q((\pi')^-)$$
   $$= \frac{|\pi'|}{|\pi'| - 1} \|\mathbf{c}' - \mathbf{a}'\|^2 - \frac{|\pi''|}{|\pi''| + 1} \|\mathbf{c}'' - \mathbf{a}'\|^2.$$

Since Π is k-means stable (see text following Theorem 2.3.1) $\|\mathbf{c}' - \mathbf{a}'\| = \|\mathbf{c}'' - \mathbf{a}'\|$, hence

$$[Q(\pi'') - Q((\pi'')^+)] + [Q(\pi') - Q((\pi')^-)]$$
$$= \left[\frac{|\pi'|}{|\pi'| - 1} - \frac{|\pi''|}{|\pi''| + 1} \right] \|\mathbf{c}' - \mathbf{a}'\|^2. \qquad (11.0.1)$$

Due to the assumption $\|\mathbf{c}' - \mathbf{a}'\| > 0$, this shows that the right-hand side of (11.0.1) is strictly positive, and $Q(\Pi) > Q(\Pi') \geq$ $\mathrm{nextFV}(\Pi)$. This shows that Π is not k-means stable, the contradiction completes the proof.

2. Let $\mathcal{A} = \{1, 3, 3, 5\}$, and $\Pi^{(0)} = \{\{1, 3\}, \{3, 5\}\}$.

In the next set of problems we shall consider two cluster partitions $\{\pi_1, \pi_2\}$ with identical centroids, that is, $\mathbf{c}(\pi_1) = \mathbf{c}(\pi_2)$. Our main goal is to demonstrate that these partitions may not be spherical k-means stable. To achieve this goal we will build "better" first variations. Assuming that $\mathbf{b} \in \pi_2$ makes an acute angle θ_0 with the nonzero vector $\mathbf{c}(\pi_1)$ (we show below that centroids of spherical k-means stable partitions do not vanish) the quality of the first variation $\{\pi_1^+, \pi_2^-\}$ obtained by removing $\mathbf{b}$ from π_2 and assigning it to π_1 is given by

$$Q\left(\pi_1^+\right) + Q\left(\pi_2^-\right) = \sqrt{\|\mathbf{s}(\pi_1)\|^2 + 1 + 2\|\mathbf{s}(\pi_1)\| \cos\theta_0}$$
$$+ \sqrt{\|\mathbf{s}(\pi_2)\|^2 + 1 - 2\|\mathbf{s}(\pi_2)\| \cos\theta_0}.$$

It would be useful to consider the function

$$\psi(\theta, a, b) = \sqrt{a^2 + 1 + 2a\cos\theta} + \sqrt{b^2 + 1 - 2b\cos\theta}, \qquad (11.0.2)$$

where $0 \leq \theta \leq \frac{\pi}{2}$ and a and b are positive scalars see Figure 11.1. Note that

$$\psi(0, a, b) = a + 1 + |b - 1| \geq a + b, \quad \text{and} \quad \psi\left(\frac{\pi}{2}, a, b\right)$$
$$= \sqrt{a^2 + 1} + \sqrt{b^2 + 1} > a + b. \qquad (11.0.3)$$

The function ψ is differentiable with respect to θ when $0 < \theta \leq \frac{\pi}{2}$ and the partial derivative is given by

181

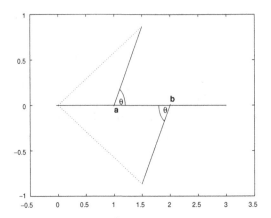

Figure 11.1: First variation of a two cluster partition with identical centroids.

$$\frac{\partial}{\partial \theta} \psi (\theta, a, b) = \left[\frac{b}{\sqrt{b^2 + 1 - 2b \cos \theta}} - \frac{a}{\sqrt{a^2 + 1 + 2a \cos \theta}} \right] \sin \theta.$$

The function ϕ is defined by

$$\phi (\theta, a, b) = \frac{b}{\sqrt{b^2 + 1 - 2b \cos \theta}} - \frac{a}{\sqrt{a^2 + 1 + 2a \cos \theta}} \qquad (11.0.4)$$

so that $\frac{\partial}{\partial \theta} \psi (\theta, a, b) = \phi (\theta, a, b) \sin \theta$ and, therefore, the sign of $\frac{\partial}{\partial \theta} \psi (\theta, a, b)$ is determined by $\phi (\theta, a, b)$. It is easy to see that $\phi (\theta, a, b)$ is monotonically decreasing on $(0, \frac{\pi}{2})$, and, as we will see later, it is of interest to examine

$$\phi (0, a, b) = \frac{b}{|b - 1|} - \frac{a}{a + 1} \quad \text{and} \quad \phi \left(\frac{\pi}{2}, a, b \right)$$

$$= \frac{b}{\sqrt{b^2 + 1}} - \frac{a}{\sqrt{a^2 + 1}} \qquad (11.0.5)$$

(when $\phi (0, a, b)$ exists) along with $\phi (0, s, s)$. The proof of the following inequalities is straightforward

If $1 < b$,   then $\phi (0, a, b) > 0$.

If $0 < a < b$,   then $\phi \left(\frac{\pi}{2}, a, b \right) > 0$.

If $0 < s$,   then $\phi (\theta, s, s) > 0$ when $\theta \in \left(0, \frac{\pi}{2} \right)$.   (11.0.6)

Problem 4.3.2. If $\{\pi_1, \pi_2\}$ is a two cluster stable spherical k-means partition, then $\mathbf{c}(\pi_i) \neq 0$, $i = 1, 2$.

Solution to Problem 4.3.2

Let $\pi_1 = \{\mathbf{a}_1, \ldots, \mathbf{a}_p\}$ and $\pi_2 = \{\mathbf{b}_1, \ldots, \mathbf{b}_q\}$. First note that both centroids cannot be 0 at the same time. Indeed, assume the opposite, that is, $\|\mathbf{a}_1 + \cdots + \mathbf{a}_p\| = 0$ and $\|\mathbf{b}_1 + \cdots + \mathbf{b}_q\| = 0$. The assumption yields

1. $p > 1$,
2. $q > 1$,
3. $\|\mathbf{a}_1 + \cdots + \mathbf{a}_{p-1}\| = \|\mathbf{a}_p\| = 1$.

Consider the first variation $\{\pi_1^-, \pi_2^+\}$ of $\{\pi_1, \pi_2\}$ obtained by removing $\mathbf{a}_p$ from π_1 and assigning it to π_2. Note that

$$Q(\pi_1) + Q(\pi_2) = 0, \quad \text{and} \quad Q(\pi_1^-) + Q(\pi_2^+) = 2.$$

This contradict the fact that $\{\pi_1, \pi_2\}$ is a two cluster stable spherical k-means partition and shows that at least one centroid should different from zero.

Next assume that $\|\mathbf{a}_1 + \cdots + \mathbf{a}_p\| = 0$ and $\|\mathbf{b}_1 + \cdots + \mathbf{b}_q\| > 0$. The assumption implies that π_1 contains two or more vectors, hence selection of a vector $\mathbf{a}_i \neq -\mathbf{c}(\pi_2)$ is possible (the condition yields $\|\mathbf{b}_1 + \cdots + \mathbf{b}_q + \mathbf{a}_i\| > \big|\|\mathbf{b}_1 + \cdots + \mathbf{b}_q\| - 1\big|$). For simplicity sake we assume that $\mathbf{a}_i = \mathbf{a}_p$. Again consider the first variation $\{\pi_1^-, \pi_2^+\}$ of $\{\pi_1, \pi_2\}$. Note that

$$Q(\pi_1) + Q(\pi_2) = \|\mathbf{b}_1 + \cdots + \mathbf{b}_q\|, \tag{11.0.7}$$

and

$$\begin{aligned} Q(\pi_1^-) + Q(\pi_2^+) &= \|\mathbf{a}_1 + \cdots + \mathbf{a}_{p-1}\| + \|\mathbf{b}_1 + \cdots + \mathbf{b}_q + \mathbf{a}_p\| \\ &> 1 + \big|\|\mathbf{b}_1 + \cdots + \mathbf{b}_q\| - 1\big|. \end{aligned} \tag{11.0.8}$$

Since $1 + \big|\|\mathbf{b}_1 + \cdots + \mathbf{b}_q\| - 1\big| \geq \|\mathbf{b}_1 + \cdots + \mathbf{b}_q\|$, one has

$$Q(\pi_1^-) + Q(\pi_2^+) > Q(\pi_1^-) + Q(\pi_2^+),$$

and $\{\pi_1, \pi_2\}$ may not be a k-means stable partition. This contradiction completes the proof.

Problem 4.3.3. If $\{\pi_1, \pi_2\}$ is a two cluster stable spherical k-means partition, then $\mathbf{s}(\pi_1) \neq \mathbf{s}(\pi_2)$.

Solution to Problem 4.3.3

Assume the contrary, i.e. $\mathbf{s}(\pi_1) = \mathbf{s}(\pi_2)$. The assumption implies that at least one of the clusters is not a singleton, and we assume that $|\pi_1| > 1$. There is at least one vector $\mathbf{a} \in \pi_1$ so that $1 > \mathbf{a}^T \mathbf{c}(\pi_1) \geq 0$. Consider the first variation $\{\pi_1^-, \pi_2^+\}$ obtained by moving $\mathbf{a}$ from π_1 to π_2.

Denote the acute angle between $\mathbf{s}(\pi_1)$, and $\mathbf{a}$ by θ_0 and $\|\mathbf{s}(\pi_1)\|$ by s. Note that

$$Q(\pi_1^-) + Q(\pi_2^+) = \|\mathbf{s}(\pi_1) - \mathbf{a}\| + \|\mathbf{s}(\pi_2) + \mathbf{a}\| = \psi(\theta_0, s, s).$$

Due to (11.0.6) one has $\psi(\theta_0, s, s) > \psi(0, s, s) \geq Q(\pi_1) + Q(\pi_2)$. This contradicts stability of $\{\pi_1, \pi_2\}$, and completes the proof.

Problem 4.3.4. Let $\{\pi_1, \pi_2\}$ be a two cluster stable spherical k-means partition with $\mathbf{c}(\pi_1) = \mathbf{c}(\pi_2)$. If $\|\mathbf{s}(\pi_1)\| < \|\mathbf{s}(\pi_2)\|$, then $\mathbf{a}^T \mathbf{c}(\pi_1) \geq 0$ for each $\mathbf{a} \in \pi_1$.

Solution to Problem 4.3.4

Assume the contrary, that is, there is $\mathbf{a} \in \pi_1$ with $\mathbf{a}^T \mathbf{c}(\pi_1) < 0$. We denote the acute angle between $\mathbf{a}$ and $-\mathbf{s}(\pi_1)$ by θ_0, and consider the first variation $\{\pi_1^-, \pi_2^+\}$ obtained by moving $\mathbf{a}$ from π_1 to π_2. Note that

1. $Q(\pi_1^-) + Q(\pi_2^+) = \psi(\theta_0, \|\mathbf{s}(\pi_1)\|, \|\mathbf{s}(\pi_2)\|)$,
2. $\frac{\partial}{\partial\theta}\psi(\theta, \|\mathbf{s}(\pi_1)\|, \|\mathbf{s}(\pi_2)\|) > 0$ when $0 \leq \theta \leq \frac{\pi}{2}$,
3. $\psi(0, \|\mathbf{s}(\pi_1)\|, \|\mathbf{s}(\pi_2)\|) \geq Q(\pi_1) + Q(\pi_2)$.

The three conditions lead to the inequality

$$Q(\pi_1^-) + Q(\pi_2^+) > Q(\pi_1) + Q(\pi_2).$$

The inequality contradicts stability of $\{\pi_1, \pi_2\}$ and completes the proof.

Solutions to selected problems

Problem 4.3.5. Give an example of a two cluster stable spherical k-means partition $\{\pi_1, \pi_2\}$ with $\mathbf{a} \in \pi_1$ such that $\mathbf{a}^T \mathbf{c}(\pi_1) < 0$.

Solution to Problem 4.3.5

Let $\mathcal{A} = \{\mathbf{a}_1, \mathbf{a}_2, \mathbf{a}_3, \mathbf{a}_4\}$ where

$$
\mathbf{a}_1 = \begin{bmatrix} \frac{\sqrt{3}}{2} \\ -\frac{1}{2} \end{bmatrix}, \quad
\mathbf{a}_2 = \begin{bmatrix} -\frac{\sqrt{3}}{4} + \epsilon \\ \sqrt{1 - \left(\frac{\sqrt{3}}{4} - \epsilon\right)^2} \end{bmatrix},
$$

$$
\mathbf{a}_3 = \begin{bmatrix} -\frac{\sqrt{3}}{4} - \epsilon \\ \sqrt{1 - \left(\frac{\sqrt{3}}{4} + \epsilon\right)^2} \end{bmatrix}, \quad
\mathbf{a}_4 = \begin{bmatrix} -1 \\ 0 \end{bmatrix},
$$

where ϵ is a small positive number (for example $\epsilon = 0.1$). Consider the two cluster partition Π with clusters $\pi_1 = \{\mathbf{a}_1, \mathbf{a}_2, \mathbf{a}_3\}$, and $\pi_2 = \{\mathbf{a}_4\}$. Note that

1. $\{\pi_1, \pi_2\}$ is a two cluster stable spherical k-means partition (check the statement with $\epsilon = 0$ and use continuity arguments to conclude that the statement holds when ϵ is a small positive number, check that the statement holds true for $\epsilon = 0.1$).

2. $\mathbf{s}(\pi_1) = \begin{bmatrix} 0 \\ \sqrt{1 - \left(\frac{\sqrt{3}}{4} + \epsilon\right)^2} + \sqrt{1 - \left(\frac{\sqrt{3}}{4} - \epsilon\right)^2} - \frac{1}{2} \end{bmatrix}$ and

   $\mathbf{c}(\pi_1) = \begin{bmatrix} 0 \\ 1 \end{bmatrix}$.

3. $\mathbf{a}_1^T \mathbf{c}(\pi_1) = -\frac{1}{2}$.

Moreover, the optimal two cluster partition $\Pi' = \{\{\mathbf{a}_1\}, \{\mathbf{a}_2, \mathbf{a}_3, \mathbf{a}_4\}\}$ is two vectors "away", and an application of the spherical k-means to Π fails to recover Π'.

Problem 4.3.6. If $\{\pi_1, \pi_2\}$ is a two cluster stable spherical k-means partition, then $\mathbf{c}(\pi_1) \neq \mathbf{c}(\pi_2)$.

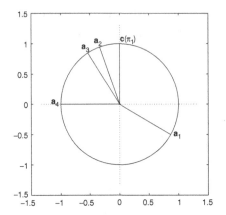

Figure 11.2: Spherical k-means stable two cluster partition with $\mathbf{a}^T\mathbf{c}(\pi_1) < 0$.

Solution to Problem 4.3.6

Assume the contrary, i.e. $\mathbf{c}(\pi_1) = \mathbf{c}(\pi_2)$. Due to Problem 4.3.3 $\|\mathbf{s}(\pi_1)\| \neq \|\mathbf{s}(\pi_2)\|$, we assume that $0 < \|\mathbf{s}(\pi_1)\| < \|\mathbf{s}(\pi_2)\|$ and focus on the following two cases:

1. $0 < \|\mathbf{s}(\pi_1)\| < 1$,
2. $1 \leq \|\mathbf{s}(\pi_1)\|$.

Case 1. Since $\|\mathbf{s}(\pi_1)\| < 1$ the cluster π_1 contains two or more vectors. Due to Problem 4.3.4 one has $\mathbf{a}^T\mathbf{c}(\pi_1) \geq 0$ for each $\mathbf{a} \in \pi_1$. This yields existence of $\mathbf{a} \in \pi_1$ so that $0 \leq \mathbf{a}^T\mathbf{c}(\pi_1) \leq \frac{\|\mathbf{s}(\pi_1)\|}{2}$, and $\|\mathbf{s}(\pi_1) - \mathbf{a}\| \geq 1$. Note that $\mathbf{a}^T\mathbf{s}(\pi_2) \geq 0$, and $\|\mathbf{s}(\pi_2) + \mathbf{a}\| > \|\mathbf{s}(\pi_2)\|$. Let $\{\pi_1^-, \pi_2^+\}$ be the first variation obtained from $\{\pi_1, \pi_2\}$ by removing $\mathbf{a}$ from π_1 and assigning it to π_2. The above discussion shows that

$$Q(\pi_1) + Q(\pi_2) = \|\mathbf{s}(\pi_1)\| + \|\mathbf{s}(\pi_2)\| < 1 + \|\mathbf{s}(\pi_2)\| < \|\mathbf{s}(\pi_1)$$
$$- \mathbf{a}\| + \|\mathbf{s}(\pi_2) + \mathbf{a}\| = Q(\pi_1^-) + Q(\pi_2^+).$$

This contradicts stability of $\{\pi_1, \pi_2\}$, and completes the proof of Case 1.

Case 2. Since $1 \leq \|\mathbf{s}(\pi_1)\| < \|\mathbf{s}(\pi_2)\|$, the cluster π_2 contains two or more vectors. We select $\mathbf{b} \in \pi_2$ so that $0 \leq \mathbf{b}^T\mathbf{c}(\pi_2) < 1$ and consider

Solutions to selected problems

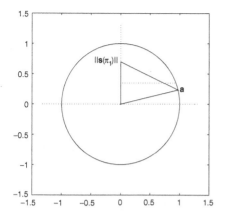

Figure 11.3: "Short positive" cluster variation.

the first variation $\{\pi_1^+, \pi_2^-\}$ obtained by removing $\mathbf{b}$ from π_2 and assigning it to π_1. If the acute angle between $\mathbf{b}$ and $\mathbf{s}(\pi_2)$ is θ_0, then

$$Q(\pi_1^+) + Q(\pi_2^-) = \psi\left(\theta_0, \|\mathbf{s}(\pi_1)\|, \|\mathbf{s}(\pi_2)\|\right).$$

Note that $\psi\left(0, \|\mathbf{s}(\pi_1)\|, \|\mathbf{s}(\pi_2)\|\right) = Q(\pi_1) + Q(\pi_2)$, and

$$\frac{\partial}{\partial\theta}\psi\left(\theta, \|\mathbf{s}(\pi_1)\|, \|\mathbf{s}(\pi_2)\|\right) = \phi\left(\theta, \|\mathbf{s}(\pi_1)\|, \|\mathbf{s}(\pi_2)\|\right)\sin\theta$$

with (see (11.0.6))

$$\phi\left(\theta, \|\mathbf{s}(\pi_1)\|, \|\mathbf{s}(\pi_2)\|\right) \geq \phi\left(\frac{\pi}{2}, \|\mathbf{s}(\pi_1)\|, \|\mathbf{s}(\pi_2)\|\right) > 0.$$

This yields

$$Q(\pi_1^-) + Q(\pi_2^+) = \psi\left(\theta_0, \|\mathbf{s}(\pi_1)\|, \|\mathbf{s}(\pi_2)\|\right) > \psi\left(0, \|\mathbf{s}(\pi_1)\|, \|\mathbf{s}(\pi_2)\|\right)$$
$$= Q(\pi_1) + Q(\pi_2),$$

contradicts stability of $\{\pi_1, \pi_2\}$, and completes the proof of Case 2.

Problem 8.2.3. Let $\phi : \mathbf{R}_{++} \to \mathbf{R}$ be a twice differentiable convex function. If for each $x, y \in \mathbf{R}_{++}$ one has

$$\phi(x) - \phi(y) - \phi'(y)(x - y) = y\phi\left(\frac{x}{y}\right), \qquad (11.0.9)$$

then $\phi(t) = c\,[t\log t - t + 1], c > 0$.

187

Solution to Problem 8.2.3

For $y = 1$ Equation (11.0.9) yields

$$\forall x \in \mathbf{R}_{++} \cdot \phi(x) - \phi(1) - \phi'(1)(x - 1) = \phi(x).$$

This implies

$$\phi(1) = \phi'(1) = 0. \qquad (11.0.10)$$

The second derivative of (11.0.9) with respect to x yields $\phi''(x) = \phi''\left(\frac{x}{y}\right)\frac{1}{y}$, and when $x = 1$ one has

$$\phi''(1) = \phi''\left(\frac{1}{y}\right)\frac{1}{y}. \qquad (11.0.11)$$

The general solution for this second order ODE is given by $\phi''(1)[t \log t - t + 1] + c_1[t - 1] + c_2$. The initial conditions (11.0.10) yield $c_1 = c_2 = 0$, and $\phi(t) = \phi''(1)[t \log t - t + 1]$.

Bibliography

[1] S. Agrawal, J. Lim, L. Zelnik-Manor, P. Perona, and D. Kriegman. Beyond pairwise clustering. In *Proceedings of the IEEE Conference on Computer Vision and Pattern Recognition*, 2005.

[2] M.S. Aldenderfer and R.K. Blashfield. *Cluster Analysis*. Sage, Los Angeles, CA, 1985.

[3] M.R. Anderberg. *Cluster Analysis and Applications*. Academic Press, New York, 1973.

[4] P. Arabie, L.J. Hubert, and G. De Soete. *Clustering and Clussification*. World Scientific, Singapore, 1996.

[5] A. Auslender and M. Teboulle. *Asymptotic Cones and Functions in Optimization and Variational Inequalities*. Springer-Verlag, New York, 2003.

[6] A. Auslender, M. Teboulle, and S. Ben-Tiba. Interior proximal and multiplier methods based on second order homogeneous kernels. *Mathematics of Operations Research*, 24:645–668, 1999.

[7] L. Douglas Baker and A. McCallum. Distributional clustering of words for text classification. In *ACM SIGIR*, pp. 96–103, Melbourne, Australia, 1998.

[8] A. Banerjee, S. Merugu, I.S. Dhillon, and J. Ghosh. Clustering with Bregman divergences. In *Proceedings of the 2004 SIAM International Conference on Data Mining*, pp. 234–245. SIAM, Philadelphia, 2004.

[9] A. Banerjee, S. Merugu, I.S. Dhillon, and J. Ghosh. Clustering with Bregman divergences. *Journal of Machine Learning Research*, 6:1705–1749, 2005.

[10] D. Banks, L. House, F.R. McMorris, P. Arabie, and W. Gaul (eds.). *Clussification, Clustering, and Data Mining Applications*. Springer-Verlag, Berlin, 2004.

[11] E. Beckenbach and R. Bellman. *Inequalities*. Springer-Verlag, New York, 1965.

[12] A. Ben-Tal and M. Teboulle. A smoothing technique for nondifferentiable optimization problems. In *Springer Verlag Lecture Notes in Mathematics*, Vol. 1405, pp. 1–11, Berlin, 1989.

[13] A. Ben-Tal, A. Charnes, and M. Teboulle. Entropic means. *Journal of Mathematical Analysis and Applications*, 139:537–551, 1989.

[14] P. Berkhin. A survey of clustering data mining techniques. In J. Kogan, C. Nicholas, and M. Teboulle (eds.), *Grouping Multidimensional Data: Recent Advances in Clustering*, pp. 25–72. Springer-Verlag, New York, 2006.

[15] P. Berkhin and J.D. Becher. Learning simple relations: Theory and applications. In *Proceedings of the Second SIAM International Conference on Data Mining*, pp. 420–436, Arlington, April 2002.

[16] M. Berry and M. Browne. *Understanding Search Engines*. SIAM, Philadelphia, 1999.

[17] G.D. Birkhoff and R. Beatley. *Basic Geometry*. AMS Chelsea, New York, NY, 2000.

[18] D. Boley, M. Gini, R. Gross, E.-H. Han, K. Hastings, G. Karypis, V. Kumar, B. Mobasher, and J. Moore. Document categorization and query generation on the World Wide Web using WebACE. *AI Review*, 13(5,6):365–391, 1999.

[19] D. Boley, M. Gini, R. Gross, E.-H. Han, K. Hastings, G. Karypis, V. Kumar, B. Mobasher, and J. Moore. Partitioning-based clustering for web document categorization. *Decision Support Systems*, 27(3):329–341, 1999.

[20] D.L. Boley. Principal direction divisive partitioning. *Data Mining and Knowledge Discovery*, 2(4):325–344, 1998.

[21] N. Bolshakova and F. Azuaje. Cluster validation techniques for genome expression data. *Signal Processing*, 83:825–833, 2003.

[22] P. Bradley, U. Fayyad, and C. Reina. Scaling clustering algorithms to large databases. In *Proceedings Fourth International Conference on*

Bibliography

Knowledge Discovery and Data Mining. AAAI Press, Menlo Park, CA, 1998.

[23] P.S. Bradley and O. L. Mangasarian. k-plane clustering. *Journal of Global Optimization,* 2(4):23–32, 1998.

[24] L.M. Bregman. A relaxation method of finding a common point of convex sets and its application to the solution of problems in convex programming. *USSR Comp. Math. and Math Phys.,* 7:200–217, 1967.

[25] P. Brucker. On the complexity of clustering problems. In *Lecture Notes in Economics and Mathematical Systems,* Vol. 157, pp. 45–54. Springer-Verlag, Berlin, 1978.

[26] G. Chen and M. Teboulle. Convergence analysis of a proximal-like minimization algorithm using bregman functions. *SIAM Journal of Optimization,* 3:538–543, 1993.

[27] E. Chisholm and T. Kolda. New term weighting formulas for the vector space method in information retrieval, 1999. Report ORNL/TM-13756, Computer Science and Mathematics Division, Oak Ridge National Laboratory.

[28] M. Collins, R.E. Schapire, and Y. Singer. Logistic regression, AdaBoost and Bregman distances. In *Proceedings of the Thirteenth Annual Conference on Computational Learning Theory,* pp. 158–169, San Francisco, CA. Morgan Kaufmann, New York, NY, 2000.

[29] I. Csiszar. Information-type measures of difference of probability distributions and indirect observations. *Studia Sci. Mat. Hungar.,* 2:299–318, 1967.

[30] I. Davidson and A. Satyanarayana. Speeding up *k*-means clustering by bootstrap averaging. In D. Boley et al. (eds.), *Proceedings of the Workshop on Clustering Large Data Sets* (held in conjunction with the *Third IEEE International Conference on Data Mining),* pp. 15–25, 2003.

[31] D. Davis and D. Bouldin. A cluster separation measure. *IEEE Transactions on Pattern Recognition, and Machine Intelligence,* 1:224–227, 1979.

[32] J. W. Demmel. *Applied Numerical Linear Algebra.* SIAM, Philadelphia, 1997.

[33] I.S. Dhillon. Co-clustering documents and words using bipartite spectral graph partitioning. In *Proceedings of the Seventh ACM*

SIGKDD International Conference on Knowledge Discovery and Data Mining(KDD-2001), 2001. Also appears as UT CS Technical Report # TR 2001–05, March, 1999.

[34] I.S. Dhillon, J. Fan, and Y. Guan. Efficient clustering of very large document collections. In R. Grossman, C. Kamath, P. Kegelmeyer, V. Kumar, and R. Namburu (eds.), *Data Mining for Scientific and Engineering Applications*, pp. 357–381. Kluwer Academic Publishers, Norwell, MA, 2001.

[35] I.S. Dhillon, Y. Guan, and J. Kogan. Iterative clustering of high dimensional text data augmented by local search. In *Proceedings of the 2002 IEEE International Conference on Data Mining*, pp. 131–138. IEEE Computer Society Press, Piscataway, NJ, 2002.

[36] I.S. Dhillon, Y. Guan, and J. Kogan. Refining clusters in high-dimensional text data. In I.S. Dhillon and J. Kogan (eds.), *Proceedings of the Workshop on Clustering High Dimensional Data and its Applications at the Second SIAM International Conference on Data Mining*, pp. 71–82. SIAM, Philadelphia, 2002.

[37] I.S. Dhillon, J. Kogan, and C. Nicholas. Feature selection and document clustering. In M.W. Berry (ed.), *Survey of Text Mining*, pp. 73–100. Springer-Verlag, New York, 2003.

[38] I.S. Dhillon, S. Mallela, and R. Kumar. A divisive information-theoretic feature clustering algorithm for text classification. *Journal of Machine Learning Research(JMLR): Special Issue on Variable and Feature Selection*, 3:1265–1287, March 2003.

[39] I.S. Dhillon and D.S. Modha. Concept decompositions for large sparse text data using clustering. *Machine Learning*, 42(1):143–175, January 2001. Also appears as IBM Research Report RJ 10147, July 1999.

[40] I.S. Dhillon, M. Subramanyam, and R. Kumar. Enhanced word clustering for hierarchical text classification. In *Proceedings of the Eighth ACM SIGKDD International Conference on Knowledge Discovery and Data Mining(KDD-2002)*, pp. 191–200, 2002.

[41] I.S. Dhillon, M. Subramanyam, and D.S. Modha. Information-theoretic co-clustering. In *Proceedings of the Ninth ACM SIGKDD International Conference on Knowledge Discovery and Data Mining(KDD-2003)*, pp. 89–98, 2003.

[42] E. Diday. The dynamic clusters method in nonhierarchical clustering. *International Journal of Computer and Information Sciences*, 2(1):61–88, March 1973.

[43] E. Diday. Some recent advances in clustering. In E. Diday, C. Hayashi, M. Jambu, and N. Ohsimi (eds.), *Recent Developments in Clustering and Data Analysis. Proceedings of the Japanise–French Scientific Seminar, March 24–26, 1987*, pp. 119–136. Academic Press, New York, 1987.

[44] W.R. Dillon and M. Goldstein. *Multivariate Analysis: Methods and Applications*. Wiley, New York, 1984.

[45] P. Drineas, A. Frieze, R. Kannan, S. Vempala, and V. Vinay. Clustering in large graphs via the Singular Value Decomposition. *Machine Learning*, 56:9–33, 2004.

[46] R.C. Dubes. Cluster analysis and related issues. In C.H. Chen, L.F. Pau, and P.S. Wang (eds.), *Handbook of Pattern Recognition and Computer Vision*, pp. 3–32. World Scientific Publishing, River Edge, NJ, 1993.

[47] R.O. Duda and P.E. Hart. *Pattern Classification and Scene Analysis*. Wiley, New York, 1973.

[48] R.O. Duda, P.E. Hart, and D.G. Stork. *Pattern Classification*, 2nd edn. John Wiley & Sons, New York, 2000.

[49] I. Duff, R. Grimes, and J. Lewis. Sparse matrix test problems. *ACM Transcations on Mathematical Software*, 15:1–14, 1989.

[50] M.H. Dunham. *Data Mining*. Pearson Hall, New Jersey, 2003.

[51] J. Dunn. Well separated clusters and optimal fuzzy partitions. *Journal of Cybernetics*, 4:95–104, 1974.

[52] R. El-Yaniv and O. Souroujon. Iterative double clustering for unsupervised and semi-supervised learning. In T.G. Dietterich, S. Becker, and Z. Ghahramani (eds.), *Advances in Neural Information Processing Systems (NIPS) 14*, pp. 1025–1032. MIT Press, Cambridge, MA, 2001.

[53] C. Elkan. Using the triangle inequality to accelerate k-means. In *Proceedings of the Twentieth International Conference on Machine Learning (ICML'03)*, pp. 147–153, 2003.

[54] B. Everitt. *Cluster Analysis, 3rd edn*. Edward Arnold, London, UK, 1993.

[55] K. Fan. On a theorem of Weil concerning eigenvalues of linear trans-
formations. I. *Proceedings of the National Academy of Sciences of
the United States of America*, 35:652–655, 1949.

[56] D. Fasulo. An analysis of recent work on clustering algorithms. Technical Report UW-CSE01 -03-02, University of Washington, 1999.

[57] E. Forgy. Cluster analysis of multivariate data: Efficiency vs. inter-
pretability of classifications. *Biometrics*, 21(3):768, 1965.

[58] W.B. Frakes and R. Baeza-Yates. *Information Retrieval: Data Structures and Algorithms*. Prentice-Hall, Englewood Cliffs, NJ, 1992.

[59] J. Ghosh. Scalable clustering methods for data mining. In Nong Ye
(ed.), *Handbook of Data Mining*, pp. 247–277. Lawrence Erlbaum,
Mahwah, NJ, 2003.

[60] J. Ghosh and A. Strehl. Similarity-based text clustering: A compara-
tive study. In J. Kogan, C. Nicholas, and M. Teboulle (eds.), *Grouping
Multidimensional Data: Recent Advances in Clustering*, pp. 73–98.
Springer-Verlag, New York, 2006.

[61] G.H. Golub and C.F. Van Loan. *Matrix Computations*. The Johns
Hopkins University Press, Baltimore, 1991.

[62] V.M. Govindu. A tensor decomposition for geometric grouping and
segmentation. In *Proceedings of the IEEE Conference on Computer
Vision and Pattern Recognition*, 2005.

[63] D. Grossman and O. Frieder. *Information Retrieval: Algorithms
and Heuristics*. The Information Retrieval Series, Vol. 15, 2nd edn.
Springer, New York, 2004.

[64] J. Han and M. Kamber. *Data Mining: Concepts and Techniques*. Morgan Kaufmann, San Francisco, 2001.

[65] J. Han, M. Kamber, and A.K.H. Tung. Spatial clustering methods
in data mining: A survey. In H. Miller and J. Han (eds.), *Geo-
graphic Data Mining and Knowledge Discovery*. Taylor and Francis,
2001.

[66] P. Hansen and N. Mladenovic. J-Means: A new local search heuristic
for minimum sum of squares clustering. *Patern Recognition*, 34:405–
413, 2001.

[67] G. Hardy, J.E. Littlewood, and G. Polya. *Inequalities*. Cambridge
University Press, Cambridge, 1934.

[68] J.A. Hartigan. *Clustering Algorithms*. Wiley, New York, 1975.

[69] Ji He, Ah-Hwee Tan, Chew Lim Tan, and Sam Yuan Sung. On quantitative evaluation of clustering systems. In W. Wu, H. Xiong, and S. Shenkar (eds.), *Clustering and Information Retrieval*, pp. 105–134. Kluwer Academic Publishers, Norwell, MA, 2004.

[70] Z. Huang. A fast clustering algorithm to cluster very large categorical data sets in data mining. In *SIGMOD Workshop on Research Issues on Data Mining and Knowledge Discovery, (SIGMOD-DMKD'97)*, 1997.

[71] A.K. Jain and R.C. Dubes. *Algorithms for Clustering Data*. Prentice-Hall, Englewood Cliffs, NJ, 1988.

[72] A.K. Jain, M.N. Murty, and Flynn P.J. Data clustering: A review. *ACM Computing Surveys*, 31(3):264–323, 1999.

[73] T. Kanungo, D. Mount, N. Netanyahu, C. Piatko, R. Silverman, and A. Wu. A local search approximations algorithm for k-means clustering. *Computational Geometry: Theory and Applications*, 28:89–112, 2004.

[74] N.B. Karayiannis. An axiomatic approach to soft learning vector quantization and clustering. *IEEE Transactions on Neural Networks*, 10(5):1153–1165, 1999.

[75] L. Kaufman and P.J. Rousseeuw. *Finding Groups in Data: An Introduction to Cluster Analysis*. Wiley, New York, 1990.

[76] J. Kivinen and M.K. Warmuth. Boosting as entropy projection. In *Proceedings of 12th Annual Conference on Computational Learning Theory*, pp. 134–144, 1999.

[77] J. Kleinberg. Authoritative sources in a hyperlinked environment. In *Proceedings of 9th ACM-SIAM Symposium on Discrete Algorithms*, http://www.cs.cornell.edu/home/kleinber/, 1998.

[78] J. Kogan. Means clustering for text data. In M.W. Berry (ed.), *Proceedings of the Workshop on Text Mining at the First SIAM International Conference on Data Mining*, pp. 47–54, 2001.

[79] J. Kogan, C. Nicholas, and M. Teboulle (eds.). *Grouping Multidimensional Data: Recent Advances in Clustering*. Springer-Verlag, New York, 2006.

[80] J. Kogan, C. Nicholas, and V. Volkovich. Text mining with information-theoretical clustering. *Computing in Science & Engineering*, pp. 52–59, November/December 2003.

[81] J. Kogan and M. Teboulle. Scaling clustering algorithms with Bregman distances. In M.W. Berry and M. Castellanos (eds.), *Proceedings of the Workshop on Text Mining at the Sixth SIAM International Conference on Data Mining*, 2006.

[82] J. Kogan and M. Teboulle. Scalable clustering with a smoothed *k*-means algorithm. Department of mathematics and statistics, UMBC 2006. Math and Stat Technical Report. http://www.math.umbc.edu/misc/technical_papers/. January 2006.

[83] J. Kogan, M. Teboulle, and C. Nicholas. The entropic geometric means algorithm: An approach for building small clusters for large text data sets. In D. Boley et al. (eds.), *Proceedings of the Workshop on Clustering Large Data Sets* (held in conjunction with the *Third IEEE International Conference on Data Mining*), pp. 63–71, 2003.

[84] J. Kogan, M. Teboulle, and C. Nicholas. Optimization approach to generating families of *k*-means like algorithms. In I. Dhillon and J. Kogan (eds.), *Proceedings of the Workshop on Clustering High Dimensional Data and its Applications* (held in conjunction with the *Third SIAM International Conference on Data Mining*), 2003.

[85] J. Kogan, M. Teboulle, and C. Nicholas. Data driven similarity measures for *k*-means like clustering algorithms. *Information Retrieval*, 8:331–349, 2005.

[86] T. Kohonen, T.S. Huang, and M.R. Schroeder. *Self-Organizing Maps*. Springer-Verlag, New York, 2000.

[87] E. Kolatch. Clustering algorithms for spatial databases: A survey, 2001.

[88] R.R. Korfhage. *Information Storage and Retrieval*. Wiley, New York, 1997.

[89] G. Kowalski. *Information Retrieval Systems*. Kluwer, New York, 1997.

[90] S. Kullback and R.A. Leibler. On information and sufficiency. *Journal of Mathematical Analysis and Applications*, 22:79–86, 1951.

[91] J. Lafferty. Adaptive models, boosting and inference for generalized divergences. In *Proceedings of 12th Annual Conference on Computational Learning Theory*, pp. 125–133, 1999.

[92] J. Lafferty, S.D. Pietra, and Pietra V.D. Statistical learning algorithms based on Bregman distances. In *Proceedings of the Canadian Workshop on Information Theory*, 1997.

[93] Man Lan, Chew-Lim Tan, Hwee-Boon Low, and Sam-Yuan Sung. A comprehensive comparative study on term weighting schemes for text categorization with support vector machines. In *Proceedings of the 14th international conference on World Wide Web*, pp. 1032–1033, Chiba, Japan, 2005.

[94] M. Larkey, L. Connell, and J. Callan. Collection selection and results merging with topically organized U.S. patents and TREC data. In *Proceedings of the 9th International Conference on Information and Knowledge Management (CIKM)*, pp. 282–289, McLean, VA, 2000. ACM, New York, NY.

[95] G Leitmann. On one approach to the control of uncertain system. *Transactions of ASME, Journal of Dynamic Systems, Measurement and Control*, 50(5):373–380, 1993.

[96] A.V. Leouski and W.B. Croft. An evaluation of techniques for clustering search results. Technical Report IR-76, Department of Computer Science, University of Massachusetts, CIIR Technical Report, 1996.

[97] Ciya Liao, Shamim Alpha, and Paul Dixon. Feature preparation in text categorization. www.oracle.com/technology/products/text/pdf/feature_preparation.pdf.

[98] F. Liese and I. Vajda. *Convex Statistical Distances*. Teubner, Leipzig, 1987.

[99] D. Littau and D. Boley. Using low-memory representations to cluster very large data sets. In D. Barbará and C. Kamath (eds.), *Proceedings of the Third SIAM International Conference on Data Mining*, pp. 341–345, 2003.

[100] D. Littau and D. Boley. Clustering very large data sets with PDDP. In J. Kogan, C. Nicholas, and M. Teboulle (eds.), *Grouping Multidimensional Data: Recent Advances in Clustering*, pp. 99–126. Springer-Verlag, New York, 2006.

[101] Tao Liu, Shengping Liu, Zheng Chen, and Wei-Ying Ma. An evaluation on feature selection for text clustering. In *Proceedings of the 2003 IEEE International Conference on Data Mining*, pp. 488–495. IEEE Computer Society Press, Piscataway, NJ, 2003.

[102] N. Trefethen Lloyd and D. Bau, III. *Numerical Linear Algebra.* SIAM, Philadelphia, 2000.

[103] M. Marcus and H. Minc. *A Survey of Matrix Theory and Matrix Inequalities.* Dover, New York, 1992.

[104] M. Meila. Comparing clustering by the variation of information. In *Learning Theory and Kernel Machines, Lecture Notes in Computer Science*, pp. 173–187, 2003.

[105] B. Mirkin. *Mathematical Classification and Clustering.* Kluwer Academic Publishers, Norwell, MA, 1996.

[106] N. Mishra and R. Motwani (eds.). Special issue: Theoretical advances in data clustering. *Machine Learning*, 56, 2004.

[107] D.S. Modha and W. Scott Spangler. Feature weighting in k-means clustering. *Machine Learning*, 52(3):217–237, 2003.

[108] F. Murtagh. *Multidimensional Clustering Algorithms.* Physica-Verlag, Vienna, Austria, 1985.

[109] O. Nasraoui and R. Krishnapuram. Crisp interpretations of fuzzy and possibilistic clustering algorithms. In *Proceedings of 3rd European Congress on Intelligent Techniques and Soft Computing*, pp. 1312–1318, Aachen, Germany, April 1995.

[110] B. Parlett. *The Symmetric Eigenvalue Problem.* Prentice-Hall, Englewood Cliffs, NJ, 1980.

[111] D. Pelleg and A. Moore. X-means: Extending k-means with efficient estimation of the number of clusters. In *Proceedings 17th ICML*, Stanford University, USA, 2000.

[112] A.L. Peressini, F.E. Sullivan, and J.J. Uhl. *The Mathematics of Nonlinear Programming.* Springer-Verlag, New York, 1988.

[113] M.F. Porter. An algorithm for suffix stripping. *Program*, 14:130–137, 1980.

[114] R.T. Rockafellar. *Convex Analysis.* Princeton University Press, Princeton, NJ, 1970.

[115] K. Rose. Deterministic annealing for clustering, compression, classification, regression, and related optimization problems. *Proceedings of the IEEE*, 86(11):2210–2239, 1998.

[116] K. Rose, E. Gurewitz, and C.G. Fox. A deterministic annealing approach to clustering. *Pattern Recognition Letters*, 11(9):589–594, 1990.

[117] K. Rose, E. Gurewitz, and C.G. Fox. Vector quantization by deterministic annealing. *IEEE Transactions on Information Theory*, 38(4):1249–1257, 1992.

[118] K. Rose, E. Gurewitz, and C.G. Fox. Constrained clustering as an optimization method. *IEEE Transactions on Pattern Analysis and Machine Intelligence*, 15:785–794, 1993.

[119] G. Salton and M.J. McGill. *Introduction to Modern Information Retrieval*. McGraw-Hill, New York, NY 1983.

[120] Y. Singer. Learning with Bregman divergences and all that brag. *In The Machine Learning Seminar*, School of Engineering and Computer Science, Hebrew University, March 2001.

[121] N. Slonim and N. Tishby. Agglomerative Information Bottleneck. In *Advances in Neural Information Processing Systems 12*, pp. 617–623. MIT Press, Cambridge, MA, 2000.

[122] N. Slonim and N. Tishby. Document clustering using word clusters via the Information Bottleneck Method. *Proceedings SIGIR*, pp. 208–215, 2000.

[123] N. Slonim and N. Tishby. The power of word clusters for text classification. In *23rd European Colloquium on Information Retrieval Research (ECIR)*, Darmstadt, 2001.

[124] H. Spath. *Cluster Analysis Algorithms*. Ellis Horwood, Chichester, England, 1980.

[125] H. Steinhaus. Sur la division des corps matèriels en parties. *Bulletin De L'Acadēmie Polonaise Des Sciences Classe III Mathematique, Astronomie, Physique, Chimie, Geologie, et Geographie*, 4(12):801–804, 1956.

[126] A. Strehl and J. Ghosh. Cluster ensembles – a knowledge reuse framework for combining partitionings. In *Proceedings of AAAI 2002, Edmonton, Canada*, pp. 93–98. AAAI, July 2002.

[127] P.-N. Tan, M. Steinbach, and V. Kumar. *Introduction to Data Mining*. Pearson, Boston, MA, 2006.

[128] M. Teboulle. A unified continuous optimization framework to center–based clustering methods, Working paper, School of Mathematical Sciences, Tel-Aviv University, May, 2006.

[129] M. Teboulle. Entropic proximal mappings with application to nonlinear programming. *Mathematics of Operation Research*, 17:670–690, 1992.

[130] M. Teboulle. On φ-divergence and its applications. In F.Y. Phillips and J. Rousseau (eds.), *Systems and Management Science by Extremal Methods–Research Honoring Abraham Charnes at Age 70*, pp. 255–273, Kluwer Academic Publishers, Nowell, MA, 1992.

[131] M. Teboulle. Convergence of proximal-like algorithms. *SIAM Journal of Optimization*, 7:1069–1083, 1997.

[132] M. Teboulle, P. Berkhin, I. Dhillon, Y. Guan, and J. Kogan. Clustering with entropy-like k-means algorithms. In J. Kogan, C. Nicholas, and M. Teboulle (eds.), *Grouping Multidimensional Data: Recent Advances in Clustering*, pp. 127–160. Springer-Verlag, New York, 2006.

[133] M. Teboulle and J. Kogan. k-means clustering by smoothing techniques. UMBC Department of Mathematics and Statistics Technical Report TR2006-17, http://www.math.umbc.edu/misc/technical_ papers/.

[134] M. Teboulle and J. Kogan. Deterministic annealing and a k-means type smoothing optimization algorithm for data clustering. In I. Dhillon, J. Ghosh, and J. Kogan (eds.), *Proceedings of the Workshop on Clustering High Dimensional Data and Its Applications* (held in conjunction with the *Fifth SIAM International Conference on Data Mining*), pp. 13–22. SIAM, Philadelphia, PA, 2005.

[135] C. J. van Rijsbergen. *Information Retrieval*, 2nd edn. Butterworths, London, 1979.

[136] S. Wang and D. Schuurmans. Learning continuous latent variable models with Bregman divergences. In *Lecture Notes in Artificial Intelligence*, Vol. 2842, pp. 190–204, 2003.

[137] P. Willett. Recent trends in hierarchic document clustering: A critical review. *Information Processing & Management*, 24(5):577–597, 1988.

[138] W. Wu, H. Xiong, and S. Shenkar. *Clustering and Information Retrieval*. Kluwer Academic Publishers, Norwell, MA, 2004.

[139] X.L. Xie and G Beni. A validity measure for fuzzy clustering. *IEEE Trabsactions on Pattern Analysis and Machine Intelligence*, 13(8):841–847, 1991.

[140] Yiming Yang and Jan O. Pedersen. A comparative study on feature selection in text categorization. In *Proceedings of 14th International*

Conference on Machine Learning, pp. 412–420. Morgan Kaufmann, San Francisco, 1997.

[141] J. Yu. General C-means clustering mModel. *IEEE Transactions on Pattern Analysis and Machine Intelligence*, 27(8):1197–1211, 2005.

[142] R. Zass and A. Shashua. A unifying approach to hard and probabilistic clustering. In *Proceedings of the International Conference on Computer Vision*, Beijing, China, 2005.

[143] H. Zha, C. Ding, M. Gu, X. He, and H. Simon. Spectral relaxation for *k*-means clustering. In *Neural Information Processing Systems*, Vol. 14, pp. 1057–1064, MIT Press, Cambridge, MA, 2001.

[144] B. Zhang, M. Hsu, and U. Dayal. K-harmonic means – a data clustering algorithm. Technical Report HPL-1999-124 991029, HP Labs, Palo Alto, CA, 1999.

[145] G. Zhang, B. Kleyner, and M. Hsu. A local search approach to *k*-clustering. Technical Report HPL-1999-119, 1999.

[146] T. Zhang, R. Ramakrishnan, and M. Livny. BIRCH: An efficient data clustering method for very large databases. In *Proceedings of the ACM SIGMOD Conference on Management of Data*, Montreal, Canada, 1996.

[147] T. Zhang, R. Ramakrishnan, and M. Livny. BIRCH: A new data clustering algorithm and its applications. *Journal of Data Mining and Knowledge Discovery*, 1(2):141–182, 1997.

[148] S. Zhong and J. Ghosh. A comparative study of generative models for document clustering. In I.S. Dhillon and J. Kogan (eds.), *Proceedings of the Workshop on Clustering High Dimensional Data and its Applications at the Third SIAM International Conference on Data Mining*. SIAM, Philadelphia, 2003.

[149] D. Zhou, J. Huang, and B. Scholkopf. Beyond pairwise classification and clustering using hypergraphs. Technical Report TR-143, Max Planck Institute for Biol. Cybernetics, August 2005.

Index

Index

Printed in the United States
by Baker & Taylor Publisher Services